A Voice for Justice

A Voice for Justice

*Sermons That Prepared a Congregation
to Respond to God in the Decade after 9/11*

Seth Kaper-Dale

WIPF & STOCK · Eugene, Oregon

A VOICE FOR JUSTICE
Sermons That Prepared a Congregation to Respond to God in the Decade after 9/11

Copyright © 2013 Seth Kaper-Dale. All rights reserved. Except for brief quotations in critical publications or reviews, no part of this book may be reproduced in any manner without prior written permission from the publisher. Write: Permissions, Wipf and Stock Publishers, 199 W. 8th Ave., Suite 3, Eugene, OR 97401.

Wipf & Stock
An Imprint of Wipf and Stock Publishers
199 W. 8th Ave., Suite 3
Eugene, OR 97401

www.wipfandstock.com

ISBN 13: 978-1-62032-808-8

Manufactured in the U.S.A.

New Revised Standard Version Bible, copyright © 1989, Division of Christian Education of the National Council of the Churches of Christ in the United States of America. Used by permission. All rights reserved.

My Special World: Poems and Photographs of Dorothy Forsythe Dale, copyright © 2005, North Point Press. Used by permission. All rights reserved.

All That We Let In
Words and Music by Emily Saliers
© 2004 GODHAP MUSIC
All Rights Controlled and Administered by SONGS OF UNIVERSAL, INC.
All Rights Reserved Used by Permission
Reprinted by Permission of Hal Leonard Corporation

The title of this book suggests that my voice has been a voice for justice, but my voice cries out from within a person who has been created by a community. I dedicate this book to some of the people who have made my life, my life: my parents Wendy and Steve Dale; my brothers Noah and Isaac; my daughters Sena, Leah and Cora; and most of all, to my wife Stephanie.

And, I dedicate it to the congregation of the Reformed Church of Highland Park who struggled with me to live out our faith in the decade after 9/11.

[God] has told you, O mortal, what is good;
and what does the Lord require of you
but to do justice, and to love kindness,
and to walk humbly with your God?
—Micah 6:8

Contents

Foreword by Allen Verhey | *xi*

Preface | *xv*

Introduction | *xvii*

Section One—Preparing the Church to Confront Other Kingdoms

1. God Gives Us Dominion, So Why Haven't We Taken the Crown? Hebrews 2:5–9 | 3

2. A Prayer Jesus Won't Answer, Mark 10:40 | 9

3. Have We Heard?: Jesus Offended the Hometown Congregation Today and I'm Trying to Understand Why, Luke 4:16–30 | 14

4. A Captive to the Spirit, Acts 20:20–24 | 19

5. Jesus Brings out the Worst in Herod, Matthew 2:7–8, 12, 16–18 | 24

6. Getting Zaccheaus into and out of the Tree, Luke 19:1–10 | 31

7. Caesar Is God's Puppet and Doesn't Even Know! Luke 2:1–7 | 37

8. Rolling the Dice: Election in the Kingdom of God, Acts 1:20b–26 | 42

Section Two—The Prepared Church Faces the Issues of Our Day

Part One: Faith Facing the Wars in Afghanistan and Iraq

9. As One after God's Own Heart, 2 Samuel 5:1–5 | 55

Contents

    10   Not in My Name, Mark 8:27–38 | 62

    11   The End Is Now, Praise God! Revelation 21:1–2, 22:1–2 | 68

    12   Christ Showed Us God, John 14:8–14 | 75

    13   Displaced but Not Disgraced, Luke 2:1–7 | 81

Part Two: Faith Facing "Enemies"

    14   Watch Out for Iran! Luke 18:35–43 | 89

    15   We're Better Off for All That We Let in, Luke 15:1–10 | 94

    16   A Corrective to the Furor over the "Ground-Zero Mosque," Luke 15:1–2 | 100

Part Three: Faith Facing Immigration Policy

    17   When a Church Loves Its Country, John 17:15–23 | 111

    18   Being Somebody in the Land That Calls You Nobody, Jeremiah 29:1, 4–7 | 116

    19   Travelers Who Expose the Truth about Herod and the Arrival of God, Matthew 2: 1–3a, 7–12 | 122

Part Four: Faith Facing Economics and Poverty

    20   The Economic Implications of the Covenant, Mark 10:17–31 | 133

    21   Tithing Is So Anti-Jesus, Luke 12: 22–34 | 140

    22   The Parable of the Talents: A Reading from the Margins, Matthew 25:14–30 | 144

    23   Fairness in the Kingdom, Matthew 19:27–30, Matthew 20:10–15 | 148

24 Devouring Widows' Houses, Luke 20:45–47,
    Luke 21:1–4 | 154

25 How Did You Respond When Herod Killed John the
    Baptist? Matthew 14:11–16 | 162

Part Five: Faith Facing Environmental Degradation

26 The Breadth of the Covenant, Genesis 9:9–11,
    Colossians 1:15–17 | 171

27 The Law, Earth, and Knowing God, Mark 12:28–34 | 178

Part Six: Faith Facing Sexual Orientation

28 The Way of the Cross: Addressing Homosexuality,
    Romans 1:18–32 | 187

Part Seven: Faith Facing American Mass Shootings

29 Don't Go Fishing Again, John 21:1–3a | 197

Part Eight: Faith Facing Natural Disasters

30 Caring before Katrina, Micah 6:8, Matthew 23:23 | 205

31 Living in Light of Rachel's Cry after the Tsunami,
    Jeremiah 31:15 | 212

Part Nine: Faith Facing Darfur

32 Darfur in Light of Easter, Acts 3:6 | 219

Part Ten: A New Day: The Election of Barack Obama

33 At What Point Do We Give up "Waiting in Anticipation?"
    1 Thessalonians 5:23–24 | 229

34 The Servant of the Lord: Does Anyone Have a President
    Who Is Bothering Them?, Isaiah 49:1–3 | 236

    Bibliography | 243

Foreword

I have known Seth since he was a student at Hope College. Already as a college student he distinguished himself as an advocate for minorities on campus and in the community. I counted it a privilege to be his advisor and teacher at Hope and an honor to give the charge to him at his ordination. I remember charging Seth to attend to the beatitudes in his work, to the blessing on those who hunger for justice, to the blessing on the merciful, to the blessing on the peacemakers, and to the blessing on those who mourn. I was sure Seth would live and minister in ways that kept faith with those words, but I did not foresee the extraordinarily creative and effective ways in which he would serve God's cause of justice, and mercy, and peace.

The remarkable sermons gathered here are evidence enough of his faithfulness and creativity as a preacher, but his words are best read in the context of the ways in which his ministry turns the gospel, not only into words but into actions and programs that serve justice, display mercy, make peace, include the marginalized, and bless the poor. His "hunger for justice" has frequently put him alongside, and taking the side of, those who are voiceless and powerless. His advocacy for immigrants and asylum seekers, described in *The New York Times* on Dec. 13, 2009, is a noteworthy example. It would have been easy enough, and safer, to stay on the sidelines when the Indonesian Christians who shared his sanctuary at Highland Park Reformed Church were arrested, detained, and separated from their families. They had come in the 90s when the economy needed cheap labor and welcomed foreign labor with a loose visa policy. September 11, 2001 changed things. Suddenly to come from Indonesia or from other Muslim countries was regarded as reason enough for the United States to demand "special registration." Now they faced discrimination and sectarian violence if they should return to Indonesia, and they faced discrimination and accusation in this country by those who were demanding a crackdown on immigrants. Seth became an advocate for them. He was able to reach an agreement—a very unusual agreement—that allowed some of the Indonesian Christians to be released from detention, to return to their families, and to work. It was a few at first, but the number grew, and became both a symbol of hope for those who are advocates of immigration reform and a model for other programs in New Hampshire (near where Seth grew up in Vermont), in New York, and in other places across the nation.

His work on immigration is only one example of Seth's commitment to social justice and of his creativity and effectiveness. Another example is his establishing a Church-Based Affordable Housing Corporation. Again it began with the church, but enlisted community support, both public and private. The outcome has been affordable housing for women "aging out" of foster care, for veterans (many of whom were formerly homeless), and for people recently released from prison. Social services are available to the residents. Again Seth's work became a model for other programs. Seth succeeded, also, in getting the classis, the regional body to which Highland Park belongs, to establish a corporation that enabled almost thirty other churches in New Jersey to utilize the tools of community development corporations to help their congregations live out dreams for justice and peace.

There are other examples that could be given, examples of his concern for the environment, examples of his work with diverse religious communities to promote understanding and friendship, especially with the Muslim community after 9/11, examples of his support for gay and lesbian people in a denomination that has traditionally not been supportive, examples of his advocacy for peace.

Seth is a man who hungers for justice, who shows mercy, and who makes peace. He is also, as I charged him to be, a "mourner," that is, one who has caught a vision of God's good future, of the world as it could be, and who mourns that it is not yet, still sadly not yet, that world. A "mourner" is an aching visionary who dreams of the hungry being fed, of the homeless having a place, of the stranger being welcomed. A "mourner" is one who hurts when he sees any victim of this world's sadness and injustice. A "mourner" is one who works to give that good future some little foothold in the city, and in the nation, and in the world.

Foreword

Seth is the best "mourner" I know. It's why he works so creatively and tirelessly for justice.

The sermons gathered here display Seth's passion for the gospel as well as justice. May they nurture in us that same passion, the passion of a church, as Seth says in one of these sermons, "rushing forward, rushing toward the kingdom of God that is moving quickly toward us. We're rushing toward it because Christ was rushing there ahead of us while he lived among us. We might have stopped when he was killed and buried, but then he got up, rushed onward, faster now, rushed onward and is now there, at the right hand of God. So we rush. We rush onward, toward the prize, joyously colliding with it throughout our lives as it breaks in upon us."

—Allen Verhey
Robert Earl Cushman Professor of Christian Ethics
Duke Divinity School

Preface

Our official office hours at our first church began the morning of September 11, 2001. My wife and co-pastor Stephanie and I had only recently finished seminary and were excited to be at the Reformed Church of Highland Park in New Jersey. We entered the church building just as the director of our seniors program yelled, "My God, one of the Trade Center towers has been hit. Somebody flew a plane into one of the towers!" Moments later he yelled again down the hall, "It happened again—another plane!—we're under attack!" The first weeks, months, and years of our ministry were a time of great turmoil in our nation.

Many voices clamored to articulate what happened on 9/11 and how we should live in response to that day. Many called for violent responses—and their perspective won out a good deal of the time. But there were others who influenced America during the first decade of the new millennium; those who guided lives, asked different questions, risked different answers, and claimed a different authority. Local preachers from many different faiths listened for God's voice and articulated God's truth in and for their communities and for the world so loved by God. Among these voices was my own.

It is my humble hope that I offered an alternative to the violent and arrogant voices of the day. A voice of humility, yes, but like the Jesus I follow, a voice also with power.

This collection of sermons from the post–9/11 decade wrestles directly with injustices, tragedies, attitudes, and worldviews of our day. Section I consists of sermons that look at how the church is to be, as it seeks to live as part of God's Kingdom. Section II is a collection of sermons that suggest how we, as a community, ought to respond to things like preemptive war, Darfur, economic disasters, and immigration turmoil. All are attempts to help a congregation of approximately three hundred people face the living of each day in light of "God's children's warring madness," as quoted from the 1930 hymn by Henry Emerson Fosdick. In providing these sermons, I have intentionally left in some references particular to my congregation that speak to certain events in our local life. This is part of what it means to speak to a congregation as together we live in the world.

May God bless you and keep you. May God's face shine upon you and grant you peace, now and forevermore. Amen.

Rev. Seth Kaper-Dale

Acknowledgments

A Voice for Justice would never have been completed without study-leave time granted by the Reformed Church of Highland Park and without the encouragement, professional assistance, and editing of Ruth Anne Phillips.

Section One

Preparing the Church
to Confront Other Kingdoms

1

God Gives Us Dominion, So Why Haven't We Taken the Crown?

October 8, 2006

> Now God did not subject the coming world, about which we are speaking, to angels. But someone has testified somewhere, "What are human beings that you are mindful of them, or mortals, that you care for them? You have made them for a little while lower than the angels; you have crowned them with glory and honor, subjecting all things under their feet." Now in subjecting all things to them, God left nothing outside their control. As it is, we do not yet see everything in subjection to them, but we do see Jesus, who for a little while was made lower than the angels, now crowned with glory and honor because of the suffering of death, so that by the grace of God he might taste death for everyone (Hebrews 2:5–9).[1]

As a kid, my favorite commercial had the great football player Lyle Alzado standing on his boat. I don't recall what he was selling, but I can picture him saying, "Get in the boat," as the fish leapt in from all sides. Try as I might, it's never quite worked like this for me at the lake in the Adirondacks we visit every summer. Not even when I tried the slightly less ambitious, "All right fish, get on my line." The lack of fish on

---

1. All Bible verse citations are taken from the New Revised Standard Version.

Section One—Preparing the Church to Confront Other Kingdoms

the end of my line was a sure sign to me that all is not right in the world, and that the last days, the *eschaton*, have not yet come.

Today's passage is about who has dominion and control on Earth and why. According to the writer of Hebrews (who may have been Paul or a follower of Paul), God left nothing outside humanity's control. Apparently God hadn't seen me fish. In Hebrews 2:8, the author writes, "In subjecting all things to them, God left nothing outside their control." Did you know that? The writer of Hebrews backs this up with a quote from Psalms 8:5–6, "You have crowned humankind with glory and honor, subjecting all things under their feet." This psalm isn't an anomaly. There are endless passages in the Bible that speak of this kind of authority granted to humanity, including Genesis 1:26 that says, "Let us make humankind in our image, according to our likeness; and let them have dominion over the fish of the sea [see that? Alzado's dominion over the fish is biblical!] and over the birds of the air, and over the cattle, and over all the wild animals of the Earth, and over every creeping thing that creeps upon the Earth."

The Scriptures of the Old and New Testament suggest that humanity in its dominion over all living things on Earth has a unique role to play in its governance. The writer of Hebrews makes a distinction between angels and humans as a way to show just how surprising this decision of God's is. The writer points out that God could have created the world and put it under the control of angels (sounds wise—put the heavenly beings in charge), but chose, instead, to place it in the control of one species made from the same dust as all the other species. In other words, God gave dominion to lesser beings, to us mere mortals.

This writer of Hebrews was aware of lots of examples of earthly dominion and control. During the writer's time, the Romans had taken over the lands of the Jewish community. Before that, this community had been forced to deal with the governments of the Selucids, Ptolomies, Greeks, Babylonians, Assyrians, Syrians, and Egyptians. Throughout the course of such a history of domination, there were other moments where control went the other way too. From time to time, Israel had been the dominating, conquering force.

The writer knew about dominion; he'd seen it and lived it, much as we have. We see dominion, and the subjugating of others, in our time and place, all the time. We could, of course, zoom in on leaders and movements all around the world. We could talk about Fascists, and

Communists, as well as terrorists, extremists, and freedom-haters. This week we could talk about the twisted dominion that has been repeated in a number of schools recently, where men with guns have demonstrated their dominion by assaulting and killing children. But today, I think this will be a much more soul-searching message if I focus on our national dominion over other nations for a minute.

The United States of America currently has so much control—and we make decisions that enable us to keep it. We decide which international treaties we will sign and which we'll decline, often based on our *own needs*, without prioritizing what is good for the world. We re-interpret the Geneva Convention so that we may be able to interrogate prisoners our own way. We refuse to sign the Kyoto Accords to help control global warming, although we are arguably the biggest propagator of the rising global temperature. We demand nuclear responsibility from Iran and North Korea while we budget for and create new nuclear bunker-buster weapons capabilities. We carry out wars on foreign soil and we seem to almost always win, one way or another. Nothing has been left outside our control. Dominion and control—we've seen it—we have so much of it.

Or do we?

Let's look at verse 8 from the second chapter of Hebrews again: "Now in subjecting all things to them, God left nothing outside their control, *but as it is, we do not yet see everything in subjection to them.*" Excuse me, writer, but what more do you want? Was it the Greeks or the Romans who you think didn't have enough dominion? Excuse me, writer, but you must not know about today. Today, the fossil fuel supplies are under human dominion. Even our DNA is almost completely charted and under our dominion. We are advancing, becoming more in control on so many fronts.

The writer knows all this, and it is in *the face of these forms of control* that he says, "not everything is subjected to them." Let's read the writer's full sentence in Hebrews 2:8–9: "God left nothing outside their control, but as it is, we do not yet see everything in subjection to them, but we do see Jesus, who for a little while was made lower than the angels, now crowned with glory and honor because of the suffering of death, so that by the grace of God he might taste death for everyone."

Jesus has dominion and control—not the United States of America nor any other nation state from today or yesterday, nor even many yesterdays ago. Jesus has dominion and control—not Donald Trump, nor any other mega millionaire. Jesus has control—not violent, twisted individuals who cause destruction in the lives of others. And Jesus has control over Earth, not because Jesus is the Son of God, but because for a little while he was fully human—and assumed dominion in the way that is proper for humanity—with humility.

Our wealth, our armies, our technology—it's some kind of power, but it's not fully human power. You get some crown for that kind of power and dominion, but not, according to this text, the human crown. Human crowns are for those who in their way of life reflect the image of God—which Jesus demonstrates with a *servant-throughout-life-and-into-death* image. The crown belongs to Christ, but it also belongs to each of us who are being sanctified and transformed into our full humanity. And Jesus is proud to call us brothers and sisters.

The kind of control that tends to dominate our communal existence as humans and define world history is actually the dominion of the powers of death, masquerading in the bodies of folks and communities and nations that have stepped away from their God-given image. Human dominion, the kind that we are *supposed* to have, is something altogether different. It still involves control. It still involves subjection. But it is servant-control that leads to a willing, self-giving subjection.

Do you want to see human dominion? Watch the way a new mother exercises dominion, waking up four times a night to nurse her baby. You want to see human dominion? Look at the way a grandmother makes homemade valentines and puts them in the mail for her grandchildren. Do you want to see human dominion? Watch the way a nation eventually responds to persistent humble servants who are elevated to prominence when the world is in crisis—Nelson Mandela, Martin Luther King Jr., Mother Theresa. Do you want to see human dominion? Watch the way a young man in love suddenly warms up to hobbies he's never cared for, watching T.V. shows that used to bore him to death, just to spend a little more time with his beloved.

In each of these cases, one can ask if these have dominion or if they've been subjugated? Human dominion, at its best, builds up all subjects to such a level that they are loved perfectly, and there is hardly a difference between *domine* and subject; in fact, it is possible to get to the place where we are all holding dominion together—maybe that's why Jesus calls us all brothers and sisters, fellow dominion holders.

But really, pastor, are you suggesting that human dominion can rule our world? My answer is simply this. My grandma's valentines look a lot more like Christ than the so-called dominion moves pulled by people in high places. I'd trust my grandmother's valentines over the closed-door meetings of world superpowers any day.

We're living in the last days. Did you know that? For some Christians the "last days" suggest that the Messiah is coming back any minute. There's a group of preachers out there pushing the idea that we are on the brink of it all coming to a head here and now. Iran's doing this, Russia's doing that, and Israel is aligned just so. Listen for one minute to Rev. John Haugee or Pat Robertson; read the Left Behind Series, and you'll see this is a common view. They mark off current events in real politics as events leading up to the Second Coming of Christ.

Others and myself, though, believe we have been living in the last days for 2,000 years. In my understanding, "the last days" and the "final coming of Christ" are not synonymous. I believe we are living in the last days now, and have been, since Jesus revealed for us the perfect love of God—but I don't know that that means we are anywhere near some sort of final coming of Christ. Sometime over the course of this extended period called the "last days" or the "end times," I imagine God doing something that might be defined as the Second Coming, but I'm not waiting around on pins and needles for it.

The writer of Hebrews, at the very beginning of his sermon/letter, gives credence to the position I've come to accept: "In these last days he has spoken to us by a Son."[2] "Last days" can also be translated as "*eschaton*" or "last days' period." The writer of Hebrews thought the incarnation of Jesus, the *first arrival of Jesus*, to be the key to this period in history. Through Jesus we have a chance to live into the fullest form of our identity, and that means claiming the dominion that is essential to who we are.

This is the good news. Jesus Christ has claimed the full dominion that God intended for humanity, subjected all things to him, and in so doing, destroyed death and the fear of death. And now, Jesus wants to help sanctify us, restore us, to that full dominion too. Jesus wants to be the pioneer of our salvation by helping us exercise proper dominion in the world. We've already crossed the deep river from death to life. We've crossed the Jordan into the promised location of the Kingdom of God. We've entered the camp—let's live with the dominion granted us!

2. Heb 1:2a.

Section One—Preparing the Church to Confront Other Kingdoms

You've been given dominion. Why don't you take it? Maybe you've forgotten where you are supposed to exercise full human dominion. Maybe you've never realized God wants you to have dominion. Here are some steps to try:

First: Challenge the things that have dominion over your life. Ask yourselves what or who dominates your time, attitudes, and opinions about all sorts of things. Is it the television? Is it political spin? Is it financial stress? Is it pride? Is it work? Is it the "norms" of your social class? Is it fear of death?

Second: Ask yourselves where you could have dominion in your life as it is right now. Be practical and start with small changes; get the feeling of human dominion that reflects the image of God. For example, as many of you know, we had a waste audit at the church a few weeks ago. Through that I realized that "the ease of throwing things out," had some dominion over my life. After the waste audit, my wife, Stephanie, and I decided we could have more dominion over what we put into the waste stream. We've gotten rid of paper napkins, have started a compost, and now, when I get those envelopes that are all paper, with a little plastic on them, I rip off the plastic and recycle that too. God has left nothing outside our control, even how we deal with waste, and I hadn't previously claimed that. We have taken a more servant-leader approach to waste and as a result, the subjugated—the Earth and all humanity—will benefit from our efforts. Small steps—but I'm beginning to exercise human dominion.

Third: Dream big and be creative—and think of sharing your dominion with a community of dominion-holding dreamers. What in the world would be better if it were within your dominion? This has been happening around this church lately, and the results have been incredible. A group at a mission meeting dreamed of a safe place for teens to come after school—and now we have "The Cave," serving fifty kids a week. It's happening again as the church wrestled with a dream to build housing for teens aging out of foster care. But what's next? I'm excited to find out. Maybe a bunch of you will come around a member of the church, and support a political run, one that brings a heavy dose of human dominion back into halls corrupted by other sorts of dominion.

God's given you dominion—why don't you take it? And let's see where that dominion takes us as a world throughout these last days. Amen.

2

A Prayer Jesus Won't Answer

O ctober 22, 2006

> But to sit at my right hand or at my left is not mine to grant, but it is for those for whom it has been prepared. (Mark 10:40)

"It's not mine to grant." That's Jesus' answer to a prayer request from disciples who had given up everything to follow him.

In Mark 11:24, Jesus tells his disciples, "Whatever you ask for in prayer, believe that you have received it, and it will be yours." But it doesn't work for James and John. When they go to him, prayerfully, asking for something, he responds with, "It's not mine to grant." What exactly had they been asking for? Something ambitious: "Grant us to sit, one at your right hand and one at your left, in your glory."[1]

There is a popular notion that suggests Jesus' disciples were *poor* fishermen. Fishermen, yes, and maybe some of them were poor, but not James and John. They were sons of Zebedee, a businessman in the fishing industry. When James and John left to follow Jesus, we are told they left behind their father's boat, and his hired men. These were young men who knew something about leadership and authority.

Just before this, Jesus had been talking strangely. Over the past week he had twice sat the disciples down to tell them that he would soon go

---

1. Mark 10:37.

to Jerusalem, be condemned to death, be mocked and spit upon before finally being killed, and after three days, would rise again.

The first time Jesus said this Peter "took him aside and began to rebuke him."[2]

Jesus' response was, "Get behind me, Satan."[3]

The second time Jesus spoke to his disciples, they wisely responded with silence—they didn't want to say the wrong thing.[4]

The third time, like the second, Jesus' words about suffering and death drove his disciples to silence, causing them to walk away and keep their distance.[5] But this third time, after the others had gone, James and John circled back into the room to talk to Jesus. They wore their power ties and nice suits. They had heard key words at the end of Jesus' strange statements, "I will rise again." While they, like the others, were horrified at the notion that Jesus would be rejected and killed, James and John knew something about what Jesus meant when he talked about "rising." They'd been invited to see Jesus transfigured on the mountain a short time before that. They'd seen him dazzle with bright light. They'd heard the voice of God.[6]

"Teacher, we want you to do for us whatever we ask of you."[7] It sounds awfully demanding, doesn't it? But remember, as I said earlier, James and John are just doing what they'd been taught by Jesus. See, they'd been good listeners—smart. They'd heard him say, on more than one occasion, things like "I tell you the truth—whatever you pray for, if you believe it in your heart, it will be granted to you." These are the kinds of guys who get ahead.

"What is it you want me to do for you?" Jesus asked.[8]

"We want the seats of power and honor, the seats to your immediate right and left, in your glory. We want to be your lieutenant governors. We want to be your special council."

They knew a glorified Jesus was worth following, and I imagine they knew that they were more qualified than the other disciples when it

2. Ibid., 8:32.
3. Ibid., 8:33.
4. Ibid., 9:32.
5. Ibid., 10:32–34.
6. Ibid., 9:2–8.
7. Ibid., 10:35.
8. Ibid., 10:36.

came to exercising power and leadership in the new kingdom—because of their family background, good business, and leadership sensibilities.

"You do not know what you are asking. Are you able to drink the cup that I drink, or be baptized with the baptism I am baptizing with?"[9]

"Yes, we are able."[10] They say it with confidence, but not arrogance. These guys are good. They've thought it out already. They know the stakes for following Jesus are high, that his cup is the cup of suffering and that joining in his baptism could mean the waters of death, but they believe the reward is worth the risk.

It is possible, of course, that James and John *were* ready. Maybe they were genuinely ready to follow Jesus to the point of total submission and to face even threats of death. Some people are, you know. Martin Luther King Jr., Harriet Tubman, Cesar Chavez—some folks risk it all to be faithful. When James and John said they were ready to follow, Jesus answered in the affirmative. You're right. "The cup that I drink you will drink, and with the baptism with which I am baptized you will be baptized."[11] You get the sense that Jesus is about to say, "Okay, if you can accept suffering and death, the seats of honor and privilege are yours."

But Jesus doesn't say that. Instead, he basically says, "Okay, you're ready to suffer and die with me, great, but sorry guys, the privilege to sit at my right and left hand is not mine to grant. Those seats are for those for whom it has been prepared."[12] They were right about the risk, they were wrong that taking a risk would lead to privilege and power in the new kingdom.

Friends, hear it well. Jesus won't grant special seats of honor and power to his disciples or anyone else. They are intended for the ones for whom they have been prepared. But who are *they*? No one knows.

Jesus, for who are the seats on the right and left of you prepared?

Jesus doesn't answer directly but instead engages in a discussion of servant leadership. Jesus gathered the disciples around him and said something like, "You know that in some leadership systems the 'Gentiles,' or rulers, hold power over others, but it is not to be so with you." Instead, "whoever wishes to be first among you must be slave of all."[13] James and John were following an outdated model—the model used by their

---

9. Ibid., 10:38 (paraphrased).
10. Ibid., 10:39.
11. Ibid., 10:38.
12. Ibid., 10:40 (paraphrased).
13. Ibid., 10:44.

Section One—Preparing the Church to Confront Other Kingdoms

oppressors. Servant leaders, those who have been found in Christ, won't lead through power chairs on the right and left of the king. Servant leaders do not belong in those chairs.

So again, who will be in those chairs to the right and left, and what is their purpose?

The Sons of Zebedee, and you and I, are told the answer to this question by Jesus time and again. The most prepared for the kingdom, and I would say the best seats in the kingdom, are for children, for the forgotten, for the prisoners, and for other victims of the world's abuses.

There is only one other time when the phrase "to the left and the right of him" is used in Mark's gospel. That phrase occurs when Jesus is hanging on the cross—revealing his glory through his non-violent suffering love—and criminals are described as being "on his left and right."[14] They are in the seats (or on the crosses) of honor. No wonder Jesus answered James and John by saying, "You do not know what you are asking."

When folks on death row along with babies are the ones at the right and left of Jesus Christ, you know the chairs of authority have a new purpose. The seats closest to Jesus are reserved not for those with great human power, but for those most in need of direct love at a given time.

When Jesus says something more than once you can bet he's serious about it. Jesus speaks of servant leadership five times in the same week, while revealing his Messianic identity and then heading for Jerusalem. You can bet he is *really* serious about it! And I think God has us repeatedly reflecting on these passages about servant leadership, and about the privileged place of vulnerable guests, because God wants us to get serious about servant leadership to help fill the seats on the right and left, the seats that God has prepared.

The Zebedee brothers were out of luck. They would lose their status if they desired to remain in Christ's glorious kingdom. But they were in luck if they came to realize that in losing their status they may be found among the multitudes for whom an expanse to the right and left of Christ have been prepared by God.

Zebedee boys, redirect your energy. Jesus' glory is something to behold. You don't need the best seat in the house—there are a lot of "great seats." But why don't you put your effort into helping those who are out of the house to get in and sit down closest to the throne? Sandwich them in, loving servants on the outside, newest and most vulnerable people on the seats between Jesus and you.

14. Mark 15:27.

And having the most vulnerable people in the world seated to the right and left of Jesus isn't just for *their* benefit. It's for everyone's—because *they* do have an extraordinary power. They have the power to articulate God's grace and the radical good news more than anyone else—and that is a form of authority fitting for the kingdom of God.

I found in this text, and my meandering thoughts about it, a particularly exciting challenge for our church. Who can we invite into our church, expecting Jesus to sit them down at the right and left? Having children participate more fully in worship is an explicit way we are giving prominence to those for whom God has reserved the best seats in the kingdom. But there are others who need those best seats too. Jesus asks us to do radically more to make this place inviting to all.

What would it look like to call a local prison, to find out if we could swing by on Sundays, and other days, to pick up inmates who may have visitation rights and who belong at the right and left in the kingdom of the fellowship of God? Or, if we can't pick up inmates, maybe the children of inmates, housed in a facility nearby. What would it look like to do that regularly? What would it look like to connect with local nursing homes, specifically reaching out to folks who are lonely and in need of fellowship, inviting them to come and sit in seats of honor in our sanctuary or at a fellowship meal? What would it look like to care for the most vulnerable immigrants, who have come here by whatever means possible, in order to feed and educate their children? What would it look like to connect with emergency foster families, to invite them to come and sit at the right and left, sandwiched in love between Jesus and the church? How about we really pursue receiving refugees from Darfur?

Such actions may just cross the line for some people—this is too much! Exactly. Jesus is too much. His next steps are through Jericho, where blind Bartimeaus is given the best seat in the house, and then on to Jerusalem, where lepers, the poor, children, and women sit all around Jesus in the temple that previously hadn't welcomed them. And then, on to the cross, with prisoners to the left and right.

Friends, a broader embrace of those in the community who are more vulnerable than we are, in ways that radically break with norms and customs, will bring those outside closer to God. And when they are seated there it is likely that they will bring us closer to Jesus, since they will be sitting in seats that are closer to Jesus than we are, and can pass his messages on to us. Amen.

3

Have We Heard?

Jesus Offended the Hometown Congregation Today and I'm Trying to Understand Why

January 27, 2007

When he came to Nazareth, where he had been brought up, he went to the synagogue on the Sabbath day, as was his custom. He stood up to read, and the scroll of the prophet Isaiah was given to him. He unrolled the scroll and found the place where it was written: "The Spirit of the Lord is upon me, because he has anointed me to bring good news to the poor. He has sent me to proclaim release to the captives and recovery of sight to the blind, to let the oppressed go free, to proclaim the year of the Lord's favor." And he rolled up the scroll, gave it back to the attendant, and sat down. The eyes of all in the synagogue were fixed on him. Then he began to say to them, "Today this Scripture has been fulfilled in your hearing." All spoke well of him and were amazed at the gracious words that came from his mouth. They said, "Is not this Joseph's son?" He said to them, "Doubtless you will quote to me this proverb, 'Doctor, cure yourself!' And you will say, 'Do here also in your hometown the things that we have heard you did at Capernaum.'" And he said, "Truly I tell you, no prophet is accepted in the prophet's home town. But the truth is, there were many widows in Israel in the time of Elijah, when the heaven was shut up for three years and six months, and there was a severe famine over all the land; yet Elijah was sent to none of them except to a widow at Zarephath in Sidon. There were also many lepers in Israel in the time of the prophet Elisha, and none of them was cleansed except Naaman the Syrian." When they heard this, all in the synagogue were filled with rage. They got up, drove him out of the town, and led him to the brow of the hill on which their town was built, so that they might hurl him off the cliff. But he passed through the midst of them and went on his way. (Luke 4:16–30)

Jesus had just come back from a trip to Jerusalem. He was finally coming home to Nazareth. His mother was excited to see him; his brothers and sisters (James, Joses, Judas, and Simon are the ones we know by name) were glad too. He'd been away for a few months to visit John the Baptist and take part in his ministry of repentance outside Jerusalem. He'd been baptized. Then, he went on a forty-day retreat in the wilderness to commit his life to God. Then, reentering Galilee, he'd begun to preach and teach in synagogues. Without any prior experience or preparation it was a bit surprising that this was going so smoothly for him. Word had it that he was "praised by everyone" who heard his teaching.[1]

The first Saturday back in Nazareth, Jesus went to the synagogue, to the congregation of his youth, the place where he was formed in faith and where he had learned the law of God. One of the elders gave him the scroll of the prophet Isaiah. Jesus hunted through the scroll, put one finger on chapter 61:1 and one finger on 58:6 and said, "The Spirit of the Lord is upon me, because he has anointed me to bring good news to the poor, he has sent me to proclaim release to the captives and recovery of sight to the blind, to let the oppressed go free, to proclaim the year of the Lord's favor."

He then gave the scroll back to the attendant and sat down. All eyes were fixed upon him. Wasn't he going to say more? This was the time to show his interpretive skills! Then he spoke, "Today this Scripture has been fulfilled in your hearing."[2]

They waited for more, but he said nothing else. Then they came up to Jesus and the well wishes flowed and sounded something like: "Oh, what gracious words you gave us today;" "Oh, it's so good to have you home again;" "Long time no see;" "Oh, I bet your mom was happy to see

1. Luke 4:15.
2. Ibid., 4:21.

Section One—Preparing the Church to Confront Other Kingdoms

you;" "Stay around here for a while;" "I can hardly believe that's Joseph's son, so confident."

And I picture them getting ready to file out of the synagogue, getting ready to spend a quiet family afternoon at home. And then Jesus said, "Doubtless you will quote to me this proverb, 'Doctor, cure yourself!' and you will say, 'Do here also in your hometown the things we have heard that you did at Capernaum.' . . . Truly I tell you, no prophet is accepted in the prophet's hometown."

The room grew quiet, an unsettled quiet. I imagine them saying, "Do you hear him? He's suggesting that we don't care what he offers now, but that we'll come begging for it later. What is he talking about? Why the tone? What does he mean we don't accept him? We listened to him. We're congratulating him. Why is he so bent out of shape all of a sudden?"

Jesus went on, "The truth is there were many widows in Israel in the time of Elijah . . . and there was a severe famine in all the land, yet Elijah was sent to none of them, except to a widow at Zarephath, [in the country] of Sidon . . . there were also many lepers in Israel in the time of the prophet Elisha, and none of them was cleansed except Naaman, the Syrian."

"*Get him.*" The now angry throng got up and chased him to the top of a hill, near a cliff, and they tried to corner him "to hurl him off the cliff." But he snuck away. Because the congregation resorted to such violence, it's easy to read this passage and end up thinking about *their* behavior, but what was with Jesus on this day? Why did he instigate this? Nobody said anything hurtful or pointed. They were gracious. They appreciated his reading. They didn't give him a hard time about giving a one-line sermon, "Today this Scripture has been fulfilled in your hearing." Why couldn't he just have let things be the way they were in Nazareth? Jesus offended his hometown congregation—why?

I half expected to find an apology from Jesus in the following verses, but there is no apology. I think he would have apologized if he had thought he was wrong, so I'm left to assume, then, that Jesus was very much "in his right mind," when he was so pointed and inflammatory in Nazareth. So, then, the question is why did he do it? Why did he speak that way to them?

We only have one thing to analyze as we ask that question: the Scripture passages he quoted from Isaiah and his one-line affirmation, "Today this Scripture [the one that says the Spirit is upon me to liberate all who suffer] . . . has been fulfilled in your hearing."

The Greek word for "ear/hearing" is frequently used, not in a literal sense, but is transferred from sense perception to mental and spiritual understanding.[3] In other words, the phrase "receiving the following words in your ear" means to take them to heart. Jesus was fed up with cheap talk. He didn't want to be patted on the back and told what a good job he was doing. He wanted his message to be understood as life altering. God had sent him for the sake of doing justice for a select group of people—the poor, captive, blind, and those who have been crushed—and to proclaim equality and restoration for all of them. Jesus was disturbed that the people of Nazareth were leaving the worship service without signs that they had really *heard* his message of justice for all.

If they had heard, *really* heard, they would have been asking how he was going to bring good news to the poor. Was he going to fight to raise the minimum wage to a living wage, rather than the proposed $7.25 an hour? How about to $9.80? That would make the minimum wage equal to the purchasing power of 1968, our previous high.

If they'd heard he was proclaiming release to the captives, they would have been asking how he was going to find a way to get three million Americans (2.5 million of them African-Americas) out of prison and into restorative programs of justice.

If they'd heard he was proclaiming recovery of sight to the blind, they would have been asking about health care and healing. If they'd heard the good news about the Year of the Lord's Favor—Jesus' reference to the biblical mandates to redistribute wealth—they would be shaking with excitement (and fear), asking how God (or Jesus) was going to bring about that radical practice of redistributing material and land equally among the people.

They weren't doing any of these things, so Jesus knew they hadn't really heard the message; and Jesus won't stand for that. Jesus, during his life, went to all lengths, including alienating his hometown, in order to ensure that the *justice reasons* for his anointing were announced. He gave everyone a chance to hear—gentle first, and then louder! And it is good news for you and me that Jesus did this and does this still by the power of the Holy Spirit.

---

3. The Greek word for ear/hearing is *"ous."* See BDAG 595.

Section One—Preparing the Church to Confront Other Kingdoms

If you live within the range of Jesus' voice, you will hear him speak of justice and peace—and if you're not hearing it, then your church has failed you and the Scripture has not spoken to you. Hopefully you are ready to *really hear him* when he speaks to you of justice. It's not a sidebar of the gospel; it's the reason for his anointing. And if his voice sounds confrontational, if you really don't like what he's saying, listen all the more closely, because maybe Christ is trying to break through a place in your life where your ears are almost entirely closed.

And maybe, maybe that most troubling place, that most difficult topic, that most serious injustice is the one about which Jesus wants *you* to then become prophet. We don't hear about the "angry crowd" in Nazareth a couple days after they tried to push Jesus off a cliff. There's a good chance that Jesus had effectively burned bridges with most of them and that most would just dismiss him as a misguided radical. However, I like to imagine that maybe a couple of them went home and thought about what they'd done, and realized that it wasn't Jesus who had the problem, it was them.

That has happened to me. The most striking time was when, as a freshman in college, I had a professor who invited an openly gay minister to come and speak to our religion and society class. Up until that point, I had been repulsed by the whole conversation about homosexuality. I could point to a couple of seemingly strong biblical statements to back up my views. I'd used gay jokes throughout my life, not knowing I was hurting people all around me. In the presentation, the gay minister talked about his hurt, and he named aloud one of the jokes that was most hurtful to him—a joke that had come out of my mouth as a youth. My eyes were stinging, and I wanted to run. I did not want to hear another word from this man who claimed to be speaking a Christian view. Even if it was the voice of Christ, I didn't want to hear it. I did not want to let his moving, personal story trump the "truth." But I tell you, within a couple of days, I had done a 180-degree turn on my feelings about homosexual persons and became, then, an advocate for the church's full acceptance of gay, lesbian, bisexual, and transgendered Christians.

Have you heard him? Have you heard the voice of Christ in the places where the rubber hits the road in our society? What's he saying to you? If you *hear* Christ, and then share Christ on matters of justice, the gospel continues to be good news. Amen.

4

A Captive to the Spirit

August 26, 2005

> I did not shrink from doing anything helpful, proclaiming the message to you and teaching you publicly and from house to house, as I testified to both Jews and Greeks about repentance toward God and faith toward our Lord Jesus. And now, as a captive to the Spirit, I am on my way to Jerusalem, not knowing what will happen to me there, except that the Holy Spirit testifies to me in every city that imprisonment and persecutions are waiting for me. But I do not count my life of any value to myself, if only I may finish my course and the ministry that I received from the Lord Jesus, to testify to the good news of God's grace. (Acts 20:20–24)

I remember the first time I read the book of Acts I was very skeptical—uncomfortable really—with many of the accounts. My skepticism was rooted in one thing: the stories sounded too much like a repeat of the Jesus narrative. Oh, I thought, early believers were just trying to celebrate their early saints, trying to make them sound like they were *just like Jesus*. What made me uncomfortable was this notion that somehow humans could live in ways that so reflected the life of Jesus of Nazareth. Jesus is my Lord and is unique. His life, death, and resurrection were unique events. Peter, Paul, and the other early amazing disciples are not my Lord. Why did the book of Acts have to make them sound so similar to Jesus in the way they lived their lives?

Section One—Preparing the Church to Confront Other Kingdoms

I was particularly uncomfortable with the chapters that told about Paul's return to Jerusalem. After preaching in cities and towns throughout the northeast Mediterranean region, Paul turns his face toward Jerusalem and prepares to face persecution and possible death. In the passages we heard this morning, Paul stops off at two towns where he has established and supported churches. He wanted to say good-bye to his friends in the faith. Did you hear the echoes of the end of Jesus' life in the two readings this morning? I did.

In Acts 20, Paul gives a farewell message to Christians in Ephesus. He says to them, and I paraphrase, "I've lived out my years testifying to the good news of God's grace; I will not see you again. Now I am heading to Jerusalem, not knowing what will happen to me there, except that the Holy Spirit testifies to me in every city that imprisonment and persecution are waiting for me." Paul sounds like Jesus there, saying farewell to his disciples. It sounds like Jesus telling his disciples in Matthew 20:18–19, "See, we are going up to Jerusalem and the Son of Man will be handed over to the chief priests and the scribes, and they will condemn him to death; then they will hand him over to the Gentiles to be mocked and flogged and crucified."

In Acts 21 the similarities between Paul's approach to impending death and Jesus' get even stronger. A visiting prophet, Agabus, enacts the way Paul will be arrested by Jews in Jerusalem, and then handed over to the Gentiles. The disciples plead with Paul not to go there. Paul, however, is convinced, saying, "I am ready not only to be bound but even to die in Jerusalem for the name of the Lord Jesus."[1] Paul's followers respond by quoting Jesus when he was praying in Gethsemane the night of his betrayal. They try to persuade Paul not to go, but then say, "The Lord's will be done."[2]

Paul is scorned, tortured, and bound in Jerusalem. He goes through great pains for the gospel. He isn't killed, but he easily could have been. He preaches in the temple and, like Jesus, is arrested by his own people. Like Jesus, he is turned over to the Gentiles. How was he able to live fearlessly, yet keep walking into the face of trouble? I think he answers the question for us when he describes himself as a "captive to the Spirit."[3]

Friends, the thing that used to bother me is now the thing that greatly excites me about the book of Acts. In the past I was bothered by

1. Acts 21:13b.
2. Ibid., 21:14b.
3. Ibid., 20:22.

the glorification of Paul and the other faithful disciples, who were treated as if they could live lives that were so much like Jesus' earthly life. But that's the shocking, good news today. Because of God's grace, because of Jesus' life and death, because he extended the Spirit to Paul, Peter, Lydia, Mary Magdalene, you, and me, we can all be captives to the Spirit. The Spirit of a loving, gracious God, the Spirit that anointed Jesus, can capture you and let you live in ways that echo the life of Jesus, even echoing his life to the point of death on a cross.

Has the Spirit captured you, leading you in ways you never could have imagined? I hope your answer is yes. I hope your human spirit is so wrapped up with the Holy Spirit that the image of being "captured" is a beautiful one. You've been captured by the Spirit of the creator, redeemer, and sustainer of every living thing! Take a moment to think of some of the ways you've been "captured" by the Spirit.

But here's the hard question: To what *extent* have you been captured by the Spirit? It's hard to measure, isn't it? I mean, what's the range? What are the possibilities? Am I asking, on a scale of one to ten—with ten being the highest—how "captured" are you by the Spirit? No, not really. What I'm really saying is this: most of the time when we are living as people captured by the Spirit, positive results occur. We have healthier churches, healthier people, happier relationships, and better social care for those who are vulnerable. Most of the time the presence of the Spirit in individual and community leads to life that seems to look more and more like the kingdom of God.

But sometimes to be captive to the Spirit means to be led to the proverbial Jerusalem, led into great risk and danger. Sometimes it means to address and challenge the church or the state, to address and challenge a wayward friend, or a bitter enemy. Paul says, "I am heading to Jerusalem, not knowing what will happen to me there."[4] Sometimes being captive to the Spirit means to have someone tell you just how dangerous the situation is going to be, and then going into it anyway.

I'm not calling for foolishness here. I'm not calling for us to rush into all sorts of trouble for no reason. But I am suggesting that Spirit-people get called to do really hard tasks. Our Spirit-captured lives can reflect the life of the Spirit-captured Jesus all the way to the cross. I think I know now why I was originally uncomfortable with Acts of the Apostles. These Christians, these followers of Jesus, are just a little too daring. They take

4. Ibid.

Section One—Preparing the Church to Confront Other Kingdoms

too many risks; it couldn't be true that they had confidence that looked like the confidence of Jesus. But I know now that it is possible. They were able to do it because they'd been captured by the Spirit of God. To what extent are you captive to the Spirit?

At a church leadership meeting recently, we were talking about a passage from John 7 in which Jesus says, "Let anyone who is thirsty come to me and let the one who believes in me drink."[5] Continuing, he says, "When you come to me and drink . . . out of the believer's heart shall flow rivers of living water."[6] Jesus goes on to say that the water he gives us to drink, and the water that flows out of us, is the Spirit. Water can be refreshing, but remember that rivers and oceans can also be wild and dangerous at times. That's what today's passage is about: It's about the Spirit being dangerous sometimes. After the meeting, I got to thinking about a kids' song I know that goes, "I've got a river of life flowing out of me. Makes the lame to walk and the blind to see. Opens prison doors, sets the captives free. I've got a river of life flowing out of me. Spring up o' well, splish splash . . ." Well, that song is sung almost like a jingle, but the content of the song is no jingle.

We're captured, and the river of life flowing out of us should make us concerned about blindness and polio and all sorts of diseases and ailments. The river of life flowing out of us should make Christians front-runners in getting health care to all people. The river of life should make us concerned about the three million people in US prisons, including those held at Guantanamo Bay without charges. The river of life should give us the confidence to organize as people of faith, to address these atrocities. We're captive to the Spirit that moved Jesus to confront the world with God's love and justice even unto death.

Maybe someday God will raise up someone from our church to be captive to the Spirit in ways that go against usual sensibilities. Maybe someone will be captive to the Spirit and lead the charge in challenging our government for spending $360 billion on war this year. Maybe someone will become a Paul, a Martin Luther King Jr., an Abe Lincoln, a Mother Theresa. Maybe someone here will say in words similar to Paul, "I do not count my life of any value to myself, if only I may finish my course and the ministry that I received from the Lord Jesus. I am captive to the

---

5. John 7:37b–38a.
6. Ibid., 7:38b.

Spirit." And if you do, I pray we will be a community of faith that, after pleading with you to be careful, finally says, "Thy will be done, O Lord."

I know why we're called "Christians," and not "Spirit-ans." God knew too. The Spirit of God has always been blowing and moving throughout the world, through occasional prophets, ancient religions, and in communities throughout Earth. But it took Jesus—it took God-in-Flesh living among us, for us to see who we could be! We needed incarnated guidance! And it still takes reflecting on Jesus, reflecting on his way of living in the Spirit, for us to make sure we are following the Spirit in a way that is pleasing to God.

I hope as we look to Jesus to open our eyes to the ways of God, we will do so knowing that all the potential of God is packed inside us, and inside this community, to follow Christ to the *fullest extent*—for we are captive to the Spirit. Amen.

5

Jesus Brings out the Worst In Herod

January 12, 2003

> Then Herod secretly called for the wise men and learned from them the exact time when the star had appeared. Then he sent them to Bethlehem, saying, "Go and search diligently for the child; and when you have found him, bring me word so that I may also go and pay him homage." . . . And having been warned in a dream not to return to Herod, they left for their own country by another road. . . . When Herod saw that he had been tricked by the wise men, he was infuriated, and he sent and killed all the children in and around Bethlehem who were two years old or under, according to the time that he had learned from the wise men. Then was fulfilled what had been spoken through the prophet Jeremiah: "A voice was heard in Ramah, wailing and loud lamentation, Rachel weeping for her children; she refused to be consoled, because they are no more." (Matthew 2:7–8, 12,16–18)

During the Christmas season the church meticulously remembers the details of the birth narrative of Jesus Christ. We hear about the interplay between angels and Jesus' various family members and new shepherd friends. We hear about a star and wise men from afar. And then, after five or six weeks of talking about the advent, the coming of the Christ child, we skip to speaking of his baptism at age thirty and his subsequent ministry. Just like that, we jump thirty years or so. It's time to move on, it

Jesus Brings out the Worst In Herod

really is. We don't spend this many liturgical weeks speaking of any other given event. But please let me have one more.

There is a detailed story woven into the gospel narrative that often gets skipped over by preachers during the Christmas season. It's the *full* story of the wise men—foreigners, who had seen the light of a holy star indicating the birth of a king, and who had accidentally tipped off Herod about the birth of the one called "king of the Jews." Herod felt incredibly threatened. That was *his* title! His political rule was, in his mind, challenged by the birth of this infant Christ. He was so anxious about what the birth of Christ implied that he tried to quell this political threat with violence.

He asked the wise men to return to him after their Bethlehem visit, to tell him the exact whereabouts of the Christ child. Then, he secretly thought, he could stop this uprising at its source. He would take the life of this child challenger. But the wise men had been warned in a dream not to return to Herod. Herod didn't get the information he was after, and his response was to lash out against the entire region.

Herod, in his anger and fear, called for the destruction of all children in Bethlehem. Every kid, from birth through two years, lost their lives, for they were such powerful and threatening rivals to the throne of Herod. The Lord had appeared to Joseph in a dream before this happened, warning him that Herod was after the baby. Quickly Joseph, Mary, and the child walked to Egypt. They must have slept on the cold ground, traveling by night, resting by day, trying to stay out of the direct hit of the scorching sun and Herod's search party. Jesus and his parents were the lucky ones. Scripture says that the weeping in Bethlehem the day Herod's army came through was like that of Rachel, who wept after the destruction of the northern kingdom of Israel, which was the lineage of her two sons, the tribes of Benjamin and Joseph. Jeremiah said that when the northern tribes fell to Assyria in 722 BC, the voice of Rachel could be heard crying out from her grave, for the lineage of her sons was no more.

Matthew tells us that the crying and wailing in Bethlehem was like *that*, just weeks after the birth of Jesus Christ, Messiah, Lord of the world.

I had been a wise man in children's pageants for years as a kid before I ever heard the full story. Somehow we decide not to talk about it. However, the story about the attempted murder of baby Jesus and the genocide carried out against innocent children in Bethlehem is the longest section of Matthew's rendering of the birth narrative. All of chapter 2 is really connected to this account. Obviously Matthew wanted the story to be told.

Why was Herod so mad? Didn't Herod know that Jesus wasn't a political leader? Didn't Herod know about the separation of church and state? Didn't he know that these foreign wise men who came asking about the "king of the Jews" were just talking figuratively? No, no, and no.

Herod saw Jesus as a political threat.

And you know what? Herod was right. That is exactly what Jesus was and is. Jesus Christ is a threat to any politician who promotes a plan for anything other than a plan of positive peace, anything other than a plan of perfect love.

Herod, the great, was from the southernmost region of Judah, the region called Idumea. Idumeans had, some sixty years before Herod's rise to power, been "forced" to become Jewish, at least in name as the result of a military loss. Therefore Herod was, technically, Jewish. Scholars disagree about whether Herod was a practicing Jew or not. Whether or not he was, there is proof of numerous ways that he helped Jewish religion and culture during his reign. His greatest achievement was to rebuild the temple in Jerusalem. Herod rose to power through military connections with Julius Caesar, and was eventually given Roman citizenship and made procurator of Judea, king of the Jews. At the time of Jesus' birth, Herod had been reigning for close to forty years. He'd maintained his rule by being faithful to Rome and to the various Caesars—first Julius Caesar and now, at the time of Christ's birth, Augustus Caesar. His efforts had helped stabilize Roman political authority along an important trade route, and helped elevate Caesar to the level of divinity.[1]

As New Testament scholar NT Wright says, "Caesar was well on his way to becoming the supreme divinity in the Greco-Roman world, maintaining his vast empire not simply by force—though there was of course plenty of that—but by the development of a flourishing religion that seemed to be trumping most others either by absorption or by greater attraction. Caesar, by being a servant of the state, had provided justice and peace to the whole world. He was therefore to be hailed as Lord and trusted as Savior"[2] The imperial cult of Rome, worship of Caesar, was the religion *par excellence*. But Caesar and his government allowed other religions to flourish, as long as they paid homage, and taxes, to Rome.

1. *Harpers Bible Dictionary*, s.v. "Herod," 385, 387.
2. Wright, "Paul's Gospel," 4.

Herod walked the fine line of being a Jew and king of a Jewish state, while at the same time acting in ways that were pleasing to Caesar. He maintained relative peace in Judea by allowing Jewish religion to operate, as long as it didn't interfere with the political and social practices advocated by Rome. He gave the Sadducees, leaders of organized Judaism, special privileges. It is clear, too, that a Jewish court—the Sanhedrin—existed and operated in conjunction with Herod's court.

First-century historians give a mixed report on Herod. There are many great achievements that he masterminded and brought to completion. But he was also in cahoots with Caesar, pushing Caesar's tax and civic policies with tremendous personal benefit. He was also brutal when stirred to anger. He would lash out militarily at anyone who challenged his rule. He had risen to power by the sword, and believed in it.[3]

The times required that the people of Israel operate within the system given them by Roman rule; but the hope for a Messiah was definitely present even during that time. In the Hebrew Scripture, the word "Messiah" ("Anointed One") was used to refer to various divine appointments to the role of priest or king. Politically, a Messiah was one whom God would appoint in continuity with the lineage of King David.

Herod was called "king of the Jews" by those who were ruling in Rome and had appointed him procurator. But the people of Israel knew the way God had worked in the past, to anoint a special one. And they were awaiting a Messiah, *one whom God would appoint*, not one appointed by the distant dictator of Rome. And he came in the form of a poor child. And foreigners passed through Jerusalem to Bethlehem to pay *him* homage. Herod, a ruler with almost forty years under his belt, was scared. The text says, "all Jerusalem" was scared—that is, all who were in government appointments and places of privilege due to Herod's reign. Herod and company responded accordingly. There was weeping in Bethlehem, and Mary, Joseph, and Jesus were driven away from their homeland and Jewish community. The one born king of the Jews wasn't even allowed to grow up near the Jews.

There is nothing good about the brutal attempt on Jesus' life. There is nothing good about genocide against children in Bethlehem. This isn't one of those sermons where I can nicely wrap things up by saying, "Hear the good news" and then feed you the punch line of one of God's eternal promises.

3. *Harper's Bible Dictionary*, s.v. "Herod," 385, 387.

Section One—Preparing the Church to Confront Other Kingdoms

However, even amidst the bloodshed and brokenness of this passage, a central truth of the gospel comes to light. Jesus brings out the worst in Herod. Let me say it more clearly. Jesus unveils, strips away, and peels back the façade of the "good king Herod" and exposes the horrors that are part of his identity. That doesn't mean that Herod was a purely evil person. But it does mean that he had qualities that didn't make him fit for being a true nation builder who had the will of the people in mind. To say that he was 100% bad wouldn't be accurate, but he did promote a "negative peace" in the land; a peace that wasn't really peace at all because it had to be maintained by brutal force and other injustices.

At Christmas we say that the Son of God came down and dwelt among us. The presence of God came upon us, bringing good tidings of great joy. But something else happened, too, at Christmas. In the birth of the infant Messiah, the truth about false gods of power, domination, and oppression were revealed for what they were. The face of the child who is prince of peace had the power to reveal all that was false, wrong, and broken in the world. And this is a gift that Jesus and the suffering babies in Bethlehem gave us. *They revealed the face of evil, that we would not stagnantly and passively accept it as a way of life any longer.*

The eyes of every family in Bethlehem were opened to the true Herod the night of the infant genocide. The ears of every surrounding community were opened to the true Herod that night when cries were heard all the way from Bethlehem. The face of abusive power, the manifestation of less-than-full life was thrown in their faces, revealed by the light of the Christ child.

The Christ child reveals what is beautiful and right, and he brings out the worst in Herod. The apostle Paul says the church of Jesus Christ is called to be "in Christ." We are called to be "the body of Christ." In the first century, those were political terms, to be "in" or "the body of" a leader was a way of talking about being part of the royal family. We are, as a community, the lineage of a royal family, the family of the Messiah, the infant Christ. And we have a responsibility to tell the old, old story of our family leader, Jesus the Christ, clearly enough that it continues to have this dual effect of bringing joy and hope and *unveiling every false politician and practice.*

Throughout the ages there are examples of churches that have lived up to the calling. They've lived the story well. I want to give two recent examples: In El Salvador in the 1970s and 80s, local Roman Catholic parishes manifested the joyful presence of the infant Christ in the way they lived out their communal lives. The Catholic Church had the inclusivity of the inn in Bethlehem. All were invited in, the poor were lifted up, outsiders were made insiders, peace was sought after, Communion was offered to all, and prayers for the world and for El Salvador were lifted up publicly. It was a church of good will. In other words, the church truly started worshiping and living for the prince of peace!

But in El Salvador in the 1980s the local Catholic church also exposed the face of evil, corruption, destruction, and hatred in the ruling class—the Herods of El Salvador. They exposed the ways that the world community, including the United States, supported that regime in various ways. And the Catholic priests and congregants of El Salvador paid for it dearly. The number of church people assassinated was stunning. Archbishop Oscar Romero, theologians and nuns, and tens of thousands of common believers were killed in El Salvador.

It was a horrific time, and *may it be the case someday that exposing Herod doesn't lead to a blood bath*. However, as Martin Luther King Jr. said about others who suffered unjustly, "They did not die in vain, God still has a way of wringing good out of evil."[4] There have been changes in El Salvador—not enough, but some—and there is international awareness about what happened.

On September 15, 1963, white supremacists placed a bomb in the Sunday School at 16th St. Baptist Church in Birmingham, Alabama. It ripped the building apart and took the life of three little girls. In a place where the prince of peace was worshiped and learned about and kids were being grounded in a life pattern of love, hope, and joy, the powers of destruction made their presence felt.

Martin Luther King Jr. gave the eulogy, and he had this to say:

> The innocent blood of these little girls may well serve as the redemptive force that will bring new light to this dark city. The death of these little children may lead our whole Southland from the low road of man's inhumanity to man to the high road of peace and brotherhood. The spilt blood of these innocent girls may cause the whole citizenry of Birmingham to transform the negative extremes of a dark past into the positive extremes of a bright future. Indeed, this tragic event may cause the white South to come to terms with its conscience.[5]

4. King, "Eulogy for the Young Victims," 18 Sept 1963.
5. Ibid.

Section One—Preparing the Church to Confront Other Kingdoms

It is a sick world where the innocent death of children serves as our wake-up call, but may the wake-up call at least come *then*. There are times when Herod, and prime ministers and presidents walk in ways that are consistent with the ways of Christ—thank God for that. There are times when communities shaped under Herod, and prime ministers and presidents and policy makers walk in ways consistent with Christ—thank God for that too. But there are times when they don't. Lots of times. We, the church, must never sell our souls to the politics of this world in a way that puts Herod and Jesus, or Caesar and Jesus, or Democrats and Jesus, or Republicans and Jesus, on equal ground. Because we only have one king and he has something to say to all the others.

For the world to be a healthy world it needs to be shaped by the prince of peace, the Messiah, and it can't do that if the church that worships him also calls Herod "Lord." If the Herods of our day are always happy with the church, always ready to come bow before the Christ child, we should be wary. If they're doing that, it's probably not the Christ child who is in the manger. If Herod comes and happily acknowledges the rising of a new prince, it's quite possible that the one in the mangers of our churches has his own face, his own little smile. There are times when this has happened.

The baby in the manger of many churches in Germany in the early part of the 20th century had an anti-Semitic smile. The baby in the manger of many churches in America had a face that accepted racism. We should always be asking ourselves, "Who's the baby in our manger?" May the only face in that manger be that of the Christ Child, the Messiah, the prince of peace.

When Christ came close as an infant, an amazing period of inclusivity, freedom, joy, and goodwill was born. But when Christ came close, the principalities and powers knew they were under siege. For a child had been born, a son had been given. And the governments will forever be on his shoulders. Amen.

6

Getting Zacchaeus into and out of the Tree

November 5, 2007

> He entered Jericho and was passing through it. A man was there named Zacchaeus; he was a chief tax collector and was rich. He was trying to see who Jesus was, but on account of the crowd he could not, because he was short in stature. So he ran ahead and climbed a sycamore tree to see him, because he was going to pass that way. When Jesus came to the place, he looked up and said to him, "Zacchaeus, hurry and come down; for I must stay at your house today." So he hurried down and was happy to welcome him. All who saw it began to grumble and said, "He has gone to be the guest of one who is a sinner." Zacchaeus stood there and said to the Lord, "Look, half of my possessions, Lord, I will give to the poor; and if I have defrauded anyone of anything, I will pay back four times as much." Then Jesus said to him, "Today salvation has come to this house, because he too is a son of Abraham. For the Son of Man came to seek out and to save the lost." (Luke 19:1–10)

Zacchaeus was a wee little man and a wee little man was he. You know, it's a cute Sunday School song, but not accurate. He might have been short, but he was not a wee little man. In fact, this story is about an incredibly strong man; the only person in all of the New Testament, the only person in all of Greek literature for that matter, called "*Architelones*," chief tax collector. Napoleon was a wee little man too.

Section One—Preparing the Church to Confront Other Kingdoms

Tax collectors in Israel were Jewish men who worked for the Roman government, collecting taxes from fellow Jews. Tax collectors were obligated to pay the Roman empire a particular tax collected from the people. I imagine it was an incredibly stressful job, with Rome breathing down your back, insisting that you meet quotas. But for your troubles, you could be well compensated. Tax collectors could charge whatever "overhead" they desired to charge.[1] This bought them some security. In case Rome upped the ante suddenly, demanding more money, they had it. And this ability to charge extra, padded their pockets. We can only imagine that a "chief" tax collector must have been even more exorbitantly wealthy due to fraud than other tax collectors. He got rich by putting financial pressure upon an already heavily taxed public.

So it must have been absolutely shocking to see Zacchaeus up in a tree. It's completely out of character. Zacchaeus is one of those guys who travel around in a stretch Hummer, driven right up to the door of fancy government buildings. Zacchaeus is one of the those guys who travels all around the world, but never see the faces of the poor, or middle class for that matter, because he's always given the biggest room at the fanciest hotel. Sycamore trees in the Middle East had long branches that dipped down, so it's not hard to think of someone getting into the tree; it's just hard to think of *that guy* in a tree, surrounded by crowds of common people. Who's the least likely person you can imagine up in a tree? That's who he was—he was dressed just like that.

But friends, Jesus got Zacchaeus to go up in the tree.

How'd he do it? Had Zacchaeus heard he was extending forgiveness to tax collectors? It was only a chapter or two earlier where Jesus told about a tax collector going to heaven! Was Zacchaeus' heart softened to think he might be given another chance by God, to make new ethical choices in terms of his vocation?

Had Zacchaeus heard of Jesus healing the sick? Maybe Zacchaeus had given coins to the blind beggar outside the city, the one who Jesus healed just before getting to Jericho. Or, maybe Zacchaeus heard about him in the board room, where tax collectors worried that a new movement among the peasant population was on the rise; a new movement claiming the rules of the "kingdom of God," a new movement with a dynamic leader. Maybe it was a little of all of this.

---

1. *Harper's Bible Dictionary*, s.v. "Publicans," 841.

Getting Zacchaeus into and out of the Tree

We will never know just what it was that got Zacchaeus up in the tree. But we *do know* that in a short time Jesus' way of living in the world was dynamic enough to reach the ears, peak the interest, even influence the behavior of Zacchaeus. A man thoroughly entrenched in "the system," broke out and climbed a tree. Another way to say it is that *Jesus' faith, Jesus' hope-filled drive toward God's good future* got Zacchaeus into the tree.

We don't talk about Jesus' faith too often. We talk more about us "having faith in Jesus." But Jesus is our Lord, not just because he is Son of God above us, but also because he displayed contagious faith in the way he lived for God. That's what got Zacchaeus up in the tree—Jesus' faith lived out in daily life.

Can you remember climbing up into the sycamore tree yourself? What was the experience of encountering Christ that was so compelling you threw off all concern about what anyone else thought, and you climbed the branches, for a better look? What was so compelling? And how did he come to you? Did he come to you through the stories about him in Scripture, or through some person in your life who knows him and emulates Christ's faith? What got you into the tree?

I think it's a good place to start, to remember how you got into the tree in the first place. Or, if you haven't ever had a compelling experience with Jesus that made you want to climb up so you could see him, maybe this sermon is, today, a call to you, to find ways to get to know him better. You need to "go sycamore" yourself, before you can hope to get Zacchaeus up there.

But the main message today is about Zacchaeus, and I want to talk about who Zacchaeus is, and about how Christian faith—our Christ-like faith—might be a way God is going to get him up in the tree. Today I want to identify Zacchaeus and talk about getting him up there—again, and again, and again.

Getting Zacchaeus in the tree was so significant to the people because to get him in the tree was to get the local symbol of an economic and political system that hurt people into the tree. The system that was warped by greed, power, insider trading, the power of a foreign empire, all this was in the tree, staring down at Jesus, as he passed through the city, surrounded by, primarily, the victims of the system.

Section One—Preparing the Church to Confront Other Kingdoms

Friends, live out your faith with such commitment to God, in all areas of your life, that Zacchaeus takes notice. If he does, he may just go up in the tree to get a better look.

This faith that we proclaim, this Jesus to whom we've given our lives, is worth climbing trees for, in business clothes, or a military uniform, or with a crown on your head. This faith that we proclaim is so radical that Wall Street executives, our president, military commanders in Iraq, bankers, and all people with Zacchaeus-like power ought to get up in a tree, just to look down at him, us, and his church, as we walk along the road.

It seems to me, most of the time Zacchaeus finds more compelling things to do, more compelling advice to follow, than the voice of the church committed to God's kingdom. Sometimes the blame there can be placed squarely on Zacchaeus himself. He wears a thick blindfold sometimes, and headphones; but sometimes I think the blame goes to Zacchaeus too quickly. Some of the blame can go to us. The faith displayed by our Lord is contagious faith. We ought to be contagious, not just to others in our neighborhoods, not just to others in our immediate circles, but to Zacchaeus and all he represents.

We followers of Jesus Christ have a role in changing Zacchaeus, converting him, and we do this when we start behaving in ways that cross Zacchaeus's path, and desk. If we believe that God wants all aspects of life to be locations for salvation, that means that our lives together, as the church, should impact all structures: economic, health care, environmental, military, political, social, racial, gender and sexual, housing, credit, education, world trade, borders, and religion.

If we believe that God wants all aspects of life to be locations for salvation to be in-breaking, that means our individual lives start being lived in ways that challenge the structures. The ethical decisions you make at work, the places where you decide to spend your money, the way you volunteer, the letters you write to Congress, the dreams you dream and build on, the people you care about and advocate for, all these things not only bless you by connecting you to God and the individuals who receive your direct service, they also get the word out to Zacchaeus.

Too often, I think, Christians give up on Zacchaeus before even giving him a chance. We assume the worst about world systems, assuming they are unredeemable, that they'll never change their minds about things. And it's true they won't change their minds—because they don't have minds or hearts—but people do! Systems are made up of people, people created in the image of God. Zacchaeus reminds us that a compelling enough faith can lead to radical transformations in systems.

If we're fortunate enough, with God's help, to get Zacchaeus up there, to a place where he can see Jesus, then there's another step to the process. He's got to be invited down. That's our job too. And that's as hard, if not harder, than getting him up there. It's hard to forgive someone who's taken advantage of you time and time again. It's hard to trust someone who steals from his own people. But Jesus doesn't seem to struggle with forgiveness, and the ease with which forgiveness flows is a healing force of incredible magnitude. "Zacchaeus, come on down, I'm coming for supper." Zacchaeus hurried, came down, and was happy to welcome him. And we don't hear anything about a conversation that passed between them. But suddenly Zacchaeus says, "Lord, half of my possessions I will give to the poor; and if I have defrauded anyone of anything, I will pay back four times as much." And Jesus said, in effect, "You've just displayed that salvation has come to this house . . . the Son of Man came to seek out and save the lost. You, Zacchaeus, are clearly found."

Whatever Zacchaeus had heard before Jesus came to town got him into the tree. And Jesus' open invitation to "come down and be in fellowship with me," was enough to not only get Zacchaeus out of the tree, but also out of a system of wrongdoing and false dealings.

This was, of course, good for Zacchaeus, but it was also good for poor people.

Zacchaeus following Jesus means more money in the pocket, more food on the table, better clothing on the kids. Zacchaeus following Jesus means more money for affordable housing so that young people and poor people can get on their feet and have a chance to succeed. Zacchaeus following Jesus means less money on guns and more money on health care. Zacchaeus following Jesus means fewer cases of AIDS in India and Africa. Friends, we've underestimated the importance of converting Zacchaeus. The world can't afford the separation of church and state, if that means the church stops bringing the will of God to bear on the "Zacchaeuses" that run the state and all the systems of the world.

Friends of Jesus Christ, today we celebrate Communion. We celebrate a meal that replenishes us, so that we might be full of Christ. As people made full of Christ, by Christ, let's live our faith with passion, not shying away from Zacchaeus, assuming there's no way he can change.

Section One—Preparing the Church to Confront Other Kingdoms

Let's not assume the worst about Zacchaeus, judging him un-redeemable, because of his many faults. Instead, let's lovingly confront the systems where he maneuvers. He may just climb a tree. And if he does, let's invite him to supper at our place. Amen.

7

Caesar Is God's Puppet and Doesn't Even Know!

December 24, 2007

> In those days a decree went out from Emperor Augustus that all the world should be registered. This was the first registration and was taken while Quirinius was governor of Syria. All went to their own towns to be registered. Joseph also went from the town of Nazareth in Galilee to Judea, to the city of David called Bethlehem, because he was descended from the house and family of David. He went to be registered with Mary, to whom he was engaged and who was expecting a child. While they were there, the time came for her to deliver her child. And she gave birth to her firstborn son and wrapped him in bands of cloth, and laid him in a manger, because there was no place for them in the inn. (Luke 2:1–7)

Once upon a time a man with an immense amount of power, Emperor Augustus, Caesar Augustus, ruler of the entire Roman world, issued a decree. I'm sure he issued lots of decrees, but this one matters to us because it intersects with the birth of Jesus.

He issued a decree that the world—his Roman empire world—be registered. It may have been an enrollment for tax purposes—there is historical evidence of a tax registration at about that time—though honestly the dating of that registration creates a bit of a conundrum, since it happened when Jesus is thought to have been ten years of age. Also, the evidence of that tax registration says nothing of people traveling to their ancestral villages. Tax enrollments were headcounts.

Another possibility was that it was an enrollment for military purposes. Caesar was always in the process of territorial expansion, and that required an ever-growing military. Quirinius, in particular, was noted for his military accomplishments in the region.[1] Maybe Caesar Augustus sent people to their ancestral hometowns to ensure that there was ethnic/tribal balance in the fighting forces he was creating.

Whether it was for tax purposes or military purposes, what we know is that his decree about a registration had poor people—all people, really—running around, getting back to their ancestral lands. It would have taken Mary and Joseph at least a couple of weeks to walk from Galilee to Bethlehem, and she was eight months-plus pregnant! No coolers, so food preparation would have been hard. No 7-Eleven along the way. No Wawa. But even with the inconvenience, the text gives us no indication of resistance or frustration. This is just how the world worked. Caesar called the shots, and his word interrupted their lives—that's just how it was.

It's a common story, isn't it? I think I heard it just this year. Decrees are issued all the time. Maybe there isn't a Caesar who is as almighty as that first-century one, but the collection of Caesars is awfully strong. Caesars of our marketplace can declare a change in interest rates and set the nation scrambling. Caesars of the *global marketplace* can create new trade agreements that result in people leaving their Nazareth, looking for a Bethlehem, because the economy of their Nazareth has disappeared overnight.

Caesars of the media market can declare a new TV series as *the best*, propping it up with intense advertising, and suddenly there is no Christmas without tickets to see Hannah Montana. Caesars of the government declare which nations are our friends and foes, and suddenly visa restrictions tighten, and people can no longer return to their countries to visit their families or just as abruptly they *have to* return—no longer welcome on this soil. Caesars can declare war, and suddenly hundreds of thousands of Americans are in Iraq—displaced, and millions of Iraqis are wandering around their country and around neighboring countries—displaced.

I used to think that Caesar Augustus's request that all the world go to their hometown to register was just an awful decree, but comparing it

1. Craddock, *Luke*, 34.

Caesar Is God's Puppet and Doesn't Even Know!

to the decrees that are made by these modern Caesars, this one was fairly low impact. We aren't told what it did to the tax situation down the road, or whether it resulted in a bunch of Joseph's peers being conscripted to do battle on the frontier of the Roman empire. But from what we know, anyway, it seems fairly low impact.

Caesars make decrees—and we scramble. That's the way the world works.

But there is another who issues decrees. In that region of Bethlehem, where Mary and Joseph traveled, there were shepherds. And one night, while they were watching their sheep, they were visited by a herald of God. Unlike the heralds who came by boat or chariot and horses from Rome, this herald came from the sky. Bright light and flashing surrounded him and he said, "Do not be afraid." (Yeah, right). "I am bringing you good news of great joy for all the people; to you is born this day in the city of David a Savior, who is the Messiah, the Lord. This will be a sign for you: you will find the child wrapped in bands of cloth and lying in a manger."[2] Then a backup choir of heralds arrived, angels all around singing, "Glory to God . . . and on Earth peace among those whom he favors."[3]

And the shepherds scrambled—set in motion, not by a decree from Caesar, but by a decree from God. "Let's leave it all behind, leave the sheep, run man! He's born in the city of David. You know what that means, right? It means God has been faithful to the covenant promises. There will be one from the house of David seated on the throne forever, just as he said! The anointed one has been born to David's line! A son of the line of King David; David, the king who started out as a shepherd like us, in these very hills!"

When they got to Bethlehem they found exactly what had been promised. They came upon a young mom, dad, and a little baby. They were out-of-towners, this couple, with ancient connections to the place. There was nothing special about the birth location. In fact, it was disturbingly humble. Not only no halo, but no bed either, for mother or baby—just animals, straw, and a feeding trough.

But they didn't need any other proof. "Mary, Joseph, everybody! We're here because God's angel told us about this child. He is going to

2. Luke 2:10–12.
3. Ibid., 2:14.

bring peace to all the people! He is the anointed one, our savior, born in the city of David!"

"And all who heard it were amazed at what the shepherds told them," about the decree from God, delivered by an angel choir.[4]

The "all who heard it" were a lot of people. Thanks to Caesar, everyone with a David connection was back in town. The little village of one hundred people looked more like Woodstock, or the parking lot at a Jets game—all the inns filled, all the fields cramped with tents, grills hot with brats and steaks. And what they heard, that day in Bethlehem, was a decree that God was making good on God's promises.

The shepherd's news wouldn't have been totally new news to Mary and Joseph. They knew, of course, that something was up. A virgin birth and angelic visits gave them a clue. But for the rest of this bulging Bethlehem, this news from the shepherds was earth shattering. What joy! They were all together in Bethlehem for the first time in ages, and God was breaking in with big news. *Thanks be to Caesar Augustus.*

Yes, you heard me right. Caesar played a key role in the birth of the Messiah. Caesar Augustus, the powerful, didn't know it, but God used him as a servant, a stagehand, a puppet, to prepare the way of the Lord. An advent tool, a handmade of the Lord, Caesar Augustus! Without Caesar Augustus' need for an enrollment, Jesus would have been born in Nazareth—a place with no historical connection to God's promises to God's people.

Without Caesar Augustus, Judeans wouldn't have been gathered from their diaspora, for a big family reunion/registration.

Without Caesar Augustus, the ancestors of David wouldn't have been in Bethlehem in force when the magi showed up, announcing that even from foreign lands they could tell, through the stars, that a new king had been born!

Without Caesar Augustus, Jesus' parents wouldn't have been close enough to Jerusalem to take him to the temple for his naming ceremony. But since Bethlehem was just a stone's throw away, they got to meet two old prophets, Simeon and Anna; prophets who, inspired by the Spirit, lifted Jesus into the air saying, "Master, now you are dismissing your servant in peace . . . for my eyes have seen your salvation, which you have prepared in the presence of all peoples!"[5]

4. Ibid., 2:18.
5. Ibid., 2:29–31.

Caesar Is God's Puppet and Doesn't Even Know!

Did Caesar know he was a puppet—a servant of God? He'll probably never know. How about the Caesars of today? I am not suggesting that Caesars, in all ways, are carrying out the will of God. I wouldn't want to be misunderstood here. The actions of Caesar need to be constantly watched and challenged, by people of faith. But also, while we challenge, we should look for God's will being worked out in spite of, and sometime through, the very disturbing and frustrating actions of Caesar. Sometimes the way God chooses to work to bring about peace on Earth are through dastardly and frustrating acts of real politics.

Luke could have told the story of Jesus' birth without bringing up Caesar Augustus or Governor Quirinius. He could have just written that Joe and Mary went to visit their cousins in Bethlehem. But he chose to say that it was by no desire of their own; in fact, it was at the whim of an emperor that the stage was set for angelic choirs, a barnyard birth, and visits from magi and shepherds. And I think he did that because he knew that God had used Caesar as an instrument of grace.

Brothers and sisters in Christ, this Christmas look a little bit differently at the decrees of Caesar. What decrees are you forced to follow? And which can you simply not avoid? What decrees are others forced to follow in our world? And instead of immediately throwing your arms up in frustration or despair at Caesar's power, look, instead, for a shepherd rushing in from the fields. Look for magi strolling in from afar. Listen for the sounds of an angelic herald, announcing a decree from God, and see if maybe, just maybe, Caesar is a servant.

The birth of Jesus came about in this way. Caesar Augustus sent out a decree that all the world would be registered. Amen.

8

Rolling the Dice

Election in the Kingdom of God

June 1, 2003

> "'Let another take his position of overseer.' So one of the men who has accompanied us during all the time that the Lord Jesus went in and out among us, beginning from the baptism of John until the day when he was taken up from us—one of these must become a witness with us to his resurrection." So they proposed two, Joseph called Barsabbas, who was also known as Justus, and Matthias. Then they prayed and said, "Lord, you know everyone's heart. Show us which one of these two you have chosen to take the place in this ministry and apostleship from which Judas turned aside to go to his own place." And they cast lots for them, and the lot fell on Matthias; and he was added to the eleven apostles. (Acts 1:20b–26)

When we were in India a few years ago, we were greatly impressed by many of the ministries and activities of the Church of South India. But one thing disturbed us about the church. We were concerned with the way the people rose to power. We heard from one observer that the push to become bishop of a region was a very costly venture. This observer had a beautiful briefcase to prove his point; a gift, he said, from one of the candidates. At the assembly meeting, once a year, when bishops are up for election, the candidates and their entourage fight and barter their way to the finals. Because, you see, to the victor go the spoils. When you become bishop, your children, cousins, and their families all suddenly have high posts within the system. But it's a democratic process; there's an election that takes place eventually, and the candidate who gets the most votes wins.

I don't mean to single out the Indian church. Our American churches have similar dirty politics. Someone in a mainline denominational office recently said to me, "Not one staff decision gets made that is not tied to someone else's quest for control and authority. Hiring and firing are always tied to power plays." Whether *that* is true or not is debatable, but what is certainly true is that power plays are at work in US denominations.

Moving from the church and into our homes, similar power plays can be seen around decision-making times. "You always get your way. We always go with your decision."

"That's not true. We always do your thing. Remember, last week you wanted to go bike riding, and we went bike riding."

"You didn't tell me you didn't want to do that!"

When we move outside the local scene and into the question of governmental systems, things get even messier. Politics has come to be a synonym for "dirty" or "ugly." When someone says, "It's so political," they are usually conveying a negative feeling. It is said that one shouldn't even attempt running for president of the United States without tens of millions of dollars in the bank. This means that if you want to run for the highest office, the policies you put forward have to be pleasing to folks with big wallets, heavy purses, and lucrative stock options. Before the public debates even start between potential candidates a lot of wheeling and dealing has happened.

Often it is said that our democratic system for choosing leaders and making difficult public decisions is not perfect, but it's still the best system. It is a good system, indeed. But I'm not sure, however, that we have to settle for the level of imperfection in behavior that surrounds the making of decisions in government or in our churches and even homes for that matter. I believe that today's strange Scripture lesson from Acts sheds some light on all decision-making systems.

In chapter 1 of the book of Acts the Christian community starts its organizational life in the "post-Jesus-with-us-in-his-humanity" period. Jesus is gone now, ascended, like a flash, before the eyes of his disciples.

Section One—Preparing the Church to Confront Other Kingdoms

They watched him ascend into the heavens, and then two messengers from God appeared to them saying, in effect, "All right, he's gone. What are you looking at? He'll come back." And with that, they went back to the ministry, to a new stage of ministry; ministry done with Jesus present in memory and in Spirit, but not in the flesh.

One of their first organizational decisions was to select a replacement for Judas. Judas killed himself, and Peter and the other eleven apostles felt the need to replace him with a new leader. Why did they need twelve? I don't know. Maybe this was to preserve the notion that the twelve apostles somehow represented the twelve ancient tribes of Israel. Maybe they thought twelve was a good number for Jesus so it was good enough for them. "Let's get off on the right foot here and keep the structures the same size." Peter quoted a random verse from Psalms 109:8 that says, "Let another take his position of overseer," giving the decision some scriptural authority among this gathering of Jews in Jerusalem.

There was a strict criterion for the replacement. It had to be someone who had been with Jesus since the time John was baptizing in the desert. In other words, it needed to be someone in place since the beginning of Jesus' public ministry.

The text says that there were 120 disciples by this point, present at the making of this decision. Who knows how many of them met the criteria for apostle? I don't imagine it was all that many. In fact, it's possible that the two proposed from among the crowd of 120 were the only ones who met the criteria—Justus and Matthias. What we do know is that when it came time to make a decision, there were two candidates, and only one slot for apostle available.

I imagine this could have been a very tense moment. People from Matthias' neighborhood could have seen the potential for some job placement for friends and neighbors, and there was the possibility that Christian service projects might be focused on their area. Justus, on the other hand, could have argued that his family was more prominent than Matthias', and therefore had more potential to bring about political change and security for this new community of followers of Jesus living under the Roman occupation. It could have been a massive duel.

"I was with Jesus when he fed five thousand."

"Oh, yeah! Well I helped carry a disabled man to see Jesus."

"Oh, yeah! Well Jesus asked *me* to read the Scripture to him."

"Oh, yeah! You may have memorized the beatitudes but I helped Jesus craft that speech." Oh, it could have been heated; it could have been messy.

But instead, the text says, Peter pulled out a pair of dice, and handed out a printed prayer to everyone present and said, "Let us pray." And they prayed together, "Lord, you know everyone's heart. Show us which of the two you have chosen to take the place in this ministry and apostleship." And I picture Peter bringing a kid to the front, asking him to shake the cup and spill the dice. "Matthias, if it's one through six, you're the apostle. Justas, seven through twelve is all you." "Four! Matthias wins!" And Matthias became the next apostle—and it was credited to the will of God. No harsh words were spoken, no money passed under the table, no punches thrown—the decision was made—and there was peace.

I hated this story growing up. Drawing straws, picking a number from behind a back, rolling dice and calling it the will of God?! What on Earth? That sounds like magic, foul play. But that's how it went. And this wasn't the first time that such a tactic was used in the community of faith that we hear about in the Bible.

"Casting lots" (rolling dice) resulted in Saul becoming king. Casting lots resulted in Jonah being thrown from the boat and making the storms cease. Casting lots resulted in the distribution of the land to the twelve tribes of Israel. Casting lots allowed Zechariah, as opposed to one of the other priests, to enter the inner sanctuary on behalf of the people in Luke 1. Casting lots resulted in Matthias being chosen over Justus to be the twelfth apostle. Casting lots was a religiously sanctioned event within the traditions of Israel. It did not fall under condemnation as did other forms of magic. It was seen as a human act that revealed a direct message from God. The dice revealed the will of God. It seems so awkward, backward, ridiculous, until you look at the results of the system. In all the examples I just gave you, the result of rolling dice resulted in a decision that led to peace and healing.

Each die had a name, *Urim* and *Thurmin*. In ancient times, and possibly even as recently as the apostle Peter, the chief priest would wear a little pouch around the neck with these two dice.[1] We don't know what these dice looked like, or how the procedure took place, but what we do know is that the chief priest would use these dice to reveal the will of God

---

1. *Harper's Bible Dictionary*, s.v. "Urim and Thummim," 1108.

Section One—Preparing the Church to Confront Other Kingdoms

in the most important, most perilous, most potentially controversial, decisions of a nation.

When the people of Israel selected their first king, around the year 1050 BC, there was the potential for serious problems: twelve tribes, all with different loyalties, families, practices and beliefs; twelve tribes, with different skills, trades, and priorities; twelve tribes with different likes and dislikes. And they wanted to be one nation. Sounds a little like the dilemmas in Afghanistan, and Iraq, or in many Central African nations. In Afghanistan today there are multiple tribes trying to trust a single leader who is part of one of the tribes, what some have referred to as "warlordistan." In the case of ancient Israel, the prophet Samuel put the names of all the tribes of Israel in a hat, and pulled out one—"Ah! The tribe of Benjamin." Then he put the names of all the families of the tribe of Benjamin in a hat, and pulled out one—"Ah! The family of the Matrites." Then he put the names of all the young men of the family of the Matrites in a hat, and pulled out Saul's name—and in that way Saul became king.[2]

That was the way a nation of twelve differing tribes was unified under one leader. It happened without bloodshed, muckraking, or money passing under the table. The same system had been employed by Joshua two hundred years earlier at the distribution of the land that was to become Israel. Twelve tribes, all coveting the same piece of land, divided it, and accepted what they were apportioned, learning to live with each other as legitimate neighbors. Eleven tribes accepted the fact that *that* tribe got a portion along the Jordan. Eleven tribes accepted the fact that *that* other got a port on the Mediterranean, and someone else was given the rainy side of the mountains. The decision of the dice was accepted as the will of God, and trusting the dice kept them from killing each other.

Whether the selected person turned out to be a great leader or not, or whether the decision brought about by casting lots held fast forever, is a secondary issue really. What is, for me, the most amazing thing about all accounts of lot casting, is that this seemingly naïve and old-school system seemed to minimize the level of back stabbing, wheeling and dealing, posturing, underhandedness, deception, and bribing that are so often found in other systems. In the moment the lot was cast, questions that were considered too much for human comprehension were left to a game of chance, an instrument of the will of God.

---

2. 1 Sam 10:20–21.

No hanging or dimpled chads. No variant in voting machines in different regions. No special interest groups. I have scoffed at this passage in the past, unsure why Jesus' followers would resort to a game of dice in decision making. They were gambling for God! Now, isn't that a bad thing? But now, I think differently. The disciples decided it was less of a gamble to roll dice to discern God's will than to try to make the decision on their own. Both candidates were qualified, but to choose one over the other was impossible for them to do without self-seeking motives.

I've thought outside the box this week, outside the ballot box even, and I've found it to be a tremendously freeing exercise. Think of what a different country we'd have if we let the chips fall as they may, if we let the dice roll as they will, to determine leadership in this nation, rather than dollars and power. We would have likely had a woman president years ago, and that would have helped us progress past the misogyny, prejudice, and glass ceiling that is still present in society. God's dice game would have led us to that realization. We would likely have had someone educated in a public school in a Bronx low-income neighborhood become president, and he would have promoted the interests of the poor, and would have unabashedly worked for the elimination of poverty. We would have likely had someone whose brother had been imprisoned, and for four years we would have had someone in power who would have taken a close look at our prison system. Quite frankly, the dice game could easily have resulted in some of the leaders of our political system being widows and orphans, from poor classes or any of the other oppressed or outcast groups—the types of folks to whom Jesus tried to give voice.

If we cast lots, and let the chips fall where they may, we would also end up with some dangerous leadership, and that would have to be addressed. Those types of situations also fall within the biblical tradition. Saul was selected by casting lots, and it was considered God's will, but he was deposed by that same community, when it became clear that he wasn't living and serving in ways that were pleasing to God, nor beneficial to the people as a whole. We'd have bad leaders sometimes, if we trusted the dice, but we would have had those anyway in our history, even with democratic elections.

We aren't going to move to a system of lot casting as the normative way to make national decisions, or church decisions, or business decisions, anytime soon. And that's fine. I'm not arguing for that, although I must say it's been fun to imagine.

Section One—Preparing the Church to Confront Other Kingdoms

There are other ways of making big decisions in the Bible. In Acts chapter 6, the community of faith gathered and selected from among themselves seven to be deacons. It sounds like they did it in a way that resonates with more modern sensibilities. The system they used to select deacons is much like the system we used recently as a church, as we selected from among our members people to be elders and deacons. The apostles told the entire body of believers to appoint seven in good standing, full of the Spirit, to engage in a ministry of care and concern. We, too, prayerfully considered who among the membership of the church, Spirit-filled, might be called to lead us in these next years. Some decisions, indeed most decisions, can be made through faithful consideration and deliberation. Hopefully most decisions can be worked out through faithful discussion, discernment, and diplomacy.

But I do think there is a word of truth behind the practice of casting lots that we can't see in other systems. *Some things cannot, for whatever reason, be decided in good faith, and they need to be left up to God—truly left up to God.* And this is good news that we as people of faith can incorporate into decision making in our homes, churches, nations, and the world.

There are some decisions that are so tedious and challenging that even a faithful community cannot come to grips with an answer that serves the common good. There are times when the level of self-benefit is so high that we are tempted to use self-serving tactics that are not befitting followers of a Lord who came to bless all people. It is in those moments that we need the wisdom of "lot casters," the wisdom that says, "Bring this one before the Lord—take it out of your own hands."

"God, my neighbor and I both want to acquire the land that's coming up for sale between our properties. Take this decision, Lord. I want it, I want it badly, but so do they. Take this decision out of my hands, and do what you will."

"God, half the church wants to start a shower ministry for homeless people in the church, and the other half wants to start a daycare for moms working third shift. They're both good things, Lord, but space only allows one to happen and people are so deadlocked. People are starting to fight about which we should do. Take this out of our hands, Lord. Both options are beautiful."

"My wife wants to take a vacation at the beach, I want to go to the mountains. We both agree that we need to be together, for our sakes, and for the kids. It's gotten ridiculous, Lord. We're not talking to each other because of our views about vacation! Both options are wonderful. Make this decision for us, O Lord."

"God, I'm running for public office and there's another wonderful candidate running against me in my same party. I think she'd be great, and I think she's got a better chance against the candidate of the other party in the next round than I do; but if I lose this, who knows what will happen to my political career. God, I've got dirt about her past that would eliminate her as a candidate, even though it isn't dirt that's applicable at all. I'm tempted to use it. I'd be a shoe-in if I did. But God, it doesn't seem right. Help me put this in your hands. I'll try my hardest in this election, but I'm not going to reduce myself and my morals in the process. Help me give this election to you—and I'll trust the result to be your will."

God, give us clean hearts at the time of difficult decisions—seeking not our own interests, but yours. God, let us encourage fairness, honesty, integrity, and compassion during times of decision making, and leave the result up to you. God, help us as a community to follow the lead of those incredibly humble eleven apostles and those other one hundred-plus disciples, who laid all self-absorbed motives, and all control of the future, at your feet and accepted your guidance with the roll of the dice. Amen.

Section Two

The Prepared Church Confronts the Issues of Its Day

Part One

Faith Facing the Wars in Afghanistan and Iraq

9

As One after God's Own Heart

July 6, 2003

> Then all the tribes of Israel came to David at Hebron, and said, "Look, we are your bone and flesh. For some time, while Saul was king over us, it was you who led out Israel and brought it in. The LORD said to you: It is you who shall be shepherd of my people Israel, you who shall be ruler over Israel." So all the elders of Israel came to the king at Hebron; and King David made a covenant with them at Hebron before the LORD, and they anointed David king over Israel. David was thirty years old when he began to reign, and he reigned for forty years. At Hebron he reigned over Judah for seven years and six months; and at Jerusalem he reigned over all Israel and Judah for thirty-three years. (2 Samuel 5:1–5)

It is the Fourth of July weekend. It's a time to celebrate nation building; a time to celebrate the events that led to our nation's beginnings including the Declaration of Independence, the fights for freedom, and the beginning of national allegiance. All these things are remembered today. I enjoyed the fireworks on Friday, especially the finale of red, white, and blue bursts of light. I hope you did too.

Here in the church we remember these events of nation building as events that happened "under God." The flag in our sanctuary reminds us that not only we as individuals, but our nation as a whole, are under God.

But what does that mean? What does it mean to be "under God?" What is the God like whom we are under?

God is, on one level, over all things. There is a very real sense in which the transcendent God—God of the beyond—is master of all things. We can say that our nation and all other nations are under God when we use this cosmic and transcendent kind of talk. God has the whole world in a divine hand.

But to be "under God" has more relational connotations as well. To recognize one's nation as being "under God" is to make a statement about the divine and human relationship. There is a connection between God and us, and it is ordered. God is over; we are under. God acts first, we respond in the way we act as a nation. In our worship service we come before God in adoration, hear the word of God, and then we respond. We go forth into the world, recognizing that our actions are to be actions under the direction of God, in whose image we were created.

On this Fourth of July weekend it is good to ponder this relationship between God and our nation. It is good to ask if, at this stage in history, we live as a nation that reflects the image of the God we know in Christ Jesus, or if we are a nation who denies God, or, even more dangerously, has recreated God in our own image. It is good to ask these questions.

I've been asking these questions of King David and his nation this week as I've wrestled with what has proven to be a very difficult biblical passage. When David was a boy the prophet Samuel came to his town on assignment from God. God told Samuel to go to the house of Jesse and anoint for future leadership one after God's own heart. Jesse, David's father, brought forth his bigger, stronger, older, handsomer sons, suggesting that one of them ought to be anointed king. They had the qualities of kings. Samuel told Jesse that God wasn't calling any of these men, and that "the Lord does not see as mortals see; they look on the outward appearance, but the Lord looks on the heart."[3] He asked if he had any other sons. Jesse answered, "Just the youngest; just David." So Samuel asked that David be brought before him. And once before him, God said, "Rise and anoint him; for this is the one."[4] Here God had found one who had a heart that resonated with the divine heart. It seemed that somehow David—in his weakness, tenderness, contentment in herding sheep and wandering the fields—resonated with the qualities found in God's own heart.

3. 2 Sam 16:7b.
4. Ibid., 16:12.

David and God apparently shared features that included simplicity, humility, and caring. Thinking that these are qualities of God might sound funny to some people, but for those of us who see God in the person of Jesus, such qualities are not so surprising. David is the man whom Samuel believed God was calling to lead the nation, because of the ways his heart was so synchronous with the humble and caring heart of the divine.

What a blessing to think that at times our human lives resonate with the heart of God! And on this Fourth of July weekend I hope you will take the time to think back over our nation's history and find moments when we, too, like the youngster David, lived with the qualities of David the youngest brother; David the shepherd; David the weak, vulnerable, and content. There are many moments over our nation's history when we have lived as one with the heart of God.

But just because a prophet once said, "Here is one after God's own heart!" doesn't mean that statement remains true throughout a lifetime. Often David is held up as being almost perfect, except for the one midlife crisis where he took another man's wife and then made sure to have her husband die on the front lines of battle. But he apologized to God for that! On the whole, we remember David's life and actions as *God inspired* and representative of very God. However, the more I read David, the more I've grown concerned about holding him up as living a lifetime "as one after God's own heart." David's rise to power and his methods for expanding and maintaining his rule did not resonate with the qualities of the heart of God that Samuel had said were reflected in David's vulnerability, humility, and simplicity of youth.

The five short verses I read this morning from Second Samuel tell of a special moment in King David's rise to power. It was the moment that the ten tribes of Israel, making up the northern region of greater Palestine, decided they wanted David to not only rule over Judah, the tribe to the south, but over them as well. Since Saul's death some seven years earlier, the ten tribes of Israel, except Judah, had been ruled by Saul's son, Ishbosheth. Read apart from its context, one would think that the northern tribes came to David on this day simply because it would be wonderful to be under David's kingship, as he was a just king whose heart was like that of God. They wanted to change national borders in order to be with him. But put in its context, it is not obvious at all that this is why they joined David. And today, I want to tell an abridged version of

Section Two—The Prepared Church Confronts the Issues of Its Day

Second Samuel, chapters 2, 3, and 4: the stories that are the immediate precursors to the ten tribes of Israel asking David to be their king.

After Saul died in battle, David had a chance to rise up in power. For years he had worked for Saul, first as a personal musician, to soothe him to sleep, and later, as a military leader—against the Philistines and others. As David grew in strength and militaristic prestige, Saul grew jealous of him. He was rightly understood as a threat to the throne. Even the prophet Samuel was in support of David. Until the last days of Saul's life he pursued David, seeking to kill him. David gained enough prestige through his military victories that in the aftermath of Saul's death David was selected to be king of the tribe of Judah. David had recently defeated the Amelekite army and had given the war plunder to that tribe, and so it was natural for him to go there first, seeking political support. At the same time that David was crowned king of Judah, Abner, the commander of Saul's army, was crowning Ishbosheth, Saul's son, as king of the other ten tribes of Israel. And with that, the nation that had been unified under Saul was unified no longer. We are not told how Ishbosheth was as a leader of his people, nor, for that matter, are we told about David's leadership during those years. But we do know that for seven years these two kings ruled and, instead of defending themselves against other nations, they turned the sword on each other. Immediately after David became king of Judah, he courted the people of Jabesh-Gilead, a city located far north of the region where David was now king. In other words, David immediately began to pursue the allegiance of a town in Ishbosheth's land. Immediately the commander of Ishbosheth's army, Abner, came with soldiers to the border between Israel and Judah and met Joab, the leader of David's army, with his soldiers. In the town of Gibeon the twelve best men from each army came together for a fight to the death. In an amazing feat, all of them died, stabbing each other simultaneously. As this more organized form of warfare proved inconclusive as to who was victorious, a huge fight ensued. The day ended with over three hundred dead from Abner's army and twenty from David's.

In Second Samuel, chapter 3, we hear that there was a long war between Israel and Judah, a civil war. And the result, we hear, is that David grew stronger, and Ishbosheth grew weaker. In the north, Abner, the commander of the army, was the strongest man in Ishbosheth's forces. To David's great benefit, Abner and Ishbosheth got in a fight over a concubine, and the result was that Abner decided to leave Ishbosheth and side with David. He sent word to David, saying he would undermine Ishbosheth's authority and try to encourage the elders of Israel to change allegiances. David met with Abner, agreed to accept his support, and then sent him away in peace. From the text it is unclear whether or not David was convinced that the commander of the rival army had truly changed allegiances.

Soon thereafter Joab, commander of David's army, came back from a raid and heard that Abner had been visiting with King David. Joab was enraged and insisted that David had been duped by the foreign military commander. David, although he was king, allowed his enraged military commander to go seeking Abner. Joab had messengers seek out Abner, and when Abner came before him, Joab stabbed him to death. David expressed great remorse, publicly, over this death, but it must be asked why he allowed Joab to leave his side while he was so clearly seeking blood.

With Abner dead, and word leaking to the public that he had died even as he tried to change allegiance, Israel's structures began to crumble. Second Samuel, chapter 4 says that Ishbosheth's courage failed. Apparently all the military commanders could see the writing on the wall—their army was crumbling, and David's was strengthening. The two leaders of the raiding forces of Israel decided that they, as leaders of the foreign fighting forces, were at great risk of their lives, and they decided to gain favor by murdering the king of Israel. They entered Ishbosheth's house while he took an afternoon nap, and killed him, cutting off his head and bringing it to David. David's response was different than the two men expected. He executed them, and hung their mangled bodies in the square in Hebron. In this way, it seems to me, he hoped to prove that he had nothing to do with the death of the king of Israel.

And now, after all these things, the tribes of Israel came to David in Hebron, which was the capital of Judah, and said, "Be our king too." After all of *that* it doesn't seem to me that they had any choice. King dead; military commander dead; heads of the raiding army dead; years of battles; militaristic power shifting 100% to David—what other choice did they have? They came to him from the tribes of Israel saying, "Look, we are your bone and flesh."[5] They came to him saying, in effect, "We remember how faithful you were to all of us back in the day when Saul ruled as our

---

5. Ibid., 5:1.

king, and you as one of his military leaders." Those statements are true. But they were always true. Why use them now as grounds for unification? If the ten tribes had wanted David as king, they could have pushed for his leadership during the last power vacuum, seven years earlier, at the death of Saul. But they hadn't. It seems they had lived happily under Ishbosheth—Saul's son and legitimate heir to the throne by the standards of that time. They came to David, it seems to me, only after a string of events unfolded that put the fear of David in them. It was too dangerous to remain his rival neighbor.

We remember David as being one after God's own heart. And he was, when he was youngest of many brothers, playing the harp, herding his sheep, and protecting them from danger. He was still acting as one after God's own heart, I would argue, when he defended his people from an attack by a stronger country, and their giant, Goliath. He displayed the heart of God when he repented after his sin with Bathsheba. But as he rose in power, some of the actions that he carried out himself, or that he allowed his commanders to carry out, were not so representative of the heart of God. He was a mighty leader, a feared king, he ended up on the throne, but did he do so through means consistent with God's own heart? Let's be careful with that one.

Why am I dragging David's name through the mud? Why so critical? I'm being critical of David because David's actions and way of being are often held up as being the actions of one who is closely walking with God, even representing the heart of God. If the actions that led to David's rise to power are representative of God's heart, then God is a violent, power hungry, manipulative, unforgiving, expansionist sort of God who cares little about people residing in any country other than those under David's rule.

If the warring and conniving of Second Samuel, chapters 2 through 4 are acts that are truly godly acts, consistent with the heart of the God who creates, redeems, and sustains heaven and Earth, then I'm not sure it's a God to whom we should commit. Jesus certainly wouldn't have committed to a God like this. Jesus was as one after God's own heart when he said things like, "Love your enemies," and when he said, "put your sword back into its place; for all who take the sword will perish by the sword."[6] Jesus was one after God's own heart when he said, "Woe to you [powerful people] . . . for you lock people out of the kingdom of heaven," and

---

6. Matt 5:44, 6:52.

when he went to great lengths to heal and comfort the sick.[7] Jesus was one after God's own heart when he shared that the kingdom of God is like a wedding banquet to which all are invited.[8] Jesus was one after God's own heart when he spoke of compassion that knew no boundaries, love that was thick as his own shed blood.

Was David a man after God's own heart? When he was a youngster, apparently he was quite consistently living this way. As he grew in power, sometimes yes, but often, when it came to his biggest political moments, he did not live consistently with God's heart at all.

Friday was Independence Day, a day for us to celebrate our nation, our citizenship, our identity. There are many aspects of our founding narrative that resonate with the heart of God. Many of our founding fathers and mothers would say that our Declaration of Independence, Constitution, and our basic structure of governance are "one with the heart of God." But may we keep asking this question about ourselves, our nation, our leadership: Do the actions of our nation, both in national and international affairs, resonate with the heart of God? If not, why not? If so, how so? Is our nation living "under God" in the sense that our actions are the actions that flow forth from the heart of God? We must keep bringing our nation before God to ask these questions, and keep from assuming that our actions are somehow automatically at one with the heart of God.

When we are truly under God, or as one with the heart of God, our self-definition comes from God—the God who resonated with the humble childhood identity of David and the lifelong identity of Jesus. And it is when we are truly living under the compassionate heart of God that we have a chance, as a nation, to beat lovingly the pulse of love, joy, and peace—for the world and for God. Amen.

---

7. Ibid., 23:13.
8. Ibid., 22.

10

Not in My Name

F ebruary 23, 2003

>Jesus went on with his disciples to the villages of Caesarea Philippi; and on the way he asked his disciples, "Who do people say that I am?" And they answered him, "John the Baptist; and others, Elijah; and still others, one of the prophets." He asked them, "But who do you say that I am?" Peter answered him, "You are the Messiah." And he sternly ordered them not to tell anyone about him. Then he began to teach them that the Son of Man must undergo great suffering, and be rejected by the elders, the chief priests, and the scribes, and be killed, and after three days rise again. He said all this quite openly. And Peter took him aside and began to rebuke him. But turning and looking at his disciples, he rebuked Peter and said, "Get behind me, Satan! For you are setting your mind not on divine things but on human things." He called the crowd with his disciples, and said to them, "If any want to become my followers, let them deny themselves and take up their cross and follow me. For those who want to save their life will lose it, and those who lose their life for my sake, and for the sake of the gospel, will save it. For what will it profit them to gain the whole world and forfeit their life? Indeed, what can they give in return for their life? Those who are ashamed of me and of my words in this adulterous and sinful generation, of them the Son of Man will also be ashamed when he comes in the glory of his Father with the holy angels." (Mark 8:27–38)

Not in My Name

There is an advocacy group called "Not in My Name" that was formed soon after the attacks of September 11, 2001. "Not in My Name" was formed by family members of victims who were concerned that America was bombing Afghanistan in the name of their deceased family members. In October 2002, our Prayer Group for Peace had one of the members from this group, Rev. Myrna, come and share with us.

Rev. Myrna told us that in one speech the president of the United States shared a story of a man who died in order to save his disabled friend in the World Trade Center. He then argued that we needed to bomb Afghanistan as retribution/payback for this man's life. It so happened that the man whose story was told had been a very committed pacifist and the family was horrified to think that the government would use his death as fuel for the raging fires of war. That family helped to start the group "Not in my Name." The families in this group believe that governments have tough decisions to make—there is no denying this. But the government doesn't know their family members, nor their radical commitment to peace. They insist that the government not use the life stories of their relatives as grounds for more destruction.

There is another name that should never be used as fuel for war—and that name is Jesus Christ. I am not arguing today for a doctrine of pacifism versus a just-war doctrine. I believe that Christians of good will can have varying opinions about war, even this impending war with Iraq. The factors of war are many, and they are incredibly complicated. I do not envy the president's position right now. He is in an incredibly difficult spot. But this I do know, Jesus Christ is the suffering Lord. Jesus Christ is not a God of warring madness. His victory over death came when as Messiah, with the potential to rule the world, he refused to play the power game played by other worldly powers. He kept his sword in its sheath, and he insisted his followers do likewise. Jesus' primary identity is as the crucified—not as "crucifier."

I believe today's gospel lesson has something to teach us about Jesus' identity. I believe today's gospel lesson has something to teach us as well about our identity and this impending war.

They had been with Jesus for some time now, that motley crew of twelve disciples. They'd witnessed his healing power and his teachings about a new kingdom. They'd even been empowered to help in his teaching and healing ministry. By chapter 8 of Mark's gospel, the disciples had been in Tyre, the region of the Decapolis, Bethsaida, Nazareth,

Section Two—The Prepared Church Confronts the Issues of Its Day

Capernaum, Gennesaret. In each town and city they'd seen him do amazing things. He was so compelling, so wonderful to follow. They were so close to him, they felt they knew him so well. Now they were heading for Caesarea Philippi, just about as far north as they could go in Palestine before touching the border with Syria. And as they approached the border, Jesus decided that it was time to cross another border with them, the border of his identity: "Who do *you* say that I am?"

It seems an odd question to ask close friends, a strange question to ask people who have given up everything—everything—to be followers. Peter burst forth with the answer, but there's no reason to believe he was alone in his thinking. "You are the Messiah!"

It's unclear whether Jesus was surprised that Peter knew his identity. Either way, I bet it was a relief for the disciples to have it out in the open and confirmed for them. All of this kingdom building Jesus had been doing through healing, teaching, and communing were just part of his coming in power as Messiah! These were all just part of the way he would establish himself as king of Israel in the triumphant establishment of God's power!

But then Jesus did the strangest thing. "He sternly ordered them not to tell anyone about him." But Peter and the others had correctly identified him, why shouldn't they share that news? As they crossed the border into Caesarea Philippi, why not let it be a coming out party, a party for Jesus to announce his true identity as the Messiah of God? Why not announce God's triumphal entry into world history?

Jesus told them not to reveal his identity, but before they would even have had a chance to tell anyone he sat them down for a discussion. I picture him saying something like, "Don't tell anyone my identity. On second thought, sit down and hear me out; it's time I tell you all about me." I imagine them sitting down on big rocks, just outside the gates of the first village within Caesarea Philippi.

"Let me teach you. Now that you have named me, let me tell you what the Messiah, the Son of Man, must go through. I'm going to suffer really badly. I'm going to be rejected by everyone who has authority in this world. The scribes and chief priests and elders will all reject me. I will be killed. And then, after three days I'll rise again."

"Jesus, come here a minute, let me have a word with you."

"What, Peter?"

"Stop this talk. You are the Messiah; you just admitted it. Stop this talk about your suffering and dying and being rejected. You are the triumphant king, the anointed one of God! Stop it, stop it!"

"No. Peter, get behind me, Satan. You are setting your mind on human things, not divine things. See why I told you not to tell my identity to anyone. I cannot trust you; you do not yet understand what it means to be Messiah."

Those who were closest to Jesus, those who had wandered on his path, bringing hope and promise to every town, didn't know their teacher's identity. He was Messiah, yes, but implicit in *his* understanding of Messiah-ship was that he would undergo suffering and rejection and even death. Jesus didn't want his disciples to say a word about him being Messiah because they didn't understand the suffering part yet—and until they did, they wouldn't accurately describe him to the world.

It's quite easy to read this passage and feel judgmental toward Peter and the others. "Peter, Peter, Peter, who do you think you are—rebuking Jesus like that? What? Do you think you can describe Jesus better than he can describe himself? Are you bent on crafting Jesus Christ in your own image?

Peter, when are you going to see the fact that this Messiah refuses to be a warrior who will use brutal force to establish his reign? Peter, can't you see he doesn't want bodyguards to keep him from danger? Peter, can't you see that rejection, suffering, and death are things that he accepts as aspects of his identity? He's going to challenge everything that is wrong in society, flip the tables of money changers in the temple, challenge the rules of the religious authorities, insist that the poor be given justice. But he's not going to be reduced to their warring tactics—even in self-defense. He is going to suffer and die—confident that God will raise him up. Peter, get Jesus' identity right!"

It was easy for me to feel judgmental toward Peter, until I got to thinking about the war again, and about the way that Jesus Christ and Christian faith have been so tied into the war talk. This has happened on all levels. Much of Christian talk radio and religious publications have confidently spoken of the United States as if it were Christ's team in this international conflict against Mohammed's team in Iraq. It seems that our nation, that has millions of followers of Christ, wants to identify the suffering Messiah with war. President Bush is doing this too.

Section Two—The Prepared Church Confronts the Issues of Its Day

Last week, in his State of the Union address, the president made a case for preemptively attacking Iraq. "We go forward with confidence, because this call of history has come to the right country..... The liberty we prize is not America's gift to the world, it is God's gift to humanity. We do not claim to know all the ways of providence, yet we can trust in them, placing our confidence in the loving God behind all of life, and all of history."[1]

Elaine Pagels, Professor of Religion at Princeton University, was quoted as saying, "The president's words may, in effect, give credence to descriptions of a 'holy war' between Christians and Muslims. At the very least, this type of rhetoric could set us up to be perceived . . . as being engaged in a holy war."[2] War may be inevitable—that is ultimately a decision for the commander-in-chief. But to put the language of faith, the language about God's will and Christ's identity so squarely into the middle of a war, and in particular, on "our side" in a war, is a question for theologians, pastors, and all people of faith. The Jesus Christ who identified himself as the rejected, suffering, and killed Messiah cannot be called upon as justification for any kind of warring—even if it is a war for righteousness' sake; because for righteousness' sake he was rejected, and he suffered and died. He refused to play the war game.

War might be necessary from time to time in a world as chaotic as this one. I said it before and I'll say it again, Christians must continually wrestle with the reality of war. But let's not act as if God is participating in and cheering for our side. Because if we identify him with our warring, we might lose the clear perspective he brings us, that violence is always a tragedy, whether necessary or not.

"Who do you say that I am?"

Do we know the identity of our Lord? We know the Lord ushers in a new kingdom, a kingdom where people of every age, race, ethnicity, and gender come together around a common table. We know the Lord is one of simplicity, caring about providing for the needs of all people. But do we know the hard part? Have we accepted the *suffering part* of his identity? Have we accepted the fact that in living unabashedly for the kingdom of God, our Lord is rejected, suffers, and dies? Have we really come to grips with the Lord's refusal to attack his oppressors?

1. Bush, "State of the Union Speech." 28 Jan 28 2003, http://www.washingtonpost.com/wp-srv/onpolitics/transcripts/bushtext_012803.html.

2. Pagels and Gaddy, "President or Preacher?" 11 Feb 2003, http://www.religionandpluralism.org/ANC_transcript_President_or_Preacher.htm.

Not in My Name

Need we go to war? What other options are there? What are we to do? All the questions of war cannot be answered. We are, frankly, in the middle of an international mess. But of this I am certain: If we do go to war with Iraq, the Messianic identity of Christ won't be on the breastplate of the "Christian army" as it marches into Baghdad. It won't be in the strategic planning rooms of the great government buildings in Washington, as they decide where to drop smart bombs. The identity of Christ won't be written on the side of the bombers. A painted cross on the side of a missile doesn't make it a Christ-like missile. Christ will not be at the front of the victory parade of one side or the other.

But Christ's identity will be written all over this conflict. The suffering and rejected identity of the Messiah will be written in the tears of soldiers, and in the tears of parents back here. The suffering and rejected identity of Christ will be written in the tears of Iraqi children hiding under their beds as bombs fall. The suffering and rejected identity of Christ will be written on the faces of despair and brokenness all around the world. The identity of Christ will be written in the tears of families who mourn their losses, as thousands, possibly hundreds of thousands, will most definitely be killed. That is where Christ will be.

Everything Jesus did, said, and taught leads me to think that he is crying out, "Not in my name!" right about now. War is crucifixion—and our Lord is not an agent of crucifixion. He is the crucified.

We know that on the third day Jesus Christ was raised from the dead. We know that God reigns triumphant and is giving signs of the kingdom, making the world better. But we also know that when Jesus walked this Earth and showed us how to live, he refused to be identified with worldly acts of violence, choosing instead a path of peace that refused to be pulled into the cycle of war. Let's not pull his name into the war. He offers a different way.

And it's a way that we're going to need a few months from now, as we try to put the pieces of our lives back together again. We're going to need the love of the Christ who knows rejection, suffering, and death. And we're going to need the hope of a Christ who God has brought through the valley of the shadow of death and into newness of life. Amen.

11

The End Is Now, Praise God!

May 20, 2007

> Then I saw a new heaven and a new earth; for the first heaven and the first earth had passed away, and the sea was no more. And I saw the holy city, the new Jerusalem, coming down out of heaven from God, prepared as a bride adorned for her husband. ... Then the angel showed me the river of the water of life, bright as crystal, flowing from the throne of God and of the Lamb through the middle of the street of the city. On either side of the river is the tree of life with its twelve kinds of fruit, producing its fruit each month; and the leaves of the tree are for the healing of the nations. (Revelation 21:1–2, 22:1–2)

This week I spent some time with a man exactly my age from Mosul, Iraq. Mosul's ancient name was Nineveh. In fact, it says "Nineveh" on his passport. His name is Rev. Jonah. Jonah from Nineveh! Jonah felt the call to ministry in the late 1990s, and began preparing for seminary. In January 2003, just three months before war broke out, he went to Egypt where he began studies at a seminary in Cairo. While there, he supported himself by doing prison ministry. He explained to me that most of the inmates in the prison where he worked were undocumented immigrants. In Egypt, if you get caught without proper papers you are allowed to go home if you can pay to go home, or you are imprisoned until someone from your home country sends the money to get you home. Most undocumented people are extremely poor Africans.

Some folks spent close to a year in immigration prison, thousands waiting in prisons for this purpose. There would be eighty people in a room the size of two containers, no proper toilet facilities, very little food, hardly space to lie down. Guards would dole out regular beatings, to keep people from rising up. Jonah was there to pray with Christians, to provide food, and try to raise financial support for those prisoners who couldn't get help from their home countries.

Jonah graduated from seminary one year ago, and planned on returning to Mosul for his ordination and to serve as associate pastor of the 160-year-old church there. But his congregation begged him not to return, saying the situation was now too dangerous for Christian clergy. "My moderate Muslim neighbors, the neighbors of my youth, have radicalized since the war began," he said. "They see this as a religious war—a new Crusade by the Christian West."

According to Jonah, the Iraqi Christian population of 600,000 has shrunk to around 150,000 since 2003. The flight of Christians is significantly higher than the flight of the general population—as persecution is coming not just as a result of the war with the United States, but also from the persecution among those who had been neighbors and friends.

After being told not to return to Nineveh, Jonah stayed in Egypt, still working as a prison chaplain. About a month later, a prisoner under his care converted from Islam to Christianity, and the government found out. "I was not talking to him about Jesus," Jonah told me. "I was giving him water and trying to get churches to give him money so he could go to his home country." The government immediately expelled Jonah from their country, trying to send him back to Iraq. The seminary interceded, helping him get a visa for entry into the United States as a religious worker. He arrived ten months ago. Four months ago, Jonah's senior pastor in Mosul was shot and killed. Jonah said to me, "I am here, now, to do peacemaking ministry."

When I asked how we could connect with Christians in Iraq at this time he said, "It's very, very hard, but how about connecting with some of the millions of refugees from Iraq that are being received in Jordan, Syria, Lebanon, Iran, [and] Egypt?" The United Nations High Commissioner for Refugees, Antonio Guterres, reported in February 2007 that 3.7 million people have fled their homes, with 2 million of those now living in nearby countries already strapped financially and socially.[3]

---

3. Scott, "Millions Leave Home," 17 Feb 2007, http://www.npr.org/templates/story/story.php?storyId=7466089&from=mobile.

Section Two—The Prepared Church Confronts the Issues of Its Day

And so this week, as I thought about Jonah and about the real and present suffering church and society in Iraq, the lectionary called me to focus on the utopian image of the New Jerusalem in Revelation 21 and 22. Around 80 AD, John, a follower of Jesus, was on an island called Patmos when God gave him a vision or a revelation. And part of the revelation, the culminating part, basically is told like this:

> Come up to the mountain with me. Let me show you the bride, the wife of the Lamb. It was the voice of an angel. And I didn't know what to expect. The church had been called the bride ever since Jesus' death and resurrection. The apostle Paul had told us to wed ourselves to Christ. Christ was called the bridegroom. Well, the angel carried me up, up a mountain high enough that I could look down on a vast city (that city was as far east to west as New Jersey is to Lincoln, Nebraska; as far north and south as New Jersey is from Miami, Florida. Or, to put it another way, the city was bigger than the entire Middle East as we define it today).
>
> And the city was landing. Yes, landing. It was coming down from God, and it radiated with the glory of God. It had twelve gates, three on each side, and they were always open. And the gates were named after the twelve tribes of Israel, acknowledging God's people who were blessed to be a blessing for the whole world. And the foundations that undergirded the walls that stretched around the 1,500-mile square—there were twelve of them—they were named after the twelve apostles of Jesus. The walls were jasper, the city itself pure gold and clear as glass! The foundations, adorned with every jewel. Each gate, a pearl— a giant, single pearl!
>
> The city was shining, like a bright light, even though it was night! And then I saw why. The Lamb of God, Jesus himself, was seated in the middle of the city that was like a garden, and from him poured light that lit up the night throughout the whole land. The city was like a garden because a river flowed directly from the throne, life-giving water spilling out. And flowers and trees sucked in the life through their roots and gave it out in the form of oxygen and fruit. Trees of life—did I tell you about these fruit trees? They flourished along the rivers that ran through every street all over the garden city universe. They were covered with fruit, and the angel told me they would produce every month— and all were invited to eat!
>
> Nothing grew that had the potential to bring a curse, as in the days of Adam and Eve. This fruit and the leaves of the trees

were for the healing and salvation of everyone! And no one was hungry, and no one was thirsty. And death and mourning and pain were no more—and no one cried.

The angel told me I was to see the bride, the church, and I looked; I looked far and wide but there was no temple, no church. I scanned the horizons, looking for one. And then I realized what I'd been shown. The whole city/garden ecosystem was the bride of Christ. The people from every nation, as well as the streams, fruit trees, forests, animals, the architecture, the artistry—it was *all the bride*. All of creation in the New Jerusalem was the bride of Christ.

And then, to my amazement, the voice of Christ, from down the mountain below spoke to me, saying, "I'm coming soon." Then the Spirit spoke, together with a voice that pulsated from the bride, from the people, trees, and streams. "Come. And let everyone who is thirsty come. Let anyone who wishes take the water of life as a gift." It was as if the Spirit was saying, "Be part of the New Jerusalem—wed yourself to Christ." No longer was I observing a future; now I was being invited to participate in it!

Though it doesn't say it, I imagine that John asked that angel to take him off the mountain and zip him right down into the New Jerusalem, so he could drink from the stream. The vision was of the future, but it was a future that he could step into, at least while in a trance.

What a clash of stories I lived with this week. Rev. Jonah of Mosul/Nineveh and his stories of suffering in Iraq and Egypt vs. the New Jerusalem described in Revelation that, ironically, would have included all of the territory of Iraq. Nineveh is only about six hundred miles from Jerusalem. It seemed wrong to be thinking about a utopian vision of God's kingdom, God's church, when Jonah had been telling me the truth of suffering today. God's going to do this, huh? God's just going to "lower down" this perfect world? Yeah, right. How about the church carrying out some realistic tasks of kindness and mercy, rather than utopian daydreaming?

It seemed like a clash of stories, and a virtually irreconcilable clash, until I started thinking more about the context in which John received his revelation. He was on the island of Patmos (which is just to the west of modern-day Turkey) when he received this revelation from God. He was living during a time of Christian persecution, either under the emperor Nero or Domitian in the late first century AD. Revelation 1:9 states, "I, John, your brother who share with you in Jesus the persecution and the

Section Two—The Prepared Church Confronts the Issues of Its Day

kingdom and the patient endurance, was on the Island called Patmos because of the word of God and the testimony of Jesus."

It's possible that Patmos was a penal colony for Rome, where John had been imprisoned for proclaiming the gospel. Or, maybe preaching in one of the churches that he writes to angered the public, and he fled to Patmos. Who knows? Either way, he was under duress. And there, in that situation, he was told, "Write in a book what you see and send it to the seven churches" who are suffering in the Mediterranean Province of Asia.[4]

Friends, God gave this utopian vision of the church—the bride flowering into a new global reality of perfected love—to a churchman who was suffering and told to share the vision with other church folks who by suffering were part of a suffering world. He is not told to give them this vision as an "escape" from their current reality. Rather, he is told to give them this vision as a motivation for standing firm in the faith. Hear the good news! Into the most despicable moments of human suffering, God gives the gift of ultimate vision—a vision of God's kingdom come and will done on Earth as in heaven. Into a society of crucifixion, Jesus announces resurrection of the entire cosmos!

Then I wished I'd asked Rev. Jonah for his thoughts about Revelation 21 and 22, because I bet it speaks to him, Iraqi Christians in Mosul, and to all in exile at this time. I bet a person like Jonah can become a peacemaker at a time like this because of a vision he has of a better world that God is bringing about. I bet he took an invitation to "come and drink."

I remembered something I read a few years back, that in Central and South America today, in the house churches that meet along garbage dump colonies in Guatemala and Peru, Revelation is the favorite and most influential biblical book. Theologian Pablo Richard of Costa Rica says, "Revelation is coming to be the preferred book of the Base Christian Communities and all the church movements in the so-called Third World that hope to transform the present situation and reform the church, movements that are born among the poor, the oppressed, and the excluded."[5] They've been drinking from the fountain too.

If an angel of God invited you up to the top of a mountain to look down on the perfected church, the New Jerusalem descending from heaven, would you go? Would you want to see it? I asked myself this

---

4. Rev. 1:11.
5. Richard, *Apocalypse*, 173.

The End Is Now, Praise God!

question this week. I had to admit that I might not go up to the mountain. Here's why.

"Angel, thanks, but I'm really busy, trying to finish this sermon. Ask me on my day off!

Angel, thanks, but the church I'm part of right now keeps me pretty filled up. I have a feeling the one you might show me from the top of a mountain will be bigger than the one I'm part of, and the one I'm part of now stretches me to my limits lots of weeks.

Angel, thanks, but no, I won't be joining you. I understand you want to give me a vision of the church as a flowering city, a church done in a whole new way! But you know, in this country we've got fairly organized cities and towns and there are municipal, state, and national governments that are to do most of the social service work, so the church, the bride, just doesn't have to be all things to all people anymore. That's an old vision, that "church-as-garden-city" thing. The church is just a part of the city.

Angel, quite frankly, I'm content as I am. I don't need a 'bigger vision' of the church. You're happy with contentment, right? We're satisfied. We're not thirsty."

I fear, sometimes, that we in the American church are shortsighted in our dreams of what the church can be because, well, *we* are doing fairly well at building a virtual reality of a "pretty good existence" as a nation. As such, the church just doesn't need to go up on a mountain to catch a view of the possibilities of a world perfectly reconciled to God because, well, have you seen the flowering trees around here? Have you seen the good road systems? Have you seen the economic activity, the social services? When we see someone falling through the cracks in society, we try to pick them up. Hey, we have our problems from time to time, but on the whole, things are good. We're not all that thirsty—or so we think.

Friends, it is good to see and appreciate the glory of the Lord all around us, as we are, but go up to the mountain sometimes, whether invited there by an angel or by walking to the top yourself, and ask God to show you the New Jerusalem descending from God. Go up in the church tower and pretend you're on a mountain and let an angel read to you from Revelation 21 and 22. Go to the top of the Empire State Building and look out. Try to imagine what New York City would be like if it were a place where death, dying, and tears would be no more. But don't get stuck on fixing what's broken; instead, imagine a *new* New York, descending and transforming the one that exists. Close your eyes and travel above Palestine and Israel. Look down and imagine it without a separation wall, and with fruit trees growing along rivers from which all people are allowed to pick and eat. Climb in a spaceship and look out at that watery ball of Earth below you, and imagine all the waters of Earth as flowing from under the throne of Christ, cleansing and restoring all things. Imagine all those scenes and say to yourself, "This is church. This is the body of Christ. This is life in God." Imagine from a distance, and then listen for the voice of the Spirit and the voice of that bride, that city, saying, "Come. If you're thirsty, come now. Take the waters of the New Jerusalem now . . . get filled up with this thing that hasn't yet descended from God."

We are people of the resurrection—we are not limited anymore to realistic pictures and obtainable dreams. We know that death can become life. So allow yourselves space to *imagine* in order to keep your resurrection vision large enough because, frankly, imagination in the Spirit is the only thing anywhere near large enough to capture resurrected life. Take a drink from John's Revelation. Drink a full glass of your own revelations. Let the waters of the future church, the end church, give you renewed bodies for life in the now-church, so that our walls might expand, or—hey!, maybe even fall to make room for all. Amen.

12

Christ Showed Us God

May 30, 2004

> Philip said to him, "Lord, show us the Father, and we will be satisfied." Jesus said to him, "Have I been with you all this time, Philip, and you still do not know me? Whoever has seen me has seen the Father. How can you say, "Show us the Father"? Do you not believe that I am in the Father and the Father is in me? The words that I say to you I do not speak on my own; but the Father who dwells in me does his works. Believe me that I am in the Father and the Father is in me; but if you do not, then believe me because of the works themselves. Very truly, I tell you, the one who believes in me will also do the works that I do and, in fact, will do greater works than these, because I am going to the Father. I will do whatever you ask in my name, so that the Father may be glorified in the Son. If in my name you ask me for anything, I will do it. (John 14:8–14)

On this Memorial Day weekend, a weekend to remember those who lost their lives during moments of heightened hostility, we are in another moment of heightened hostility. I spent time this week praying and reflecting on Memorial Day, and our current crises. What do these current events mean for Christians? What do they mean for people who speak about the "will of God?"

These are troubled times. We are saturated with thoughts about the presence of war, terror, prisoner abuse, revenge killings, political uncertainty in our country, and insecurity in Iraq's new governing council. These are troubled times, and I see a lot of people shaking their heads, wondering how we got into this mess, and how we're going to get out of it. I've heard a lot of Christians say, "I feel completely helpless. I don't know what is right or wrong in this situation. All we can do is pray, and leave it in God's hands."

There are many days when I, too, throw up my hands in despair, folded in prayer, and call out to the heavens, asking for the mysterious presence of God. "God, don't you have something to say about all this? God, what is your will? Show us yourself, Lord God, show us yourself and your way and we will be satisfied." It usually doesn't feel that God gives answers to that question.

The situation that the disciples of Jesus were facing around the year 30 AD gave rise to similar despair, over a similar spiritual crisis. You see, the disciples had followed Jesus for two or three years now, participating with him as he tried to redeem and transform a troubled, impoverished, occupied nation. He taught radical love, he healed, and he worked for justice. They were by his side as he challenged those in power in both politics and temple life. He gave them hope of a life lived in conformity to God. But now it was clear that many wanted him dead. In John 10 we hear about a plot to kill Jesus, and in chapter 12 Jesus talks with his disciples about his impending death. In chapter 13, Jesus serves his disciples a special meal, foretelling the details of his death.

And all of this talk of Jesus' death must have been terribly troubling. How could anyone want to kill this man who was bringing healing and perfection to the world? How could anyone want to stop the social progress that was being made in a troubled society? But that is exactly what was going to happen, and the disciples could see the writing on the wall.

In the face of that spiritual crisis Philip said, "Lord, show us the Father, and we will be satisfied!" And, as I interpolate that phrase, I hear Philip asking, "Jesus, show us God, let us see the will of our Creator, and then we'll come out of this despair, and know how to face tomorrow. Jesus, show us God, and then you will have really calmed our troubled hearts, you will have really prepared us for your death and for how we are to keep on living."

And I've been asking the same thing that Philip asked. "Jesus, show us God, show us the Father/Mother/Creator of all things. Show us the will of the one who brought all things into being! Show us what God wants us to do, how God wants us to live, in the face of this present hostility. Then, and only then, will I be satisfied."

> Philip, I have shown you God. Have you been with me all this time, Philip, and you still do not know me? Have you been with me all this time, Seth, and yet you still do not know me? I am in the Father and the Father is in me. If you have seen me, you have seen God. I came to you as the good teacher. I was one of your own, a simple man of Galilee, but I came to you with wisdom and teachings that were like nothing you'd ever experienced. I taught rejection of accumulation. I taught love for Samaritans (your "enemies"). I taught gender equality, and I taught that serving was the greatest way to be rewarded, to be humble was the greatest way to be exalted. I sat and listened to strangers. I took the time to get to know the sick and disenfranchised. In my teaching, you have seen God. Be satisfied.
>
> I came to you as healer, inviting you to cast your diseases, sicknesses, and brokenness upon my shoulders. I entered your homes, paying house calls. I stood in your square, inviting folks to come from far and wide. I recognized the touch of a bleeding woman when she reached out in a crowd and touched my cloak. I recognized the pain in the face of a hurting father, as his daughter was on the verge of death. I drove out the demons and powers in your life that were leading to destruction. In me as healer you have seen God. Be satisfied.
>
> I came to you as forgiver and reconciler. I dined with Zaccheaus, the chief of all financial cheats. I restored the blind and lame, leading them not only out of their disease, but into restored reality. I forgave the world, even those who put me in chains, even those who hung me on a cross. In my forgiving, you have seen God. Be satisfied.
>
> I came to you as prophet, demanding that justice be done. I cleaned out the temple, insisting that the poor be treated fairly by the religio-political establishment. I prophesied about a new social reality, one defined by a different president and country than the one in which you lived. Caesar wasn't king and president of what I proclaimed, and the kingdom wasn't defined by the limited geographical boundaries of the Roman empire. God is king, and the boundaries of God's kingdom are limitless. It is a kingdom that is ruled by love. In fact, love is another name I gave you for God. As I proclaimed the kingdom, you were seeing God. Be satisfied.

Section Two—The Prepared Church Confronts the Issues of Its Day

I came to you and committed to a path of perfect peace, a path of nonviolence, even when it led to my death. In these acts, too, you have seen God. Be satisfied.

Philip, Seth, Reformed Church of Highland Park, I have shown you the Father. Whoever has seen me has seen the Father. I am in the Father and the Father is in me. Through me the Father who dwells in me does his works.

Friends, hear the good news, *we have seen God*. We have seen God in the life and person of Jesus Christ. God and God's will are on display for us.

But the good news today is one step more radical. Today is Pentecost Sunday. It's the day when the church was born. Jesus told his disciples that the Spirit of God, the same Spirit that rested on him, empowering him to embody God and God's will, was coming to all of them. "You are the salt of the Earth . . . you are the light of the world," he said to them.[6] And in Acts 1:5b he said, "You will be baptized with the Holy Spirit not many days from now."

When we really consider what this means, it is an incredible promise. *The presence of the Spirit, together with following the path of Jesus, enables us to see God in ourselves.* The Spirit of God blends with our human spirit, empowering us to be Christians, people who, like Christ, have the power to display God and God's will in our own lives.

Try saying the promise to yourself right now. It's scary. "In me is the presence of God. By the power of the Spirit, I and the Christ and the Creator are one." It almost sounds ridiculous, and yet, that is what Jesus says to his disciples.

So, during this time of great hostility, Philip and I, and you, need to stop throwing our hands up in despair while we ask, "God, show us yourself, show us your will," assuming that we can't possibly get that chance to see into the great beyond. Instead, we need to ask that question, believing with absolute certainty that God already has shown Godself and God's will—in Christ. And when we see God in Christ, a lot of the murky waters start to clear, and it becomes easier to discern the will of God in the world, and easier to embody it in ourselves.

And if God and God's will are in us, then we can become what Christ told us to become, the light of the world, the salt of the Earth, embodying the fruits of the Spirit. In terms of politics, in terms of the

---

6. Matt 5:13a, 5:14a

Christ Showed Us God

global situation, our nation is incredibly far from the fruits of the Spirit right now. "Love, joy, peace, patience, kindness, goodness, faithfulness, gentleness, and self-control" are in short supply.[7]

Friends, studies show that at the time the Iraq war broke out, only 15% of churchgoers heard their pastors mention the war in a sermon or in prayers. I think this is a terrible statistic. The Christian church, a community that claims to embody the presence and will of God, has disconnected faith from world events, especially anything that seems "political."

For a community that claims to have seen God and already knows the will of God, this seems downright irresponsible. If we know it, we ought to be sharing it in ways that influence the world scene! It is the will of God that we treat all people in the world as our brothers and sisters, being especially respectful to our enemies. As Christians, we should be forerunners in terms of insisting on the right treatment of prisoners. We should be outraged by demeaning the enemy by putting their faces on a deck of playing cards, making a mockery of their lives. We should refuse to believe negative blanket statements made about people, about nations.

It is the will of God that we practice humility, and recognize that arrogance only leads to destruction. As Christians we should be insisting that our nation listen to the wisdom of others; that we sit and engage in dialogue. We should insist that we exercise our ears before we exercise our military muscle. It is the will of God that our central citizenship be in the kingdom of God—a country without geographical borders into which all people are invited, even now. The interests of the kingdom of God should always be bigger than any national interest. We should speak out boldly whenever "national interests" drive us into hostility. We should always insist that our national behavior lead to a kingdom where the afflicted are comforted, the poor are helped, and the suffering have a place to be healed.

It is the will of God that we practice nonviolence, that we avoid warfare and killing. It is the will of God that we become willing to suffer for righteousness sake. We should raise our voices in a loud "no" whenever dropping bombs from 15,000 feet becomes the norm, whenever driving into towns in large tanks with guns a-blazing becomes all right.

For those of us who know the will of God as revealed in Christ, it is clear that our nation is behaving in ways that are far from our maker. The result has been a loss of credibility in the world, and most dramatically,

---

7. Gal 5:22–23.

the loss of American soldiers and civilian contractors as well as Iraqi soldiers and citizens. On this day I want to remember the eight hundred American lives that have been lost. Many of those lost were much younger than I am, just getting going on the new and exciting stage of life defined by marriage and children.

I also want to remember the loss of thousands of lives of the grown children of Iraqi mothers and fathers, pulled in to fight a war they didn't choose, but that came inside their borders, into their communities. They, too, are somebody's child, somebody's husband, somebody's wife, somebody's Mommy or Daddy.

Jesus says that in him we know God's will. Jesus says that through the Spirit that will is to be made manifest in our lives. Is it? If so, there is love, and there is God. Maybe it will be through you who look to Christ and therefore know that God is love, that one day we will truly beat weapons into garden tools. Maybe it will be through you, and through your sharing the will of God, that our nation will stop having names to carve into walls of remembrance for those who died in battle. May it be through seeing God in you, and in Christ, that the heart of the world may soften into instruments that stream with the love of God.

God did appear, in Christ, and now in you. See God and confront this world with love, for God is love. Amen.

13

Displaced but Not Disgraced

D ecember 24, 2003

> In those days a decree went out from Emperor Augustus that all the world should be registered. This was the first registration and was taken while Quirinius was governor of Syria. All went to their own towns to be registered. Joseph also went from the town of Nazareth in Galilee to Judea, to the city of David called Bethlehem, because he was descended from the house and family of David. He went to be registered with Mary, to whom he was engaged and who was expecting a child. While they were there, the time came for her to deliver her child. And she gave birth to her firstborn son and wrapped him in bands of cloth, and laid him in a manger, because there was no place for them in the inn. (Luke 2:1–7)

"Everyone to your hometown! The emperor is taking count!"
"What. What did he say? Does he know what that means?"
Farmers leaned on their rakes, bakers stopped kneading their bread, children stopped playing in the pathways. "To our hometowns, huh?"
And so the citizens of the occupied provinces of Galilee and Judea began wandering. Streams of people passed each other in all directions, heading away from their current homes and back to their ancestral lands. All headed away from crops they had started, but would never enjoy and from systems of care they had established with their neighbors. This wasn't just a one-day jaunt back to the ancestral village. This probably

Section Two—The Prepared Church Confronts the Issues of Its Day

took a season, at least a couple months. They left their homes unguarded—who knew what they might find when they got back.

In those days, a decree went out from the emperor in Rome that all people who lived within the occupied lands in Palestine had to go to their hometowns for a census. The purpose of the census is debated (tax purposes or a military draft?) but it is clear that it wasn't a census for the sake of helping the common woman and man. This wasn't some way to make sure everyone got a health care card, or food rations. The purpose of the census was so that the emperor, living in a far away place, could get something that he needed.

Mary and Joseph had to travel at least forty miles by foot, most likely, to get from Nazareth to Bethlehem. Theirs was far from the longest journey. There were some who had to travel at least 120 miles or more. They had to bring enough food for weeks. And so, for weeks the roadways that usually only carried traders, moving goods between Egypt and Syria, were flooded with lines of common folks—folks who weren't traveling for fun, but because of the political decisions of a foreign ruler. Unlike the traders, who traveled on well developed chariots, these travelers moved on well developed calluses.

How did they do it? How, especially, did Mary, and all the other pregnant mothers of the day, do it? How did the sick and the lame do it? Is it any wonder that there was no room for them in the inn in Bethlehem? With all of Galilee and Judea on the move, there were few indoor sleeping spaces available.

I'm having an easier time in these times today imagining what it must have looked like during the weeks and months that Mary and Joseph were traveling to Bethlehem. I think it must have looked like lines of Afghanis, trying to get out of Kabul before the bombings. You've seen the pictures in the media, haven't you? Lines of old Toyota pickup trucks, stacked fifteen feet high with mattresses, cooking utensils, and children. And people walking, en masse, with everything they can carry, down dusty paths.

I think it must have looked something like Iraq in the weeks before the war, where streams of families headed out of Baghdad and Takrit. I think it must have looked something like the lines of Mexicans, moving by the cover of night across the US border, in order to make five bucks an hour, so their young children can afford school tuition and supplies. I think it must have looked something like the lines of Palestinians trying to get past a checkpoint, so they can be day laborers in Israel, so that their families can eat. It must have looked something like the lines of the 30,000 or so of our national guardsmen and women who are lining up, as we speak, to be shipped out of town, and into towns on the other side of the world in Iraq and Afghanistan.

We live in a world where common people move en masse, in lines, from one place to another because of Caesar Augustus and the census, and policies, and wars.

We often display pictures of Joseph and Mary traveling alone, on their way to Bethlehem, but that was surely not the case. Mary and Joseph were common people in the common line, trying to meet the demands of an emperor who really didn't care about them, and certainly didn't care that she was pregnant.

During the census, I picture the sleepy town of Bethlehem as a place transformed and damaged. As one of the central ancestral homelands, the homeland of all who linked themselves to David's line, many would have been traveling there. For those months, I picture Bethlehem as a tent city of displaced people. Or, if not a tent city, then at least like an outdoor Grateful Dead concert, just, without the concert. People were sleeping in barns, and on the open ground—not enough food, not sufficient sewage facilities for that many people.

But then . . . the concert did start. It was an angelic concert. The stage was lit up, with light from heaven. A child was born, whose birth was the topic of the songs. Shepherds rushed in to join the mosh pit of peasants. And everyone spent the night streaming into the stable to see a newborn—a little seven-pound boy.

Emmanuel, God-With-Us, entered the world through a displaced woman, in a tent city of displaced people; God came into the world through one woman who spoke for Every-Man and Every-Woman who is tired of being put out of her village because of forces beyond her control.

When Jesus was born, God brought hope and significance to every Afghani line of Toyotas, every underground railroad traveler, every tractor trailer truck full of migrant workers, every asylum seeker, every frustrated soldier. In this act, God showed that divine favor rested on the displaced. God gave hope to those who sleep beside their wagons.

People often say to me, "Pastor Seth, it's easier to pray and imagine God is with me when times are tough." As we all know, severe turbulence on an airplane can quickly transform travelers into praying saints who promise to devote themselves to God if God will just guide this thing to the ground.

Some people feel badly about this, that they feel closer to God when they are in moments of weakness, vulnerability, and need. But I don't think it's something to feel bad about. Jesus came to those who were displaced. Maybe, instead of feeling guilty about seeking God only in a weakened state, it would be good practice to spend more time thinking about the ways we are displaced. We can hide it better than those who are in lines of peasants leaving Baghdad, but that doesn't mean we are free from the experiences of displacement.

There is the displacement of loneliness. There is the displacement of inadequacy. There is the displacement of a broken heart. There is the displacement of addiction. There is the displacement of rejection. There is the displacement of unreal expectations. There is the displacement that comes from feeling completely at odds with the direction of one's government. There is the displacement that comes from the guilt of being a silent beneficiary of unjust world politics. There is the displacement that comes from feeling like you can never get ahead, that rent and school will always be a struggle.

These are just some of the forms of displacement that I encounter on a weekly basis as a pastor. We tuck these things away sometimes, but it seems to me that it is when these things are laid bare, when they are exposed, when we realize our displacement, that it becomes easier to find the manger, and the baby who was born as grace to the displaced.

The angel sings, "Glory to God in the highest heaven, and on earth peace among those whom he favors!"[1] I think God's favor rests on those who are displaced, because they are the ones who seem to find him.

So, where is Jesus born this year? Where is God-with-Us alive and effective? I hope he's born in Baghdad hospitals. I hope he's born to a mother waiting in a Liberian food line. I hope he's born in an AIDS clinic in South Africa. I hope he's born for the children and parents of our soldiers who are having a hard time sleeping tonight. I hope he's born under the bridge in our town, to those who are cold tonight. And I hope, as your eyes are turned to the world, you are able to witness his birth in all these places.

---

1. Luke 2:14.

But I hope, too, tonight, that Jesus is born right here, in the midst of your own displacement. I hope he's born for you as your eyes are turned in upon yourself.

Jesus Christ can come to any he chooses. But he often seems to choose those who are displaced, and who know they are displaced. As Jesus said later in his life, "Those who are well have no need of a physician, but those who are sick."[2] Jesus came for those who knew they needed a doctor. He was too young to talk those first nights in Bethlehem, but if he could have, I bet Jesus would have said to the tent city of Bethlehem, "You've been displaced, and I've come to bring you grace." Amen.

---

2. Mark 2:17a.

Part Two

Faith Facing "Enemies"

14

Watch Out for Iran!

M arch 6, 2005

> As he approached Jericho, a blind man was sitting by the roadside begging. When he heard a crowd going by, he asked what was happening. They told him, "Jesus of Nazareth is passing by." Then he shouted, "Jesus, Son of David, have mercy on me!" Those who were in front sternly ordered him to be quiet; but he shouted even more loudly, "Son of David, have mercy on me!" Jesus stood still and ordered the man to be brought to him; and when he came near, he asked him, "What do you want me to do for you?" He said, "Lord, let me see again." Jesus said to him, "Receive your sight; your faith has saved you." Immediately he regained his sight and followed him, glorifying God; and all the people, when they saw it, praised God. (Luke 18:35–43)

"What is that sound? It sounds like a happy crowd. It sounds like a confident crowd. This isn't a typical crowd. It's not time for the markets to be open. Hey, who's going by?"

"Jesus of Nazareth."

"Jesus, Jesus the prophet! Jesus the teacher! Jesus the healer! Jesus, Son of David, have mercy on me!"

"Hey, stop that. Don't bother him, he's talking."

"Jesus, Son of David, have mercy."

"Hey, stop that, don't bother him, he's walking."

"Jesus, Son of David."

Section Two—The Prepared Church Confronts the Issues of Its Day

"Hey, stop that. Don't bother him . . . he's special."

And Jesus stood still, stopped in his tracks, not making a sound. Jesus stood still, didn't rush to judgment, didn't put him down. Jesus stood still, collected himself, and asked that he be brought to him. And with his request you can feel Jesus saying, "Bring him near to me, close like he matters, close like I love him, close like I'll listen, close like there is no one else in the world, on whom I'm focusing. Just him." We aren't told, but I bet he asked him his name. I bet he asked how long he'd been sitting there. I bet he asked where he slept at night, if he had eaten. I bet he asked about his family and friends.

"Just you, I'm here for you. What do you want me to do for you?"

"Lord, let me see again."

Friends of Jesus Christ, as we travel the way of the cross we are called to hear unwelcome voices above the din of a crowd. We are called to humanize "the blind man," "the murderer," "the terrorist," "the regime."

The crowd, the crowd of this culture, that claims to have Jesus in it, might sternly order our enemies to be silent, might refuse to take "enemies" seriously, might leave them as a labeled group, but we can't do that. We've got to stop and listen to the blind man.

We are in the midst of a war that is being waged, in large part, because of American failure to listen to the blind man—Iraq. Rather than humanize the "enemy," we dehumanize it. We are attacking "a man who gassed his own people;" we are attacking "a country that stands against every kind of freedom that we hold dear;" we are attacking a country that "harbors terrorists." So many voices are saying phrases like this that it's impossible to choose who to quote!

Be quiet, *be quiet, be quiet*, blind man. No we won't negotiate, no we won't let you articulate. No we don't want to hear your voice. We don't want to hear your view. We don't want you to explain. We don't even want to ask your name. We know who you are. Be quiet, blind man.

It's too late now, to go back and meet the blind man—Iraq. We're in too far. Too much has happened. But there is another unwelcomed stranger on the street today. Another who is crying out to be heard, another that longs to be understood, another nation that feels so misunderstood that it feels blind. It can't see light; it can't see hope. That nation is Iran. And I want to preempt this looming confrontation with loving conversation.

Friends of Jesus Christ, the way of the cross in 2005 includes stopping, standing still, listening, and asking about Iran. What is going on in our national relationship with Iran? How can Iran be invited into the crowd so that we might hear its voice?

We should listen to Iran, for Iran's sake. But if that doesn't feel relevant, if that feels too distant to you, just wait. Wait until your sons and daughters are being sent to fight the "enemy blind man" whom we haven't even been invited to get to know.

As I was starting to think about Luke 18 this week, an amazing thing happened. I was on the Internet, looking for the most recent information on Iran, and while I was doing so, news broke that Iran had not allowed UN inspectors into one of their military sites, Parchin, for a second visit. As I sat there and watched, new document after new document appeared on my Google search. New articles about the situation were coming in faster than I could read them. Here are the kinds of phrases that I found in articles published on March 2, 2005, between the hours of 2 and 4 pm: "US Accuses Iran of Deceiving UN Inspectors;"[1] Iran Was Willing and Apparently Able to Manipulate the Nuclear Nonproliferation Regime in the Pursuit of Nuclear Weapons; Iran Shuts out Nuclear Inspectors; and Military Action against Iran Possible.

And the media and government sternly ordered Iran to be quiet. The media and the government tell us the blind man is armed and dangerous, too dangerous to discuss things with, too dangerous to be invited into the crowd. There seems to be a lot to be said about this lurking enemy, but not much listening going on. Why listen to those terrorists? We're told, "If you listen to them, you're supporting them."

Stop, followers of Jesus. Stop and insist that the crowd stop too. Stop, and insist that Iran be allowed to explain its reason for not letting UN Inspectors into the Parchin base. Mr. Naseri, head of the Iranian delegation, explained to *The New York Times* that "'notions of threats of attacks against Iran's safeguarded and other facilities by a major nuclear-weapon state [i.e., the United States] . . . [was the reason] for Iran's unwillingness to allow further inspections at Parchin.'" The first inspection of the base showed that no nuclear material was present, so further inspections that could result in leaks of military secrets were, in Iran's estimation,

---

1. Bernstein, "US Accuses Iran," http://www.nytimes.com/2005/03/02/international/europe/02cnd-nuke.html; ens_newswire.com/ens/mar2005-03-01-02, archivesdawn.com/2005/01/19/top17.htm.

unwarranted.² Stop and learn about Iran, about its political system, about its cultural and religious climate. Stop and read the headlines carefully, from many different sources. Start doing the work yourselves. The crowd isn't stopping—but you need to—for the love of God. Stop and listen and ask, "What do you want me to do?"

Maybe Iran will say, "Help me see again. Help me see that we need to not live in fear of an attack. Help me see that I am somebody to you. Help me see that I can come close and work for the restoration of all things. Help me see that the West, so influenced by Christianity, has come back to God."

We can help the blind man, and we can help the crowd, our national crowd. When we stop, and listen, and love we have the chance to help our government, media, and culture to stop and listen.

Luke tells us that upon being heard and received in love by Christ, "immediately he regained his sight and followed him, glorifying God."³ And all the people, when they saw it, praised God. I think that the Iranian government might also walk in the love that is seen in Christ if it were listened to.

The blind man had a lot to learn after all those years of isolation. There are things that Iran needs to learn too. That nation would do well to walk with the global community, to be influenced by some of the freedoms of Western democracy. And we would do well to walk with Iran, learning many things ourselves.

Who would you least want to invite for dinner? In Jesus' day it was the blind, lame, diseased, tax collectors, and Samaritans. Who is it for you? This week, invite someone to dinner who you really don't want to get to know; someone you really don't want to listen to. Maybe literally invite someone, maybe figuratively. Invite that hated ex whom you haven't spoken to in years. Maybe "invite" an Iranian, by reading an Iranian love poem at the table. Maybe sit at the table, and write a gentle note to someone you've never stopped to listen to before—asking questions. Write to George Bush, or Bill Clinton, whichever one you don't like, and say, "What do you want me to do for you? How can I love you?"

This is not an easy teaching. But it comes to us from one who not only stopped for a blind man, but also from one who sat at table with

---

2. Bernstein, "U.S. Accuses Iran," http://www.nytimes.com/2005/03/02/international/europe/02cnd-nuke.html.

3. Luke 18:43a.

Judas, Peter, Pharisees, and Sadducees. Followers of Jesus, this meal today is for you. May it feed your soul, and let you know that you are a friend of God. Extend the table to the world. Stop and listen to your enemy, sit at the table with him or her. That is the way of the cross, the way that leads to resurrected life. Amen.

15

We're Better Off for All That We Let In

September 12, 2004

> Now all the tax collectors and sinners were coming near to listen to [Jesus]. And the Pharisees and the scribes were grumbling and saying, "This fellow welcomes sinners and eats with them." So he told them these parables: "Which one of you, having a hundred sheep and losing one of them, does not leave the ninety-nine in the wilderness and go after the one that is lost until he finds it? When he has found it, he lays it on his shoulders and rejoices. And when he comes home, he calls together his friends and neighbors, saying to them, 'Rejoice with me, for I have found my sheep that was lost.' Just so, I tell you, there will be more joy in heaven over one sinner who repents than over ninety-nine righteous persons who need no repentance. Or what woman having ten silver coins, if she loses one of them, does not light a lamp, sweep the house, and search carefully until she finds it? When she has found it, she calls together her friends and neighbors, saying, 'Rejoice with me, for I have found the coin that I had lost.' Just so, I tell you, there is joy in the presence of the angels of God over one sinner who repents." (Luke 15:1–10)

Some issues just don't seem to go away. Jesus and the Pharisees and scribes locked horns about so many things. Four times in the book of Luke we hear that the Pharisees and scribes were grumbling about Jesus welcoming sinners and tax collectors. To repeat a story four times in one fairly concise gospel suggests that this issue was like garlic breath during Jesus' ministry—it just wouldn't go away.

Who were these folks with whom Jesus insisted on sharing meals? To share a meal with someone, by the way, was the ultimate cultural way of showing full acceptance. Before I move on, a word about tax collectors and sinners. Tax collectors were Jews who worked for the Roman government, the government that ruled Palestine. Tax collectors were required to pay a certain amount to Rome, and then they could keep what was left over for themselves. They set the levy, so they were able to control how much was available to skim off as a keepsake. Tax collectors were seen as sneaky and, even worse, traitors of their own people.

And then there were the sinners. I spent a great deal of time this week exploring the Greek word "*amartolos,*" or "sinner." What is a sinner? Today's text doesn't refer to a group of people who sometimes sin; this is a group that was defined by sin. There was an amazing diversity of definitions that I found when I explored this word. Some definitions suggested that "sinner" arose in later Judaism as a term to define anyone whose life is not defined by careful observance of the Torah. Others said it referred to all non-Jews. Others said that a sinner, according to Pharisees, was anyone who did not subject himself or herself to pharisaic interpretation of the Torah. Some said an *amartolos* was anyone who lived an extremely immoral life. Others included the sick and lame as sinners, as their diseases were thought to be attributed to their sins or the sins of the previous generations. But while there seemed to be disagreement about what constitutes sin, there was one consistent theme. A sinner was one whom the local religious authorities had deemed unworthy to be part of the synagogue, too unclean to participate in the central institution of the community.

By chapter 15 of Luke's gospel, Jesus has repeatedly responded to questions regarding his inclusive actions. They said things like, "Why Jesus, why do you spite us, by welcoming those that our upright religious community has decided are undesirable?" Usually his answer focused on the *recipient* of his surprising hospitality. In chapter 5, when asked why he dines with sinners and tax collectors he says, that it's "because those who are well have no need of a physician, but those who are sick."[1] In chapter 7 of Luke, when asked why he let a sinful woman put ointment and her tears on his feet, he said it was because "her sins, which were

1. Luke 5:31.

Section Two—The Prepared Church Confronts the Issues of Its Day

many, have been forgiven; hence she has shown great love."[2] Usually his answer focused on the recipients. He does these things out of love for the lost, forgotten, and excluded.

But today, Jesus gives us another answer about why we should welcome the sinner and tax collector—and this answer took me by surprise. This time when the Pharisees grumble, asking why Jesus welcomes sinners, Jesus told two stories that focused not on the *recipient* of love, but rather on the *joy that comes to the one who seeks the sinner and tax collector.* The recipients in his two stories are a sheep and a coin, two rather indifferent recipients. The sheep *may* care to be found. But who knows? It might not have even known it was lost. The coin certainly doesn't care if it is lost or found. Jesus seemed to choose two stories in which the recipient is of secondary focus—and I think he did it to make a point. He wanted to focus on the joy that the *seeker* experiences when finding something that is lost.

If you lost a sheep, and you left all the others in pursuit of the one, and you found it, think about *your* joy! If you lost a coin worth ten days' wages, even if you had nine others, you'd look all over. And when you found it, *the joy!* The rejoicing! There is great joy in looking for what is lost, in trying to include what has been excluded, in trying to heal what has been broken.

Jesus' answer in this passage to why he cares for sinners and tax collectors is this: to find a person who is lost is a memorable, incredibly joyful experience. Beyond that, he says that even God has a different level of joy when someone who is lost becomes someone found.

Friends, Jesus is saying something here that I would be afraid to admit without his saying it first. To extend love to the unlovable, to the forgotten, to the person in the questionable occupation, or with the troubling reputation, will result in joy for you, as well as for God. Giving love, like receiving love, results in heavenly joy. So give love!

Jesus felt the Pharisees were keeping themselves from great joy by not inviting in those who have been left out—and in this passage he called them on the carpet for it. In guarding the gates, being unmoved keepers of what seems pure, they had missed endless chances for joy. And how about you, dear friends? Have you given love recently to someone who is excluded—someone called "sinner" or "untouchable"? Have you given yourself the potential for great joy?

2. Ibid., 7:47a.

We're Better Off for All That We Let In

The title of my sermon this morning is inspired by the most recent album of one of my favorite bands, The Indigo Girls. In the title track, "All That We Let in," they sing of the pain in the world, and just how hard it is to face it all. But in the middle of a melancholy song, they suddenly sing *"you may not see it when it's sticking to your skin, but we're better off for all that we let in."*

This is what I believe Jesus is saying to us today through two stories that emphasize the joy experienced by givers of love as they seek out the lost. We are living in an age where there are serious parameters drawn around who we are to love and not love. There are a lot of assumptions made about people, ethnic groups, religions, and political parties. It might seem completely counterintuitive, based on what the talk shows, and the TV stations and the politicians tell us, but according to Jesus, we're better off for all the "sinners" that we let into our lives.

I hear a lot of references to "bad," "evil," "terrorist," and "radical." I hear a lot of name-calling, a lot of people referred to as "sinners," but not a lot of attempts at getting to know those "sinners." Assumptions are made, but people aren't welcomed or sought out, and when that happens I'm afraid that the world is missing out on opportunities for joy.

A couple of our church members, Joan and Elaine, didn't miss their opportunity this past weekend when they attended what was billed as an "interfaith retreat"—a retreat hosted by Muslims precisely to invite into their lives people whose religion and culture was non-Muslim. Last year it was fairly well balanced between Muslims, Christians, and Jews. This year, however, they were the only two non-Muslims at this large camp. They shared a room with Muslim women, learned about "the veil," observed 5 am morning prayers, and had theological conversations. They opened themselves to a group that has been largely driven out of American communal life since the events of September 11, 2011. Joan and Elaine received great joy by being open.

One of the tasks my wife, Stephanie, and I feel called to in ministry is to constantly encourage our congregation to examine how we can be more inclusive. Who doesn't yet feel welcomed here? Who avoids us altogether, and why? What can we do about it? We want to be more open for the sake of the person who feels uninvited, but we also want to be more open because, as Jesus tells us this morning, inviting *the uninvited, the sinner, the tax collector* to commune with us is to experience great joy as a congregation.

Section Two—The Prepared Church Confronts the Issues of Its Day

This week I watched members of the Highland Park community and our church community come together to welcome a family that recently moved here from Sierra Leone, Africa. This family had no affiliation with community members, or with the church, and I watched as numerous people put time, energy, and resources into helping them get rent money together, and begin the process of furnishing an apartment. The family was clearly grateful, but I saw a glow on the faces of givers this week, too, experiencing the joy that Jesus said they would experience.

If you want heavenly joy in your life, it's going to take risk; it's going to take inviting in those who are currently uninvited into our lives and communities of faith. Maybe, like Jesus and his followers of old, we'll find that some who were called "sinners" were poorly labeled. Maybe, like Jesus and his followers of old, we'll find some of those called "sinners," and who lived in ways to properly earn the title, will be loved right out of that identity.

Sometimes there will be uncomfortable moments—but I rest on the promise that giving love will bring the giver joy too. Two years ago I went to the Sonora Desert, west of Tucson, Arizona, to meet up with a group of Christians in a group called "Humane Borders" concerned about border issues. I spent one full day of that trip in a water tanker, stopping occasionally to wheel big jugs of water to strategically placed cisterns. As government helicopters hovered overhead, zooming in on us to see if we were hiding anyone, we filled water cisterns, placing big white flags on them. These Christians take "giving-love" very seriously. They especially take Jesus' words seriously about giving a cup of water to the stranger. The director, Robin Hoover, explained to me that the agency isn't encouraging illegal immigration; rather, it just wants to prevent death. Hoover underscored for me that people don't come into this country for our cup of water. They come here because of economic injustices promoted by governments on both sides of the border. People come into this country for food; they come so that they can send money back for their kids to attend school. Some people come with bad intentions, but they are the minority. Humane Borders gives water, but more importantly, it seeks out those who are lost, considered "sinners" by some, for entering the country illegally.

Especially in these terror-frenzied times, people have mixed feelings about border issues. Maybe you do too. That's precisely why I told this story. It's not always comfortable to reach out to the excluded. I bet Jesus didn't feel comfortable at all the first time he invited the tax collector to dinner who overcharged his family at a tax checkpoint every time he tried to travel out of town. But I can tell you that the folks at Humane Borders, like Jesus himself, experience joy on a daily basis as they say "yes" to the stranger despite the discomfort.

When a federal agency praised Humane Borders for saving the lives of forty-five Mexicans in 2002, forty-five of whom would have died of dehydration had they not come upon a cistern in the desert, I saw that the joy already experienced by those in Humane Borders was spreading into places its participants had never dared dream it would. The INS, through its statement, was starting to show a humanitarian face, and with it, joy.

We aren't told how the Pharisees responded to these stories. I hope they started letting people into their lives, not only so that sinners and tax collectors could receive the joy of a community of faith, but so that the Pharisees themselves could experience the joy of giving love. Amen.

16

A Corrective to the Furor over the "Ground-Zero Mosque"

September 12, 2010

> Now all the tax collectors and sinners were coming near to listen to him. And the Pharisees and the scribes were grumbling and saying, "This fellow welcomes sinners and eats with them." (Luke 15:1–2)

Brothers and sisters in Christ, we gather today, on this twelfth day of September 2010 having just acknowledged the ninth anniversary of the 9/11 attacks. We, the public, still haven't pinned down the reason for the attacks. We were told that "they" were against our freedoms; we were told this was a "Muslim crusade;" we were told that there was no rational reason and that we can't reason with those folks. In other words, the truth—whatever it was—was covered up with blanket statements that, for some reason, the nation seems to have accepted.

We gather today, ten Septembers since the day we were together in this sanctuary in tears and with fears, calling on God. We gathered then to ask for guidance, to ask for forgiveness, to ask for help, to ask for healing for devastated children, spouses, and parents. We asked, too, that we might come to understand what happened that led to 9/11. We also wanted to understand how anyone could give his life in a devastating suicide mission that wreaked such havoc? We asked that God help us

A Corrective to the Furor over the "Ground-Zero Mosque"

better understand Islam, to get to know Muslim brothers and sisters, that we might be able to differentiate between those who committed these horrific acts and the rest of the Muslim community in our country and around the globe.

And here we are, nine years later, and the eyes of the nation are once again on that same section of lower Manhattan, and the hearts of the nation are once again stirred over something that has to do with Islam and 9/11: Park 51, or the so-called "Ground-Zero mosque."

We've got real estate mogul Donald Trump offering to buy the property, with a serious markup, just to make the whole issue go away.[1] We've got a Christian pastor in Florida ready to try to broker a deal to stop the mosque, saying that if it isn't moved he'll hold a Quran-burning ceremony. We've got Mayor Bloomberg saying that "denying religious freedom to Muslims would play into terrorists' hands."[2] We also have Newt Gingrich declaring that "the Ground-Zero mosque is an Islamist cultural political offensive designed to undermine and destroy our civilization."[3]

All of this controversy, believe it or not, over a Muslim cultural center that is open to all people for activities including basketball and swimming, and that is being planned by an Imam who was a spokesperson for George W. Bush and the US Department of State, and who is a key player in the American Society for Muslim Advancement. Imam Feisal Abdul Rauf, spokesman for the project, said the organization pledges to promote, "integration, tolerance of difference and community cohesion through arts and culture," based on the Islamic values of "compassion, generosity and respect for all."[4]

Hatred, fear, religious tension, and broken American communities are alive and well this September—and that's why I'm talking about Christians and Muslims and America today. Brothers and sisters, what is going on?

I've read scores of articles on the mosque/cultural center in recent weeks—you probably have too. Many, written by Christian leaders, are so

---

1. Mangan, "Donald Trump Makes Bid," 4:34.

2. Karen Matthews and Beth Fouhy, "NYC Panel," http://www.salon.com/2010/08/03/panel_clears_way_for_ground_zero_mosque/.

3. Ratnesar, "Ground Zero," http://www.time.com/time/nation/article/0,8599,2011400,00.html.

4. Joseph Phillips, "Tolerance and the Ground Zero Mosque," http://townhall.com/columnists/josephcphillips/2010/08/16/tolerance_and_the_ground_zero_mosque/page/full.

hate-filled and uninformed about Islam that I feel ashamed to share with these authors the title of Christian pastor.

Other articles, by those who think the mosque should be permitted, argue for it on rational grounds: 1) the mosque isn't actually being proposed to be built on one inch of the sixteen blocks that once held the Twin Towers. It's not a Ground-Zero mosque and never claimed to be; 2) Muslims live in lower Manhattan and have been worshiping, meeting, and carrying out Muslim lives for decades there. If they want to build a community center, then why shouldn't they be allowed to do so?; 3) The zoning board approved it, with twenty nine of thirty voting "yes." That rationale seems right to me, but most of the articles sound like they would be convincing only when preached to others in the same analytical and passionless choir. Their answers won't even be considered by those holding the "Don't-Build-the-Ground-Zero-Mosque-in-My-Backyard" signs in places as far away as Washington State, California, and Florida.

Many of you have known me since 2001. September 9, 2001, was our very first Sunday in Highland Park as your pastors, just two days before the awful attacks. As you probably guessed, I stand firmly with those who say, "Let them build it;" but today I want to address this situation from a specifically Christian place, a place that comes from a careful reflection on today's lectionary passage from Luke 15.

Now, the tax collectors and "sinners" were all gathering around to listen to Jesus, but the Pharisees and scribes were muttering and grumbling, saying, "This man welcomes sinners and eats with them."[5] Muttering about Jesus and the company he kept is a central theme in the gospels. Jesus kept all the wrong friends.

Now, those tax collectors and "sinners" had names, and families and positive identities. They are named here; not by their mamas, or their favorite uncles, but by those who despised them. We know that some in first-century Palestine were called "sinners" simply because the jobs they did made them ritually unclean. Others were called sinners because of skin, blood, and body conditions they were born with, or acquired through no fault of their own. While tax collectors were despised, they were key to keeping a healthy relationship between Palestine and Rome—hated, but you had to have 'em. It is true that Jesus can and does welcome those who had committed grave sins; but it doesn't appear to me, here in Luke 15, that was the situation with this particular group of people. This

5. Luke 15:2.

wasn't a "big-time-sinner convention." No, here *the Pharisees are making a judgmental blanket statement about all the people who didn't fit the Pharisaic description of acceptable—which happened to be most of Jesus' friends!*

The text continues: "Then Jesus told *them* this parable." Now, it is unclear who the *"them"* is. To me it sounds like he is talking to the entire group, those who are gathered close (those who were "sinners" in the eyes of the establishment) and those who won't get near those people (Pharisees and Scribes/"the establishment"). I picture Jesus saying these parables very loudly, so that everyone there could hear.

> Let me tell you something: Which one of you, having one hundred sheep and losing one of them, does not leave the ninety-nine in the open field and go and search for the one until he finds it—and the rejoicing over finding the one who is lost is greater than the rejoicing over the ninety-nine who didn't need to be found! You'd carry it home and call your friends and neighbors together to celebrate! I tell you the truth, there will be more joy in heaven over one sinner who repents than over ninety-nine righteous persons who need no repentance.

The word translated for "repent" is "*metanoia.*" Metanoia literally means "turn around." "Repenting," for these so-called sinners, is about turning around and walking back into a warm welcome of the full community.

Jesus goes on, and I paraphrase: "Picture a woman who loses a coin. She's got lots of other coins, but she will search high and low for that missing coin, and oh the rejoicing, when that one is found!"

Notice first that as far as Jesus is concerned, all one hundred sheep belong together; all ten coins belong together. They are all beloved of the same shepherd and the same woman. *Together* is what is normal and right. The fact that one is not there with the established group is the problem that needs to be corrected—and not passively. All efforts need be directed toward full restoration!

I wonder how the tax collectors and sinners felt, having been identified here as "lost sheep," and "lost coins." It's a bit presumptuous of Jesus, isn't it?—to categorize people this way, or maybe not. Maybe this group, named so unfairly by the establishment, knows exactly how it feels to go through town with judgmental eyes staring them down. Maybe this group knows just how it feels to choose to "stay lost" and separate from the established society because it is surely safer off by themselves, among their own, rather than being close to the ones who will call them sinner and write them, their spouse, and their children off as different and weird.

Hopefully they could hear that Jesus was saying something like this:

> Pharisees and scribes, there have been some lost from the full community for some time. I am one who looks for them. I will seek them until they are found. And I am happier, and God is happier, about finding these people than God is about seeing you at the table—for it is wonderful to reclaim someone who has been gone! I want to welcome, include, get to know, and learn from those who have been outside. I don't call them "lost" any longer. I call them "beloved dinner guests." Pharisees and scribes, you are still invited too—if you are willing to sit at the table with all of us!

I have, in the past, read this passage out of context. The passage in Luke (and the almost identical version in Matthew 18) suggests that God is a shepherd who loves us so much that God seeks us out! I've usually used this passage as one that speaks to personal faith—when I'm lost, God finds me and brings me back to faith. But it never really says explicitly that it's a passage about finding "faith." Reading this passage out of context, I've never thought to ask, "God found me, but for what purpose?" Read in context, however, the answer shines through: "Pursue people who are excluded so that we can sit and eat together and can welcome one another."

Through his actions, and with these parables, Jesus was *effectively redefining who "fits" within community*. And this is important. This isn't a passage about finding someone to make them a Christian, or to get them to accept certain doctrines or beliefs. No, Jesus was seeking those who were marginalized, so he could get everyone around the table of a new, healthy, and restored community.

Brothers and sisters, the God who we have gotten to know through the person of Jesus Christ is a God who should make the authorities of politics and religion mutter, because God is always standing with the oppressed and judged and inviting them in! And we are ambassadors of the one God.

Right now it seems that some loud misguided Christians in this country are the self-appointed gatekeepers, not afraid to use hate-filled and judgmental language when referring to Muslims, and especially

A Corrective to the Furor over the "Ground-Zero Mosque"

when referring to this Muslim Community Center in New York City. Those loud Christians seem to have quite a following—though the media helps make it feel larger than it (hopefully) really is. Most of the rest of the Christian population seems silent or passive on the matter. *Neither option is the way of Jesus Christ.*

It is time for the politicians, the talk show hosts, and the cable channels to stop muttering about Muslims. It is time for them, instead, to start muttering about Christian friendship, support, and solidarity with Muslims! For Muslims are, within our society and context, among those currently being pegged "sinner," "radical," "violent," and "suspicious." By their vulnerable place Muslims are God's priority, and we Christians are to be ambassadors for God.

But have you heard any muttering? I haven't.

My biggest concern about this whole ordeal in Manhattan is that I've heard so little grumbling, so little muttering, about Christians who walk hand in hand with Muslims. With their way of thinking, there should be finger pointing and judgment *aimed at us* by these right-wing talk show hosts. Instead, all of the name-calling, hatred, and misconstrued facts, have been directed at Muslims. Even those Christians who have been supportive of the "mosque" have been sure to say things like, "If *they* want to do this it is entirely up to *them.*"

Followers of Jesus Christ, we should firmly state that Muslims building a community center and mosque is exactly the kind of activity that should happen in the kingdom of God that was announced by Jesus Christ. Let's speak our support using religious language, religious convictions. And then we ought to sit at the table with Muslim brothers and sisters ourselves—and play hoops in their community center.

Why is there so little muttering? I believe it's because even though we are years past September 11, 2001, most Christians haven't gone out of their way to seek friendships, relationships, and connections with Muslim neighbors. Part of "seeking" our Muslim brothers and sisters, and joining in table fellowship, would be to seek real people, our real neighbors. Here in New Jersey this is a real option for us. We should be doing a much better job with interfaith fellowship efforts. I hold myself accountable for the lack of movement on that front. Also, the efforts that *are unfolding* should be highly publicized, a reminder to us of the importance of these connections.

Section Two—The Prepared Church Confronts the Issues of Its Day

Part of seeking to connect with Muslim brothers and sisters in our particular context should be for Christians *to demand* that our government give us the truth about what happened on 9/11. Those attacks on the World Trade Center and Pentagon were largely the result of American policies overseas, and the result of what at that time was a forty-year war waged by the CIA against the Bin Ladin family and others in Afghanistan. While I do not claim to have any insights into the details, I feel sure that 9/11 had more to do with covert policies involving government than it had to do with your common Muslim family in America. We cannot settle for not knowing the truth.

Our complete failure to learn the truth, coupled with our failure to become real friends with American Muslims, has kept anti-Muslim sentiment high for the past nine years. It has been hidden, most of the time, just below the surface, until it is exposed again with all its horror, with situations like the "Ground-Zero Mosque."

It would be easy this week to stand up here and pass blame. It would be easy for us to look at the actions of Pastor Terry Jones in Florida and think, "Wow! That guy is out there." We could dismiss him and say, "We're glad we're not that kind of Christian." We could look at the US flag burning around the globe, and the anti-American response to Terry Jones and we could think, "Wow! Those Muslims are really scary. That's way too strong a response to burning a sacred book." But I think we would do best, instead, to look at ourselves this week and ask, "Why isn't anyone muttering about us and about our deep connections with the Muslim community?" Why aren't they muttering? Well, because we haven't been doing our job of seeking those who have been lost from table fellowship—those who, on the whole, have not been welcomed as brothers and sisters in America.

Let's change that, okay? I want to encourage you this week to connect with Muslims at work, at school, in your neighborhood. I want to encourage you to begin what should be a long process of developing relationships. I want to encourage you to stick up for Muslims in any conversation where people without one Muslim friend are making blanket assertions about a whole people.

I want to encourage you to start asking for facts about 9/11. Not "facts" about security failures, but facts from a "longer history" that might help—once and for all—separate 9/11 from regular, ordinary followers of Islam.

A Corrective to the Furor over the "Ground-Zero Mosque"

And every time someone mutters about you, as you are victorious in terms of forging an interfaith friendship, or sticking up for a Muslim in a political or social context, or getting a new bit of truth about 9/11, rejoice like the woman who found the coin, or the shepherd who found the sheep, and know that God in heaven is rejoicing right along with you. Amen.

Part Three

Faith Facing Immigration Policy

17

When a Church Loves Its Country

M ay 28, 2006

> I am not asking you to take them out of the world, but I ask you to protect them from the evil one. They do not belong to the world, just as I do not belong to the world. Sanctify them in the truth; your word is truth. As you have sent me into the world, so I have sent them into the world. And for their sakes I sanctify myself, so that they also may be sanctified in truth. I ask not only on behalf of these, but also on behalf of those who will believe in me through their word, that they may all be one. As you, Father, are in me and I am in you, may they also be in us, so that the world may believe that you have sent me. The glory that you have given me I have given them, so that they may be one as we are one. I in them and you in me, that they may become completely one, so that the world may know that you have sent me and have loved them even as you have loved me. (John 17:15–23)

On May 30, 1868, after the Civil War ended, Memorial Day was formalized. Flowers were put on the graves of both sides in order to help heal the nation. It was later expanded to include all who died in America's wars. But Memorial Day, throughout the generations, has also been a day for prayer and Spirit-driven action. It's a day to mourn the loss of young men and women of our country, called into battle over the course of our

Section Two—The Prepared Church Confronts the Issues of Its Day

national history. But it's also a day for prayer—for connecting with God about peace, about the end of war, and the end of division.

Vice President Lyndon Johnson's remarks on May 30, 1963, in Gettysburg, Pennsylvania, illustrate that Memorial Day spirit:

> On this hallowed ground, heroic deeds were performed and eloquent words were spoken a century ago. We, the living, have not forgotten—and the world will never forget—the sacrifices or the words of Gettysburg. We honor them now as we join on this Memorial Day of 1963 in a prayer for permanent peace of the world and fulfillment of the hope for universal freedom and justice . . . as we maintain a vigil of peace, we must remember that justice is a vigil too—a vigil we must keep in our own streets and schools and among the lives of all our people—so that those who died here on their native soil shall not have died in vain. One hundred years ago, the slave was freed. One hundred years later, the Negro remains in bondage to the color of his skin. The Negro today asks for justice. We do not answer him—we do not answer those who lie beneath this soil—when we reply to the Negro by asking, "patience." It is empty to plead that the solution to the dilemmas of the present are in the hands of the clock. The solution is in our hands. Unless we are willing to yield up our destiny of greatness among the civilizations of history, Americans—white and Negro together—must be about the business of resolving that which confronts us now . . . The Negro says, "Now;" others say, "Never." The voice of responsible America—the voice of those who died here and the great man who spoke here—their voices say, "Together." There is no other way.[1]

I bring up these words from Lyndon Johnson's Memorial Day speech today in this sermon, because the speech tells us about the power of the church. For eight years leading up to that day in 1963 the church had been the church Christ calls every church to be—a church set apart for God so that it is then prepared to be sent into the world. The church impacted the president's speech, and national attitudes, and legislation.

The black church in Montgomery, Alabama, started it. From the very first day of the Montgomery bus boycott in December 1955, the church was at the center of the Civil Rights Movement. When so many voices in society, in the "world," seemed to be against the actions of

---

1. Johnson, "Remarks at Gettysburg on Civil Rights," http://www.lbjlib.utexas.edu/johnson/archives.hom/speeches.hom/selected_speeches.asp.

When a Church Loves Its Country

"Black America," black churches, and then some white churches, held prayer meetings, hymn sings, and rallies for peace and justice every single night. Christian communities let their relationship with God in Christ define them and redefine them over and over; they let God protect them, and they were able to wake up the next morning and behave in non-violent confrontations with the "world." As evidenced by Lyndon Johnson's speech, in time they changed the world—saved it.

At the Last Supper, Jesus prayed at length for his disciples—so John tells us.[2] After Judas got up from the table, to go betray Jesus, Jesus turned his face toward the sky, and prayed out loud in the midst of his disciples, saying something like, "God, the hour has come; I'm going to you. But I want to pray for those whom you gave me to be disciples. I have been glorified in them. They are one, like you and I are one. I have protected them, cared for them; God, bless and protect them now that I am going to you. Also, God, give them the ability to stand firm against the world that is going to attack them. I have given them your word, and the world has hated them because they do not belong to the world, just as I do not belong to the world. God, don't take them out of the world; don't set them apart permanently. Just protect them from the evil one. God, I in them and you in me, they can be completely one with us—and through them, then, the world may know that you have sent me and have loved them even as you have loved me."

Friends of Jesus Christ, if we the church want to love our country, the first thing we need to do is ground ourselves in the reality that we do not belong to the "world"/"country;" we belong to God. If we are grounded in the radical love that is God, we begin to practice love. We begin to shine. If we want to love our country, we've got to "have [his] joy made complete in [ourselves]."[3] We've been given the living word, Jesus Christ, and a living community of friends with whom to define a new and alternative reality. If we love our country, we cannot let the policies and practices of our country own and define us; we can only let Jesus Christ define us.

But being set apart is just the beginning. Jesus says so, right in this prayer. If we want to love our country, we need to stay in it, even though we are alien to it. You, friends, are undocumented in this country, you are resident aliens. You do not belong to this country—this world. Your

2. John 17.
3. Ibid., 17:13b.

Section Two—The Prepared Church Confronts the Issues of Its Day

only true papers are stamped by God. You belong to God. And Jesus says in his prayer that our vocation is to stay in the "country," or "world," so that the world might know the love of God. What we have to offer our country is our very best selves and congregation, formed in the image of Jesus Christ.

This Memorial Day weekend our congregation has a special opportunity to love our country through the way that we choose to love people who are caught up in the throes of immigration chaos. Of particular concern are our Indonesian brothers and sisters who are in this country and in serious crisis.

For those of you who haven't yet heard, in the early hours of Wednesday morning, the Department of Homeland Security raided an apartment building near here where many of the members of the Indonesian congregation, and one family from our congregation, live. They went door-to-door, kicking doors, yelling, "Everybody out with your hands up!" They slapped handcuffs on fathers in front of their children; they took away a father who was home alone with a three-month-old baby while his wife was working the third shift in a factory. They took a man away from his wife who is eight months pregnant. The next morning the papers read, "Feds Round up Fugitives: Edison, Metuchen, Woodbridge Raids Net 35 Illegals."[4] Not one of these people had any crime larger than that they had overstayed their tourist visas. The paper bragged of 797 "fugitives" having been caught in New Jersey since last October. I wondered if the other 762 were as harmless as these thirty-five. I imagined so. Many members from this community are now in hiding, not sure what to do. I am generalizing here, but the "country's" assessment of this situation, and similar situations, is if they don't have their papers, they shouldn't be here. And that's about the kindest assessment out there. Other labels are also attached to these communities, such as "terrorists," and "leaches."

But you, friends, do not belong to this country, nor are you defined by government rhetoric, the public opinion polls, nor even by the laws of the land. You have to abide by them, but you're not defined by them, and, therefore, you can always challenge them! You are from God, and since you are from God, broad sweeping terms that generalize and dehumanize are just not acceptable. You are from God, and you get your way of life from the community of faith as we love each other, pray together, wrestle with Scripture, and listen attentively to our neighbors. Because you look

4. Harrison, "Feds Round up Fugitives, p. 1.

for the definition of things from the very source of life, the odds of your assessments being superior to that of the news headlines, or the government spokespersons are very high.

Pastor Stephanie spoke last week about the way the Spirit often acts in a surprising and compelling way, and then we are invited to respond. She said, "The Spirit has acted; the ball is in our court now!" Do you remember that she used an example in her sermon about immigration? She asked how we could tolerate a fence being built through the border if God's Spirit was at work in a church that straddled that border. I thought a lot about her sermon this week.

I do not know what the Spirit of God has in mind in terms of the situation unfolding with the Indonesian community. All I know is that this week the Spirit of God told me this is the most important thing on my agenda, and I've seen the Spirit say the same thing to many others within our church. Raids like the one the other night happen all the time in our country—and they should never happen.

The Department of Homeland Security is upping its number of nationwide "raid teams" from thirty-six to fifty-two in a couple of months. It seems that most raids happen against undocumented workers from countries without a large American population. It's a way for the government to give the image of "coming down hard on terror" without offending any block of voters. It also seems that raids happen against undocumented workers from primarily Muslim countries, so that the government can play off the country's bias against Muslims, and the association of "Muslim" with "Al Qaida." These policies are not making us safer; they are so unloving that I am ashamed they are practiced by the country of my birth.

It's Memorial Day. Let's remember today all the people who gave their lives for this country and what it stands for and stood for during their lives. And, also, let's remember that when it has stood for good things, positive things, it's often been because the church has been nudging it along. For all who have gone before, and all who will come after, let's nudge the country along to welcome our neighbors. Amen.

18

Being Somebody in the Land That Calls You Nobody

O ctober 14, 2007

Jeremiah, prophet of old for new—we've been learning from you. Jeremiah, you sure have challenged us. You called us to awaken from our slumber about justice and to recommit to our covenant with God. Then you surprised us, telling us that sometimes there is no healing that God can bring about, no balm in Gilead; but you surprised us even more by telling us that God will be a suffering God with us, when there is no relief, and God will suffer with us on the road of pain and exile. Jeremiah, you've brought us hope when we've least expected it. Buying property in Jerusalem while the city is under siege? Would you buy a condominium in Baghdad, or Bethlehem? How about Darfur? Would you? I bet you would. Today Jeremiah, you keep pushing us—with words to people living in exile:

> These are the words of the letter that the prophet Jeremiah sent from Jerusalem to the remaining elders among the exiles, and to the priests, the prophets, and all the people, whom Nebuchadnezzar had taken into exile from Jerusalem to Babylon . . . Thus says the Lord of hosts, the God of Israel, to all the exiles whom I have sent into exile from Jerusalem to Babylon: Build houses and live in them; plant gardens and eat what they produce. Take wives and have sons and daughters; take wives for your sons,

and give your daughters in marriage, that they may bear sons and daughters; multiply there, and do not decrease. But seek the welfare of the city where I have sent you into exile, and pray to the Lord on its behalf, for in its welfare you will find your welfare. (Jeremiah 29:1, 4–7)

The Babylonian exile was one of the most formative moments in Judah's history. It was an exile that happened in two different phases. Jeremiah's words today were given to the exiles sent away in phase 1. In 596 AD the Babylonian army marched on Jerusalem for the first time, taking into exile the king, his court, the priests, and its creative heart, the artisans. Most of the buildings, and most of the population were spared *for now*, and a puppet governor was placed on the throne.

The exiled leaders knew what they wanted. They wanted to get back to Jerusalem! They wanted to get back there because, well, that's where they were from. That's where they had families. And, that's where they had power. And there was another reason they wanted to get back. That was the place their religious life made sense. For four hundred years the people of Judah had been practicing a faith that found God to be located in that particular place—Jerusalem. In the temple and in the God-ordained monarchy, David's line, God resided. For generations the mandate from God had been to "tear down all other high places of worship—don't confuse matters—God lives in Jerusalem!" But now, the people of Judah didn't live there anymore—they wanted to get home.

In Jerusalem they were somebody—in Babylon, nobody. In Jerusalem they were powerful—in Babylon, powerless. In Jerusalem they were connected—in Babylon, disconnected. In Jerusalem they were shapers—in Babylon they were the misshapen. In Jerusalem they felt the presence of God. In Babylon they had no God.

And the result of all this was despair; and the result of their despair—a fluctuation between depression and a desire to mount an insurrection. For this particular crowd, insurrection at least felt like a choice. They were people with friends in high places around the region, whose support they might have been able to muster.

But Jeremiah, that's when you spoke up. Two years after the exile you heard murmurings that Jews in exile were going to mount an insurrection and you just couldn't keep quiet. Don't fight! You had the gall to basically say, "No way! Don't fight for your nationalistic freedom. God is sovereign and brought you into exile. Don't fight God's decision. You will

Section Two—The Prepared Church Confronts the Issues of Its Day

get back some day, but don't fight for your return. To fight Nebuchadnezzar would be to fight your God." But Jeremiah, you didn't stop there. You didn't stop with telling them what NOT to do. You offered an alternative.

Build houses and live in them, plant gardens and eat what they produce, get married, have children. Encourage your children to marry and have children. Multiply here and do not decrease. Seek the welfare—the *shalom*—of the city where I have sent you into exile, and pray to me on behalf of the city. If you seek the city's *shalom* you will find your own *shalom*. Jeremiah, your words must have been met with anger. How dare you, a prophet still in Jerusalem, still having dinner with your family, ask displaced exiles to stay put and love the city that took them from their homes? How dare you?

You dared to say it because it was true—and you spoke the truth. I don't think I'd ever feel comfortable saying to someone who has ended up in Highland Park because of duress in the world, and who felt down about being here, "No, stay here, build a life. This is God's plan for you." It's not my place—I sit too comfortably to say something like that.

But you know what? Jeremiah's words about living a free life in exile are true. I know this *not* from Jeremiah, but because of the witness of many of you. A few years ago, I tried to start a Spanish Bible study here. I put advertisements up all over Highland Park, and then I'd come and sit in the quiet room, singing Spanish praise songs and reading the Bible in Spanish at church, by myself, week after week, hoping someone would show up. I did this for about two months. No one came. Congregants would ask me how it was going. "Great!" I'd say. "Everyone understands my Spanish!" I finally decided this wasn't a great use of my time, so I told God I'd sit there one more week, and if nobody came, I was done. And just as I got to church that Tuesday night, so did Vicente Alverde. He'd seen the sign in the Laundromat, and had decided to come over. Vicente was here in this country, by himself, to work. He'd come across the border from Mexico, through the desert, risking his life. Why? He risked his life because he had two daughters, ages four and six, and a wife, in Oaxaca. He was working hard, and sending virtually all his earnings home to save for a little house, and to pay for school fees for his six-year-old girl.

When I asked him why he decided to come to the Bible study he answered, "Well, I'm here alone. I'm lonely and depressed. I live in a tiny room of an apartment. I'm not able to enjoy life day to day. Out of my loneliness, I'm starting to make bad decisions. I thought maybe coming to church would help me feel more connected to God and to others in this place." You know, for the next two years or so Vicente worshiped here with us and became part of us. Church members helped him land a job. He cleaned the floors and rooms of patients in our local hospital. He connected with God and invested in the city where God had put him. He missed his family to no end; his situation was still unbelievably hard. But by praying to God for *shalom* in the city, and working for *shalom*, he experienced *shalom* himself.

I just told a story about Vicente; but in this congregation today there are endless people who've undergone similar journeys, similar "moments of exile" that landed them here, in this town. While not dragged to the United States, like those first exiles were dragged off to Babylon, the imbalance of economic power between nations does almost *force* people to be on the move. Small and weak economies all over the globe are at the mercy of market decisions in the United States, Europe, and China. England stops buying bananas from a Caribbean Island and suddenly half the population is out of work and family members, to ensure survival, travel the globe. Sonia and Daren, can I get an "Amen"? The price of cotton in Kenya or Mali drops dramatically, due to overproduction in the United States and a flood of cotton in the international market, and Kenyans and Malians are jumping boats to Europe in order to live. Grace, can I get an "Amen"? War wreaks havoc in Sierra Leone. People flee for their lives. Hawa, can I get an "Amen"?

And when you get here, you're not what you were. There you were a surgical nurse, here you can't get a nursing license. There you were a radiologist, now you don't have papers and can't even take the exam. There you had a family; here you are alone. There everyone spoke your language; here nobody does. What do you do? There you never needed a car; you could walk to everything. Here you need a car, but can't get one. There you praised God in one way; here they praise God with different songs and rhythms. There is where your heart is; here is where you are.

And over and over again you are left with the choice. How am I going to live in the city or town where I've landed while I'm in exile? Am I going to close off from this hard-to-enter society? Will I rebel somehow, or will I choose to plant gardens and seek the *shalom* of the city?

Time and again I've seen you, my global teachers whom I have just highlighted, choose to seek the *shalom* of the city. You've lived out Jeremiah's advice day in and day out. Sonia and Daren, for the past two years, you have cared for one of our most needy homebound congregants. Hawa and Grace, you both care for homebound seniors as well, giving yourselves to needy individuals and families. And this place has gone from being a strange land, to being a home away from home—a second home.

You know, Jeremiah? You were right. In the long run, you were exactly right. The reason why the people of Judah survived the forty years of exile is because they learned to connect with God, and God's work of *shalom* for Babylon.

There is another exiled one I'd like to mention today, who also chose to seek the *shalom* of the city, and of every little fishing town and country village he entered. There was another exile who, while in Palestine, stopped for lepers in lands that lay between Samaria and Galilee. He came from a distant place, and while we can only speculate about whether he had any choice in the matter, we know that from the moment he arrived in this strange land he was mistreated. He was born among cattle, a feeding trough as his bed, to parents dismissed because they were not married. As an infant he was chased out of one foreign country and into another by a king who already felt threatened by him. Jesus Christ left his home and came into this world connecting with God everywhere he went. Throughout his ministry he contextualized his interactions, bringing food when food was needed, bringing healing when healing was needed, acceptance when acceptance was needed, critique when critique was needed. In all ways, this exile from heaven sought the true *shalom* of human cities.

And while I fear trivializing the horrors of real exile by making this comparison, I want to suggest that we too—all of us who live with Jesus—are also exiles now, like he was. Whether we were born in Highland Park, Houston, or Haifa, we are not fully from here. And we know our homeland, and we love are homeland. Our homeland is the kingdom of God. Our homeland is the kingdom of peace. Our homeland is the kingdom where lion and lamb lie down together. The place where there are no more tears. The Bible sometimes calls this place the New Jerusalem. We are exiles from there.

But God challenges us today. God challenges us that our homeland includes Highland Park and surrounding towns among its provinces. God is at work in our city, and it, too, is becoming a territory impacted by, and maybe even becoming part of, the kingdom of God.

So engage, exiles! Engage the world around you. Plant a garden or a planter on Main Street. Build a house, or a housing complex for young women aging out of foster care. Organize a walking route to school. Bring a fair trade business to town. Start a toy store. Serve in the food pantry. Deliver meals on wheels. Teach poetry. Staff the thrift shop. Work for telecommunications. Care for children. Raise our children. Engage fully in the community as an act of faith. Seek its *shalom*!

But do all this with an eye toward home. It's possible—isn't it, Elsie?—to love Highland Park and give your life for it, and to simultaneously love your home island of Jamaica and celebrate it. And it's possible, also, to fully give yourself to the community you're in, and simultaneously keep your eye on the home God has for you—the kingdom that is out before us and breaking into time and space.

Build gardens; eat the food that grows there. Build a house. Pray for the peace of this place where you are. Find peace yourself. Maybe, just maybe, as you look out on the horizon of the place where you are building and planting, you'll see the kingdom of God descending upon our city—and it will feel like home—and it will be home, for now. Amen.

19

Travelers Who Expose the Truth about Herod and the Arrival of God

January 9, 2011

> In the time of King Herod, after Jesus was born in Bethlehem of Judea, wise men from the East came to Jerusalem, asking, "Where is the child who has been born king of the Jews? For we observed his star at its rising, and have come to pay him homage." When King Herod heard this, he was frightened.... Then Herod secretly called for the wise men and learned from them the exact time when the star had appeared. Then he sent them to Bethlehem, saying, "Go and search diligently for the child; and when you have found him, bring me word so that I may also go and pay him homage." When they had heard the king, they set out; and there, ahead of them, went the star that they had seen at its rising, until it stopped over the place where the child was. When they saw that the star had stopped, they were overwhelmed with joy. On entering the house, they saw the child with Mary his mother; and they knelt down and paid him homage. Then, opening their treasure chests, they offered him gifts of gold, frankincense, and myrrh. And having been warned in a dream not to return to Herod, they left for their own country by another road. (Matthew 2:1–3a, 7–12)

"I saw a sign, and it brought me here. I had a hunch, and I went with it. I got a chance, and I took it. Something unfolded that let me know that faithfulness to the sign would lead me to encounter God." These words could have come straight from the mouths of the magi when they were talking about their journey with curious locals in Bethlehem. They caught a glimpse of a God-given star. Their desire to be faithful led them to take risks and travel far.

What heroes, these travelers from afar—and what a reward they received for their faithfulness! They arrived at a stable and recognized a simple child as Lord—bowing down before him!

"I saw a sign, and it brought me here. I had a hunch, and I went with it. I got a chance, and I took it. Something unfolded that let me know that faithfulness to the sign would lead me to God's good news. God was with me in this decision." These could just as well be the words of many recent immigrants who are now in this church who we call brothers and sisters in Christ. Dozens of you have shared with me, and with us, stories of your journey. For many of you, it was no more than a faint constellation from God in the sky that got you moving toward the United States.

You came here from Sierra Leone, escaping civil war. You came here from the Windward Islands, after changes in the world economy bankrupted your island. You came here from Ghana, escaping personal persecution; you came here from Indonesia, when a major political change suddenly put you at great risk. You came here from the Philippines, following work opportunities that came your way.

Some of you came with the right papers, others with some papers, some with the wrong papers, still others, no papers. You came because you had a need. Sometimes you came because someone here, some business, some elderly shut-in, needed you to come. You got a break and you went with a hunch; you followed God.

You are heroes, travelers from afar—traveling because God sent you—following a star that sometimes only you could see. You trusted the traveling would result in some epiphany—some manifestation of God for you at the end of your travels. What rewards you have received! You have had an epiphany—some of you, an abundance of them. You've had moments where your faithfulness to the journey allowed you to find the baby in a manger, to find Christ in some opportunity, to find Jesus here among us. You've had moments since your journey, where you've been brought to your knees in adoration of the Creator, Christ, and Holy Spirit.

And those of us who are not travelers—at least not travelers to the extent you are—have been encouraged to travel more, to follow stars, to listen to the Spirit's prompting, because we've seen that such trips are particularly capable of leading to epiphanies. For some of us, the closest we've ever been to having our own epiphany is connecting with you as you have had some dramatic encounter with the living God that grows out of your journey.

But the similarities between the experience of the traveling magi and you, our travelers, run deeper still; for most of you have encountered Herod somewhere along your journey. And this encounter with him has impacted—might I even say "enhanced"?— the manifestations from God you've experienced. Your journey started when you followed a sign from God, and you have come to a place where you are encountering God made manifest. In between God-at-the-start and God-at-the-epiphany you have encountered Herod who is pursuing you now, even beyond your epiphanies.

I like to imagine that there was a good-sized group of magi—the Bible doesn't say three—three was determined by some clever Christmas pageant organizers who decided that that was as many costumes as they wanted to make. "Tell you what!—three gifts, three wise men—that does it!"

I like to picture this large group of foreign faces showing up in Jerusalem, speaking unrecognizable languages. I like to picture that as Herod pieced together they had come far for a royal visit—for someone other than him—a knot formed in his stomach. This sounded like a threat to the throne. Maybe it was or maybe it wasn't.

Herod's response was to send the magi out of the room and to call in his own staff to discuss this topic in a way that made sense to him and his people. He went from personal conversation with magi moved by a sign from God, to reading old prophesies, getting answers from old important papers. Despite the fact that his holy books agreed with the magi's searching, he never considered the possibility that something good might be occurring.

His only use for the magi after that was as informants. He never listened to the magi again, never considered that it was amazing that a star had guided them to Jerusalem, and to Israel's God. He never wondered if this child might be a blessing, rather than a threat—maybe a way to bring new relations with the hostile nations to the East, just beyond the border of Palestine.

Travelers Who Expose the Truth about Herod and the Arrival of God

"When you have found him, bring me word so that I may also go and pay him homage." You can feel the insincerity of his words making your skin crawl—the kind of troubling thing that haunts a good night's sleep. The text says after they saw the baby they were warned in a dream not to go back to him. I'm sure the warning came in the form of a nightmare.

Herod's eventual response to a few amazing visitors showing up from other countries was to kill children, ruin families, and create havoc. Brothers and sisters in Christ who have traveled here from afar, following signs from God, following a star—watching you confront Herod has been one of the hardest experiences of my life and one of the hardest experiences ever faced by this congregation.

Herod, our government, hasn't taken the spirituality of your journeys seriously enough. He hides behind phrases like "rule of law," when he could rewrite that law if he desired to do so. Herod picks and chooses what laws to uphold. Herod picks and chooses what he wants to see and ignore, what he wants to enforce. Herod picks and chooses when it is beneficial that you found your way here; and if it serves Herod, he'll let you stay for a while, as long as you live in silence.

Doesn't Herod know that God has been at work in your travels? Doesn't Herod know that many of you have become part of the way God is working out God's loving way for the future of America? Herod is too busy talking to the wrong staffers in a back room to ask you why you came without all the papers. Rather than singing "Praise God from whom all blessings flow" that you are here and safe, that you are you, and that you are making us *us*, Herod (or a whole lot of Herods) is choosing to ruin your families and create a culture of fear.

Friends of Christ, I want to say, today, that while the suffering you have faced here as undocumented immigrants is horrible and wrong, your suffering has not been in vain. In addition to blessing us by your journey here and by sharing the epiphanies that you've experienced, you are blessing us by exposing the Herod who lives and works in our government and society. Tucked into this great democratic society, a society for which we are grateful and frequently proud, Herod is alive and well, and he lashes out with brutal and manipulative force—and many of us didn't know just how bad it was. You are exposing the godlessness of our infrastructure. You are exposing the way that fear, power, and the lack of listening to stories of stars and epiphanies is leading us down the wrong road in this country. We can't seek a remedy until we have a diagnosis; and you have helped us make the diagnosis.

Section Two—The Prepared Church Confronts the Issues of Its Day

And speaking now as an American, I want to apologize to you. I'm sorry that as you bless us by exposing our nation's brokenness, you are facing such suffering. I'm sorry for any day you have lived in fear. I want to say sorry to all the children in this country who are growing up without dads because Herod sent your dad away. I want to say sorry to the Harapah family. I want to say sorry to Lilly for Herod sending away the love of your life. I want to say sorry to Sandra for the months you have lost with Resheidio. I'm so sorry; but sorry is not enough.

When I read the story about the slaughter of the innocent babies in and around Bethlehem by Herod, I was disgusted with Herod. But I was also saddened by the lack of fight. I'm sure Herod's power was overwhelming; but when Herod comes to ruin your village and kill your children, shouldn't there be a story of resistance, or flight? Sorry doesn't cut it.

Immigrant friends, you have blessed us by your faithful traveling and by the epiphanies you see. You have blessed us by exposing Herod's fear and waywardness. But you have blessed us in yet another way. Unlike the magi, who saw an appearance of the Christ and then left, you have experienced Christ and Herod and have stayed here—stayed among us. By becoming one with us, by becoming part of this expression of the body of Christ, and by allowing us to get to know you, and love you, and pray with you, you have allowed us to share in your struggles and become a resistant people.

We are not just sorry about what is happening. No, we are sorry *and* we will not let Herod come for your children, your spouses, nor your friends without serious non-violent resistance. We will not let the media get away with only telling stories such as the one that recently reported that 70 percent of Americans now think children of undocumented parents should be denied a public school education. We'll insist that they also tell stories of the millions who think this whole argument is shameful.

We will not submissively allow Herod to keep children down who were brought to this country as children, that they can never go to college here or get a legal job.

We will not let anyone who, by the grace of God, has escaped a dangerous setting, be sent back to that setting simply because Herod doesn't care.

We will not let those who came here because of the conniving of rich business and government be called "law breakers," instead of "victims."

Travelers Who Expose the Truth about Herod and the Arrival of God

We will not let states around the country write discriminatory laws without hearing from our pews and pulpit.

We will not let families be broken up without sharing the story over and over and over.

We will not let immigrant detainees languish in detention without visits and cards of support.

As I prepared to preach this sermon, I explored more about the recent announcement that Essex County, New Jersey, just up the road from us, has quietly been presenting, for the past eight months, a proposal to the Department of Homeland Security, calling for a detention facility for 2,700 new immigrant detainees in New Jersey. This would be added to the 1,600 beds for this purpose we already have in this state, spread among five facilities. The reason for entering the contract is job creation—county economic growth. The county will earn $105/day for each inmate housed. That is touted as good for the economy and yet "affordable" by detention standards.[1]

In the articles I read there was never mention of the fact that most of the 2,700 inmates are tax-paying, non-violent family people with mortgages or rents (that's already the case with most of the 1,600 who are locked up). In the articles I have read there was never mention that the children of these inmates will need more help at school, that their now-single moms or dads will be broke and broken-hearted. There is no mention that after a stay inside, the family members will suffer from PTSD, depression, or deep resentment—having been through a family trauma. What's the cost of all of that? What's the cost in terms of the soul and in terms of dollars?

There is no mention in the articles about the Essex County detention proposal that most detained individuals *could* stay with their families while being monitored by the government, if monitoring was deemed necessary. There is no mention that those who are truly alone, with no contacts in the United States (which is a very small number), could be housed in loving, caring, yet "security minded," options run by faith communities or social service organizations at a fraction of the cost.

Brothers and sisters in Christ, together as a congregation, we have recently completed an advent journey. We sought our Lord with advent candles—flames that look a bit like the faint star that the magi followed.

---

1. Khavkine, "Essex County to Receive New Detention Center," http://www.nj.com/news/index.ssf/2010/12/essex_county_to_receive_new_de.html.

Section Two—The Prepared Church Confronts the Issues of Its Day

Then we arrived together, bowing before the manifestation of God named Jesus Christ.

And now it is time to notice that Herod is in pursuit of some of the travelers who are part of our body. He's only in pursuit of travelers whose journeys started in other countries. These targeted travelers are part of the human family and part of the American family now. These targeted travelers need an army of peaceful and hardworking resistance fighters who aren't afraid of Herod. Are we up for defending undocumented immigrants in our Bethlehem? There should be no need for Mary and Joseph to flee to Egypt, nor any need for the other families in Bethlehem to flee to Egypt.

While Herod is in the back room, making plans for a new detention center, let us be shouting in from the windows, "The Jesus in me loves the Jesus in you! Herod! Herod! Wake up to the presence of the living God!" When Herod is signing contracts with construction companies and private correction agencies, looking to get rich off people's pain, let us sing "Amazing Grace," and start our own construction of housing for those immigrants who need housing. Let us fund our own services for those who need support through immigration trials and tribulations. While Herod looks to write legislation that gives legality to his brutality, let's race Herod to the floor of Congress, creating loving legislation that needs to be taken seriously too.

Let us grow a wall of love and peaceful resistance that is so strong around our Bethlehem that it protects those who are suffering and brings Herod himself to his knees—or not.

It's hard to get Herod to his knees. It's always possible, indeed likely, that our resistance will be resisted by him. But if it is, look then for epiphanies, for God is made manifest most clearly when we are facing crosses. For we've learned something about crosses. We've learned that they are tools of Herod's reign that cannot succeed. We've learned that they become the occasion for resurrection. We've learned that death has been swallowed up in victory!

We saw a sign, and it brought us here. We had a hunch, and we went with it. We got a chance, and we took it. Something unfolded that let us know that faithfulness to the sign would lead to an encounter with God. God was with us in the decision.

Brothers and sisters, those could be words of magi, or words of the immigrants among us, but they are also words of our whole congregation

Travelers Who Expose the Truth about Herod and the Arrival of God

as we journey together in a world with broken immigration policies and anti-immigrant opinion.

Sometimes it feels like we follow a faint star in the sky, and at other times, the whole sky lights up. And sometimes, sometimes we've had the great fortune of seeing God come down and be made manifest. Let's hope, someday, we can rest from this journey, together with Herod, and with all the immigrants of the world, together around the manger of love. Amen.

Part Four

Faith Facing Economics and Poverty

20

The Economic Implications of the Covenant

M arch 12, 2006

> As he was setting out on a journey, a man ran up and knelt before him, and asked him, "Good Teacher, what must I do to inherit eternal life?" Jesus said to him, "Why do you call me good? No one is good but God alone. You know the commandments: 'You shall not murder; you shall not commit adultery; you shall not steal; you shall not bear false witness; you shall not defraud; honor your father and mother.'" He said to him, "Teacher, I have kept all these since my youth." Jesus, looking at him, loved him and said, "You lack one thing: go, sell what you own, and give the money to the poor, and you will have treasure in heaven; then come, follow me." When he heard this, he was shocked and went away grieving, for he had many possessions. Then Jesus looked around and said to his disciples, "How hard it will be for those who have wealth to enter the kingdom of God!" And the disciples were perplexed at these words. But Jesus said to them again, "Children, how hard it is to enter the kingdom of God! It is easier for a camel to go through the eye of a needle than for someone who is rich to enter the kingdom of God." They were greatly astounded and said to one another, "Then who can be saved?" Jesus looked at them and said, "For mortals it is impossible, but not for God; for God all things are possible." Peter began to say to him, "Look, we have left everything and followed you." Jesus said, "Truly I tell you, there is no one who has left

house or brothers or sisters or mother or father or children or fields, for my sake and for the sake of the good news, who will not receive a hundredfold now in this age—houses, brothers and sisters, mothers and children, and fields with persecutions—and in the age to come eternal life. But many who are first will be last, and the last will be first." (Mark 10:17–31)

We're on the road with Jesus now, and he is heading toward Jerusalem. We're traveling with him; we're his disciples, and he's told us that he knows what awaits him there. "I will undergo great suffering, be rejected, betrayed, and killed, and after three days I will be raised." And as Jesus walks toward Jerusalem, and we gather each Sunday in Lent, I have been preaching about a theme that hardly comes up at all in Jesus' last days—at least not explicitly. We're talking about covenant. We're talking about the special relationship that God has with you and with every person and every living thing—and we're talking about various implications of this covenant relationship. And this is why we're talking about it; Jesus and the God he referred to as "Father," were in an intense covenantal relationship. That relationship is at the core of Jesus' loving way in the world.

Doctrinal theologians love to speculate about how God the Father and God the Son worked out their relationship within the Godhead. Such speculation doesn't interest me. I'd rather stick with the biblical narrative. At Jesus' baptism, when the voice of God came from the clouds saying, "You are my Son, the beloved, with you I am well pleased," that was the moment when we hear that Jesus began to live fervently in light of his covenant with God.[1] God spoke. God said "yes" to Jesus; God sent the pulsing power of the Spirit into Jesus. And Jesus' immediate response was to spend forty days in the desert, wrestling with what it meant to be in a father-son covenantal relationship with God. What was it going to look like to live bound up with God in an intensely personal relationship? Whatever happened out there in the desert, Jesus came out of that place aware that his covenantal relationship with God was not going to be a two-person covenant, Creator to Christ. Rather, if it was going to be a covenantal relationship that honored the depth of God's character then Jesus' life was going to have to impact every living thing.

The idea of covenanting with God was not a new concept for Jesus. The Torah was full of talk of God's covenantal promises. The broader covenantal promises were to Noah and then to Abraham. But for the people

---

1. Mark 1:11b.

of Israel, it was the Mosaic covenant that came to hold such incredible weight. The Mosaic covenant grew out of the wilderness-wandering period, soon after God had led the Israelites out of Egypt. It was the language of "deal making," between God and that particular people. God would promise to love, and care, and protect the people of Israel, but they needed to adhere to particular laws—614 of them, in fact, in order for the covenant to be maintained. Jesus knew that law, the covenant law between God and Moses. But Jesus didn't come out of the wilderness spouting the Mosaic covenant. No, Jesus came out reinterpreting aspects of that covenant, wrestling with old laws and creatively enhancing them for a more radical ethic. Jesus came out engaging the world in fresh ways.

Jesus came out of the desert with a way about him that sounds much more like the covenantal prophecy of Jeremiah, who said in the 6th century BC, some 700 years after Moses:

> The days are surely coming, says the Lord, when I will make a new covenant with the house of Israel and the house of Judah. It will not be like the covenant that I made with their ancestors when I took them by the hand to bring them out of the land of Egypt—a covenant that they broke, though I was their husband, says the Lord. But this is the covenant that I will make with the house of Israel after those days. I will put my law within them, and I will write it on their hearts; and I will be their God, and they shall be my people."[2]

God had *that kind* of covenantal relationship with Jesus. God wrote it upon his heart. Jesus responded to God's initiative by infusing covenantal care for all things. When Jesus touched somebody with his healing, it was experienced as God's healing, for the covenant between the father and the son was so perfect that it was indeed God who brought the healing touch. Friends, we're talking about "covenant" this Lenten season because the covenantal relationship with God written on Jesus' heart motivated his actions and behaviors in every area of human life, with all people he encountered, even until death on a cross. We're talking about it because truly knowing yourself, as a child of the covenant, will motivate your response to God as well. For these forty days of Lent, step into a space with God where you can be grounded in the covenant and prepared to respond creatively in all things.

2. Jer 31:31–33.

Section Two—The Prepared Church Confronts the Issues of Its Day

In her article "Covenant and Care: From Law to Loving-Kindness," Margaret Whipp says that "*motivation* remains the chief contribution of the covenant concept. The relevance of the covenant concept lies in the tremendous care that is given to decision-making."[3] Today I want to take some time to talk about how being in covenant with God and, by extension, all people, impacts the way we reflect on economics. I want to do this by reflecting on the interaction between Jesus and the young man in Mark chapter 10.

A young man came to Jesus and said, "Good teacher, what must I do to inherit eternal life?"

"You know the commandments: you shall not murder; you shall not commit adultery; you shall not steal; you shall not bear false witness; you shall not defraud; honor your father and mother."

"Teacher, I have kept all these since my birth."

"Jesus looked at him, *loved him*, and said, "You lack one thing; go, sell what you own, and give the money to the poor, and you will have treasure in heaven; then come, follow me."

When he heard this, he was shocked and *went away* grieving, for he had many possessions.

Unlike many of the people who had come to Jesus at this point in Mark's telling of the gospel, this man is not an antagonist trying to get Jesus in trouble. This is a man who comes with a sincere question; a man who wants to live a morally upright life and be confident about his future in God. The young man didn't come to Jesus asking, "What should I do with my money?" He was asking about eternal life. Why did Jesus respond by addressing him about money?

Mark tells us that Jesus looked at him, and he *loved him*. This is a unique statement in the gospels. I think Mark is saying here that it was precisely because Jesus *loved him* that he responded as he did. He told the young man to give away all his possessions and money and to come follow him. I think he did so because Jesus knew that money was the thing keeping him from truly covenanting with God and other people. Jesus didn't answer the question about inheriting eternal life; instead he told him what he should be doing *now*, and simply alluded to heavenly treasurers in the future. And the man *went away* grieving, shocked, for he had many possessions.

3. Whipp, "Covenant and Care" 117.

The Economic Implications of the Covenant

Friends, he missed a chance to experience the covenantal love of Jesus. He missed seeing that the statement was prompted by love and a deep care for his life! *He went away grieving*—for he had many possessions—instead of following Jesus.

This passage is troubling, but tolerable, when we read it as Jesus' statement to someone else. But how do we respond if we read it as Jesus' words to us? "Jesus is looking at you, loving you, and saying, 'Go, sell what you own. Give it to the poor; you'll have treasure in heaven. Come follow me.'" He's saying it to you; he's saying it to me. Regardless if you make $500,000 or $5,000 a year let these words be words of love for you today. They are spoken to you by Jesus, who was in perfect covenantal relationship with the creator who loves you with steadfast love. Jesus is asking you about one of the most sensitive areas of your life. He's asking you about the thing that has been known to preoccupy you, whether you have lots of it, or too little of it. He's asking you about your money. He's asking you to think about the way possessions keep you from the fullness of your covenant with God and with the entire world that is "in God." Don't go away grieving—please don't. Jesus loves you, and he's bringing it up out of love.

The message sounds pretty clear. Young man, if you want to follow me, give away your possessions, for they're weighing you down, and come follow. If there is any economic model that is identifiable with Jesus' early community, and the community of the church formed at Pentecost, it is voluntary socialism. Especially in the book of Acts we hear that the early church "shares everything," and nobody owned their own property. It is too simplistic to think that we should cut and paste the specifics of Jesus' teaching into our current economic reality. But motivated by our covenantal relationship with God, that motivates us to care for all people, this passage should challenge us as believers to linger in questions about money and possessions, and to respond creatively.

What are the money issues that Jesus needs to address to you? I decided this morning to share with you the kind of money questions I've been dealing with, since I really started letting Jesus say to me, "Sell what you own; give the money to the poor, then, come, follow me." Since we came to this church, you all have been putting money into our pension fund. We are so thankful for that. Because of you we have some small investments. Well, about three years ago, I started asking about denominational investments because of a committee I was serving on; I realized that the money in our pension funds was potentially causing harm to people and the environment. I had been totally oblivious to financial market issues before that point. The mutual funds of the denomination were not screened. It was entirely possible that money was being invested in nuclear weapons development or other weapons development, pornography, tobacco, and companies notorious for environmental degradation. It was shocking to realize that our retirement funds were potentially causing harm in the world.

I was talking to one friend in the church last week who said that he had made an ethical decision not to invest in the stock market because of his concerns about the inability to track how his money was being invested. I admire that, but it's a step further than I've been willing to go (at least so far!). What my wife and I did was to research socially screened funds. Socially screened mutual funds are transparent about their holdings in companies, and about the ethical principles they use to make investment decisions. They do not invest in war projects, environmentally destructive companies, sweatshops, pornography, or tobacco. Additionally, most socially responsible investments are proactive about investing in companies that give back to their communities, and that have racial, ethnic, and gender diversity on their corporate boards and in positions of particular power. Whether the return on our investments will be as high as the "non-screened" funds is debatable. But there is something that is not debatable. As a Christian, asked to "give it all up" by Jesus, the least I can do is to ensure that the money is not causing harm and might even be doing good. I have lingered with the question of pension funds, and now feel that I am following Christ more closely with this investment.

Additionally, beyond the stock market, there are other ways to invest. In 1975, the World Council of Churches formed a micro-bank called "Oikocredit" (meaning "belief in the whole house of God"). Oikocredit is a "bank for the unbankables," formed on the premise that while God is in a covenant relationship with the whole world, many are not able to get loans to start businesses because of extreme poverty. Oikocredit now has four hundred million dollars, 75% of which is currently loaned out, and all of which has been collected from churches and individual Christians around the globe. Loans of $50 to $200 can get a family in many parts of the world on track for a successful business. In one slum city in South India alone, there are 128,000 families that have received Oikocredit loans. The neighborhood is being transformed. A few years back, Stephanie and

I decided that every January we would look at the previous year, and, if possible, invest a few dollars in Oikocredit. We get 2% interest on the money, and have the pleasure of knowing that the money is going to fund micro-businesses around the world.

Another issue I currently struggle with is how to be ethical as I shop. How can I be sure that I'm not participating in sweatshop abuses when I buy a new shirt for $5 on sale at Wal-Mart? There are websites out there that track the ethics of retail stores, both the treatment of employees and the environment, but I haven't really put the time in to transform shopping habits. One of the things I feel really good about in this regard, though, is being part of a church that birthed a fair trade store: a store that intentionally focuses on making purchases that do justice to workers and communities. When I purchase coffee at the fair trade store I am covenanting with God through caring for coffee growers in Africa and Latin America.

Another constant question is where to contribute money. How much should we be giving to the church? How much should we give to political groups that fight to reduce hunger worldwide? How much should we give to local ministries and groups that meet the needs of the most vulnerable citizens? My money decisions are best when I make them in the presence of Jesus saying to me, "Sell what you own, and give the money to the poor. If not, you're going to be lacking." Each person in this room will hear something different when they ask money questions before Jesus. I imagine some of you will feel you can be a lot more generous and a lot more intentional with your money. I imagine others will hear Christ saying, "Keep what you have, and go to your church and ask for financial help." Maybe your "possession" that you need to give up is your pride, and you need to ask for help at this time. It is my prayer that if you come to the church for help, we'll creatively respond to you, for we are in this covenant together.

Following Christ involves selling all you have, even as Christ sold all he had for the sake of his covenant with God. Be motivated by the covenantal promises that you've received from God. God's endless grace is for you, and your response is pleasing to God. Amen.

21

Tithing Is So Anti-Jesus

O ctober 22, 2006

> [Jesus] said to his disciples, "Therefore I tell you, do not worry about your life, what you will eat, or about your body, what you will wear. For life is more than food, and the body more than clothing. Consider the ravens: they neither sow nor reap, they have neither storehouse nor barn, and yet God feeds them. Of how much more value are you than the birds! And can any of you by worrying add a single hour to your span of life? If then you are not able to do so small a thing as that, why do you worry about the rest? Consider the lilies, how they grow: they neither toil nor spin; yet I tell you, even Solomon in all his glory was not clothed like one of these. But if God so clothes the grass of the field, which is alive today and tomorrow is thrown into the oven, how much more will he clothe you—you of little faith! And do not keep striving for what you are to eat and what you are to drink, and do not keep worrying. For it is the nations of the world that strive after all these things, and your Father knows that you need them. Instead, strive for his kingdom, and these things will be given to you as well. "Do not be afraid, little flock, for it is your Father's good pleasure to give you the kingdom. Sell your possessions, and give alms. Make purses for yourselves that do not wear out, an unfailing treasure in heaven, where no thief comes near and no moth destroys. For where your treasure is, there your heart will be also. (Luke 12:22–34)

At various times in my life I've heard phrases from this text being brought into discussions with poor people: "Don't worry;" "Don't be anxious;" "Don't worry about tomorrow." The overall message has been that everyone, including the poor, should not live with worry or anxiety of any kind, including about money or security. Someone good of heart was trying to bring comfort to someone "down-and-out," the comfort of knowing that God would provide. When used in this way, this passage sounds trite and condescending to me. But Jesus was not talking to homeless mothers with children. He was not addressing folks who had just lost jobs and were anxious to find work. He was talking to his disciples: some of them boat owners; one of them a tax collector; all of them articulate enough to be given leadership roles within the newly forming kingdom community.

Jesus' teaching here about "not worrying about provisions for tomorrow" is directed at those who are able to store things up in barns, IRAs, pension plans, or properties, and for those who, though they might not yet have obtained such things, have goals of obtaining them someday. He's not just saying, "Don't worry about tomorrow;" he's defining "worry" for us as "personal preparation." So, if you are preparing financially for tomorrow, you are, by Jesus' definition, "worrying about it." That activity, according to Jesus, is a form of idolatry—you cannot serve both God and wealth.

When read as a directive to people of means, this passage becomes a strong challenge. If I really let Jesus speak here and bring his words to bear on today, Jesus is taking a long and critical look at the stock market as a concept. He's challenging savings accounts, CDs, and pension plans. He's taking a long look at those of us who see ourselves as "responsible," even "wise" for investing in such things. If I really let Jesus speak here, to today, Jesus is scoffing at *individual* planning for the future and the idea of putting money aside for a rainy day. I do not want you to leave this morning saying, "Pastor Seth told me to get rid of my savings account and sell all of my stock." I'm not ready to do that in my own life—how could I ask it of you? But I do hope you leave wrestling with the fact that this is what Jesus is saying. He really doesn't want his disciples storing things up for themselves on Earth. Don't worry, I'll try to soften the blow this morning, tease out a gentler message, but I don't want to do that before first saying that Jesus' message about money is always going to be more radical than I'm ready to live up to—and I imagine the same is true for you.

Section Two—The Prepared Church Confronts the Issues of Its Day

I cannot resolve the tension for you, and I wouldn't want to. I can only suggest that you keep the tension alive between Jesus' ideal and your material realities and goals, truly praying about it all the time. For the challenge to part with all your money comes from Jesus, the one who parted with all his material possessions and even his own life, for the sake of perfect love. His voice about "giving up everything and not worrying about it," is a voice of authority that should constantly resound in our ears.

Is Jesus simply anti-material? Does he want destitute disciples who have no contingency for tomorrow? No, he loves the Earth, the matter. He just wants the *whole world* to experience the very best material world—the world that could come about if we ever could allow the kingdom of God to fully reign. Jesus wants anxiety and worry that lead to the amassing of personal wealth to get out of the way so that God's kingdom can thrive unhindered.

The birds don't worry and try to store up excessive amounts for themselves, and the kingdom thrives for all birds. The lilies don't worry and amass for themselves; yet the fields of lilies thrive. Jesus wants us all to stop worrying about ourselves and letting that worry lead to massive individual "storing," because such actions don't add a day of life or joy to the person who focuses on storing; nor does it add life to those who have legitimate material concerns—those who do not have enough food to eat, a safe place to sleep, or clothing to cover themselves or those in their care.

Instead of personal anxiety, Jesus wants us to turn our entire selves over to the kingdom of God. "Strive first for his kingdom!" Striving first for the kingdom is the antidote for worry about tomorrow. Jesus is calling for us to bring our wealth and to deposit it in the radical communalism of the kingdom of God that he says is near—that is forming right in this world. When we put our treasure there, in the kingdom, our heart will be with God also.

I imagine that Jesus was against tithing—percentage giving. Sure, he knew it was the practice of ancient Israel up until his day to give 10% of one's money to God, for use for worship life and for widows and orphans, but based on today's passage and others, I bet he didn't like it. Tithing isn't nearly radical enough for Jesus.

Remember the rich young ruler who asked: "What must I do to be saved?" Jesus said, "Sell all your possessions, give them to the poor, and come, follow me." To be part of the church—the manifestation of God's in-breaking kingdom—he had to give it all away in a manner that reached those in material need. He had to sell all his possessions, not to become devoid of possessions, but to show his true trust in the communalism of the kingdom of God. Giving it all away would lead to having a lot more, as he came to be part of everyone else's life.

We hear that people will see their possessions increase one hundredfold when they give it all away in response to Jesus' teachings. Jesus says in Matthew's gospel, they will "receive a hundredfold . . . and will inherit eternal life."[1]

But is it true? Will I really feel less worried, less anxious, if I give it *all* away? Jesus says, "yes." Will I really be provided for materially, when *I'm* in need in the future, if I part with all my material treasures? Jesus says, "yes." However, he doesn't want us to focus on that question—that's a question borne of worry. Just worry about today. If we'd all stop asking that question and accept that we are all part of God's family, and care for each other, such questions would become unnecessary. We'd be taking care of today for all of us, and dealing with tomorrow for all of us when tomorrow comes.

So give away your wealth, enough so that it hurts. Give it away to non-profits that find cures for disease and that care for children. Give it to your government for roads and schools and infrastructure—and then use your voice to insist the government stop using it for war and violence. That's my biggest problem with taxes, by the way. The way they are used to fund wars borne of worry—wars that protect and worship earthly treasure America. Give it to your church like the early disciples did. Make sure we spend it on spiritual formation and on peace and justice. Give it away to families around you who are struggling. Shower them with gifts—this is their day!

There is no perfect place to give hard-earned material wealth, but don't let that stop you from giving until it hurts. Jesus' words today are for you, givers. When givers give instead of storing up, the giver experiences the kingdom of God. When givers give instead of storing up, givers' hearts are in the right place and they are in the kingdom of God. When givers give, and gifts are received by those in need, the kingdom of God is made manifest. Put your treasure where you want your heart to be, right beside God. Amen.

---

1. Matt 19:29.

22

The Parable of the Talents

A Reading from the Margins

M arch 31, 2008

> For it is, as if a man going on a journey, summoned his slaves and entrusted his property to them; to one he gave five talents, to another two, to another one, to each according to his ability. Then he went away. The one who had received the five talents went off at once and traded with them, and made five more talents. In the same way, the one who had the two talents made two more talents. But the one who had received the one talent went off and dug a hole in the ground and hid his master's money. After a long time the master of those slaves came and settled accounts with them. Then the one who had received the five talents came forward, bringing five more talents, saying, "Master, you handed over to me five talents; see, I have made five more talents." His master said to him, "Well done, good and trustworthy slave; you have been trustworthy in a few things, I will put you in charge of many things; enter into the joy of your master." And the one with the two talents also came forward, saying, "Master, you handed over to me two talents; see, I have made two more talents." His master said to him, "Well done, good and trustworthy slave; you have been trustworthy in a few things, I will put you in charge of many things; enter into the joy of your

The Parable of the Talents

master." Then the one who had received the one talent also came forward, saying, "Master, I knew that you were a harsh man, reaping where you did not sow, and gathering where you did not scatter seed; so I was afraid, and I went and hid your talent in the ground. Here you have what is yours." But his master replied, "You wicked and lazy slave! You knew, did you, that I reap where I did not sow, and gather where I did not scatter? Then you ought to have invested my money with the bankers, and on my return I would have received what was my own with interest. So take the talent from him, and give it to the one with the ten talents. For to all those who have, more will be given, and they will have an abundance; but from those who have nothing, even what they have will be taken away. As for this worthless slave, throw him into the outer darkness, where there will be weeping and gnashing of teeth." (Matthew 25:14–30)

I am servant #1. No, call me steward #1. That's more accurate. My master is one of the most powerful people in the land. His holdings are incredible. He owns field upon field—and the amount increases every day. His portfolio puts him in the upper echelons of society, a "fortune-500" type of guy.

I don't like to call myself servant because, well, there is a huge difference between my situation and the situation of those under me. I, too, am financially bulging, not to the extent of my master's portfolio, but my wealth makes me more like my master than other servants. My master treats me well. I receive a lucrative salary as a result of making him loads of money.

There is a high cost, though, for what I do. I am hated by my own people. You see, the land of my master was once the ancestral land of thousands of citizens. Now, at best, people are servants on the land they once owned. Yes, I'm a steward for a master who buys up land that was once inhabited by common folks. He "reaps where he does not sow, he gathers where he did not scatter seed," as the people like to say. But you know, it is actually me, not my master, who swings the deal. He doesn't even have to be here, and he makes money. The guy takes off on long trips time and again, and leaves me in charge. His "hands are off" the actual transactions; I am the one who does the dirty work of land confiscation and peasant removal. When you hear people refer to tax collectors and "sinners," and you wonder who the "sinners" are, often it is me they are talking about.

Section Two—The Prepared Church Confronts the Issues of Its Day

The other high cost is that I constantly need to produce for my master. I live under the weight of needing to constantly acquire, regardless of the ethics of the acquisition. It is exhausting to live under constant pressure. My master is gone now on a journey to another land, and he left me with five talents of money this time—the equivalent of 32,000 days' worth of day labor pay! And you know what? By the time he gets back, only a few months after he departed, I will have doubled that money. I will! I will work tirelessly to ensure this is the case.

I am servant/steward #2. I agree with everything servant/steward #1 said. He is the best, though, at making money for the boss. The master trusts him with more money than me because, time and again, servant #1 proves he can make great things happen financially. He can work the markets; see the next big merger. He pulls the strings most of the time. I aspire to be like him, and I'm getting there. When my master comes back I will be proud to show him that I've doubled the two talents he entrusted to me. That is my goal, and I will come through—I aim to please!

I am servant #3. I buried the money that the master entrusted to me. He gave me a lot, one talent, less than the other two stewards, but still a tremendous amount of money. He gave me less because I have no track record yet as an investor. And I promise you, he'll never give me money again. And you know what? That's fine. I'd just bury it again. I don't want his money. I can't work for him. I am afraid of the way he behaves. I am afraid of the fact that he is a harsh man, reaping where he does not sow, gathering from where he did not scatter seed. I will not be a steward of a man like that. I am afraid that he hurts families, destroys lives, and steals jobs, that his greed is destroying Palestine!

I am afraid that he has no regard for the teaching of the prophets who call for justice and mercy for all. I will not participate in this destructive economy anymore! He will call me wicked and lazy, guaranteed. He will say I stole his money by not turning a profit. "You could have at least kept up with inflation!" he'll say to me. He will take the talent from me, and give it to servant #1. He will punish and abuse me. He will say, "To all those who have, more will be given, but for the have-nots, they will have less."

Throw me in jail if you want. I won't play those games. Throw me in jail. I follow Jesus Christ. I am steward of but one master. Jesus said that I cannot worship God and money. I choose God. I cannot be awake for the coming of the Lord if, while waiting for his coming, I choose to abuse and monopolize at the expense of others. I will not let my love grow cold. I will keep my lamp trimmed and burning.

Jesus Christ is coming again, and he told me that to be a steward of God I need to be ready to feed the hungry and give the thirsty something to drink. I need to care for the sick. I need to clothe the naked. My earthly master isn't doing that. I will seek to treat the last like they are first. These are the teachings that frame my life. Call me a worthless slave if you'd like, but so, too, have they called my Lord, who suffered endlessly for love, refusing to be a steward to anyone other than God almighty.

Friends, take your money, time, and energy out of systems that corrupt, and bury it—bury it away from what corrupts. Bury it—bury your treasure. Take it out of circulation, if the circulation is causing destruction and death. We are stewards of God, and yet time and again in our lives we are asked to be stewards of earthly masters, stewards of social, political, familial machines that go against the very gospel of our Lord. Pull your money, time, and skills away from systems that corrupt and do injustice. Pull your money from pension plans and mutual funds that grow fat on endless war, bunker buster nuclear weapons, child pornography, and child labor. You'd be amazed how many of them do.

Boycott injustice, even if your portfolio dips. Bury your money, and stand back and get clear eyes to see the hungry, thirsty, naked, and diseased. Then, with clear eyes, dig it up and invest it in businesses that seek to do justice, even as they make a buck. Dig it up, and then bury your money in the pockets of businesses that, through healthy business practices, build up communities. Bury your time, treasure, and skills in civic- and faith-based projects that take account of those who are left out of society. Contribute to the Red Cross. Donate to the food bank. Drive someone to an appointment. Give to your church and insist that it commits to investing in the work of our only master.

Put your time and energy into projects that reflect your master, who, in the resurrection and ascension, has gone away on a journey but has not left you orphaned, sending the Holy Spirit—the very presence of God—to be within you. Take money, time, and energy out of the system that corrupts, and redirect it into systems that promote the weighty matters of the law: justice, mercy, and faith. Amen.

23

Fairness in the Kingdom

September 22, 2002

> Then Peter said in reply, "Look, we have left everything and followed you. What then will we have?" Jesus said to him, "Truly I tell you, at the renewal of all things, when the Son of Man is seated on the throne of his glory, you who have followed me will also sit on twelve thrones, judging the twelve tribes of Israel. And everyone who has left houses or brothers or sisters or father or mother or children or fields, for my name's sake, will receive a hundredfold, and will inherit eternal life. But many who are first will be last, and the last will be first." (Matthew 19:27–30)

> Now when the first came, they thought they would receive more; but each of them also received the usual daily wage. And when they received it, they grumbled against the landowner, saying, "These last worked only one hour, and you have made them equal to us who have borne the burden of the day and the scorching heat." But he replied to one of them, "Friend, I am doing you no wrong; did you not agree with me for the usual daily wage? Take what belongs to you and go; I choose to give to this last the same as I give to you. Am I not allowed to do what I choose with what belongs to me? Or are you envious because I am generous?" (Matthew 20:10–15)

The kingdom of heaven is the kind of place where those who work hard all day are paid the same amount as the ones who show up in the fields for only one hour of work. Yes, that's what the passage says, loud and clear. And, yes, believe it or not, that is good news.

I grew up in a town and in a social situation where all the people I knew worked an eight- or nine-hour day. Good stock, hard-working folks. These were people who did their work, punched the clock, and got their just reward—decent pay, a 401(k) and two or three weeks' vacation every year. The apostle Peter felt like he was this hard-working type himself. He'd given up a lot to follow Jesus. He worked a hard day each day for the Lord. He expected, like the hard-working folks I knew as a child, that hard work for the Lord would result in special rewards for him and the other disciples.

So one day, Peter said something like this to Jesus, "We've given up everything to follow you, what's in this for us?"

"You are going to receive great things," Jesus says. "Everyone who has left houses or brothers or sisters or father or mother or children or fields, for my name's sake, will receive manifold gifts, and will inherit eternal life. I can picture Peter breathing a sigh of relief and thinking, "Ah, I knew hard work would pay off."

But then Jesus went on. You'll receive great things, Peter, but so will everyone else. Actually, Jesus said it much more severely than that. "Many who are first [like you, Peter] will be last, and the last will be first." And then Jesus illustrates what he means with the parable. He launched into a description of the kingdom of heaven being like the happenings in a certain vineyard. In this vineyard, some workers worked long, hard hours. Some worked short hours. At the end of the day, the owner paid everyone the same wage. He gave each worker a denarius, the amount promised to the full-time workers. He started by paying those who worked the least, and then paid the full-time workers the same amount.

Jesus focused in on how the workers who worked the longest grumbled about the newcomers being paid the same amount. And he ended the parable by saying, in essence, "The landowner wants to pay a fair wage to all." At the conclusion of the parable, Jesus says the same thing to Peter that he said at the start of the parable: "See, many who are first will be last, and the last will be first." The central theme that Jesus wants Peter, and all full-time, long-term disciples to know, is that in the kingdom of heaven *everyone* receives what they need for healthy living. Everyone receives manifold gifts.

Section Two—The Prepared Church Confronts the Issues of Its Day

It was while living in an environment where everyone I knew worked hard and received a fair wage and decent benefits that I first read the parable of the laborers in the vineyard. The kingdom of heaven must be a strange, unfair kind of kingdom with a strange and unfair God, I thought. It's the kind of place where people who don't do much work end up getting equal pay and benefits. What kind of a God promotes this? I sympathized with Peter.

I perceived the folks in the parable who didn't work full days as being lazy. Why don't they get a job? Why don't they earn their keep? But due to opportunities that I've had to see and understand the world in recent years, the perspective I approach this passage with is now very different.

Many mornings, while I sip coffee on the porch, I watch people zip by on bike or foot, past the corner of Raritan and Second Ave. I know where many of them are going. It's a forty-five minute walk from Highland Park to a labor line on the other side of New Brunswick. Day laborers from our town go and wait for someone to hire them for a day of mowing, raking, cleaning, or whatever work is available. A couple of hours later many of the same people come back up Raritan, having been forced, by the lack of work opportunities, to take another "day off." These aren't lazy people. They are people who desire to do hard work; they just can't find any. Employment is difficult for people in a lot of different situations.

Almost every week someone comes into the office to tell us that the factory they work for is moving to another country, or to another town, and they are being left without a job. Others tell us of working a full-time job, plus a half-time second job just to make ends meet. These people aren't in a vocational crisis because they are ineffective workers. They are victims of an always in-flux, global economy that prioritizes profits for shareholders above all else.

I read this parable from a different angle now. I've seen the world a bit more, and I've come to *know* people who literally and figuratively wait anxiously in the market all day, waiting for someone to hire them. I've gotten to know the guys who commute by bike across this town each day for the chance at day labor. I've come to know more of the single parents in our society who are trying to find work that adequately provides for their family's financial needs and allows them to be home when their children need them.

Fairness in the Kingdom

The thing that's *not fair* in the story about first-century workers in the vineyard that Jesus describes and *not fair* in our world, is that some people can't find work—hard as they try. What's also not fair is that a person can work a seventy-hour week at a fast-food restaurant and still not pay for a decent apartment in many towns in America. That's *not fair*.

There's a lot of unfair vocational distress around here and in the world at large. And it is from knowing the reality of vocational unfairness that this parable becomes one of the most beautiful in all of Scripture. Jesus says the kingdom of heaven is the kind of place where people in power go out of their way to find jobs for everyone. It's the kind of place where people who are unable to find full-time work are still paid a living wage for the part-time work they do. The kingdom of heaven is the kind of place where all people go home with money to pay for food, clothing, and the basic necessities of life.

The kingdom of heaven is a "fair" place—but fair/just as defined by different standards than most economic systems. It's fair and just when looked at from the perspective of the people who can't find work and who are unable to make ends meet. Jesus Christ looked at the fairness question from that perspective. He looked from the perspective of the "last," not the "first."

This is our Lord. He cares about the murky waters related to questions of underemployment.

Jesus Christ, the Son of God, had his eyes open to the vocational hard times of the people of first-century Palestine. He was troubled that day laborers waited out the day in the market, and went home at night without a denarius, the basic wage needed to feed the family. Jesus, the Son of God, the one who we believe had his mind solely focused on the ways of God, had his mind on the victims of the job crisis. And he didn't just notice it and shrug his shoulders. Being faithful to God meant responding to the vocational turmoil he saw around him by describing and promising a new situation.

He describes a kingdom where CEOs go cubicle-to-cubicle, asking workers if they are making a living wage. He describes a situation where powerful people make multiple trips to the labor line, all day long, to make sure there are none in town who are unable to find work. He describes a world where bosses go out to create new jobs at their own expense in order to provide an income for families.

Section Two—The Prepared Church Confronts the Issues of Its Day

That's the kind of Lord we have, a Lord who is concerned about people getting work and making a livable wage. He's bringing about a kingdom that's fair for all—and his understanding of "fairness" comes from the perspective of those who are left out, those who are last.

Jesus says in Matthew 13 that parables are given for the sake of revealing the secrets of the kingdom of heaven, or the kingdom of God, as Mark and Luke refer to it. There was a time when I used to read parables and automatically read them as interpretations of God's identity. That's not a wrong reading. I believe that God *is* like a landowner who makes sure that everyone has a job and wants everyone to get paid a living wage. God *is* like a person who invites everyone to the wedding feast. God *is* like a person who forgives debts. God *is* like a shepherd who goes after lost sheep. But Jesus doesn't say, "Hear this parable about God's identity." No, Jesus almost always says, "Hear this parable about the kingdom."

A kingdom is made up of people, and the kingdom of heaven is made up of God's people. We are that people. When we read the parables in the Bible, we are reading about the qualities that we are to exhibit as we live as members of the kingdom that claim Jesus Christ as Lord.

The parable of the vineyard is about Peter and it's about us. The understanding of fairness exposed here by Jesus Christ is an understanding that is meant for us. In all aspects of life, whether we're thinking about "eternal benefits," like Peter was, or if we're thinking about vocational justice, we live for the kingdom when we embrace God's kind of fairness—fairness that starts with the last. Fairness that includes the excluded, raises up the lowly, invites those who are left off the party list, raises the salary of the underemployed.

We are kingdom people. The parables of Jesus describe our community. We are called to be the characters in Jesus' story—in every walk of life. Sticking with the vocational issues put forth in the parable, we express our kingdom identity when those of us with hiring power live like the landowner, going out of the way to care for people, to help them find work and a fair wage.

We express our kingdom identity when those of us who are full-time workers at our jobs embrace new people and rejoice when the minimum wage is raised, even though we had to work years before we got that much. We are expressing our kingdom identity when we humbly accept from God and from those in the community more than seems our due.

Fairness in the Kingdom

As we go through our days, let's try to impose Christ's kind of fairness in every walk of life. As a church, let's rejoice when a person who has lived a rough-around-the-edges life decides to call this place home. Let's give them all the perks and privileges of full membership. Let's be thrilled when newcomers feel just as comfortable and blessed here as those who have been members for life.

Peter asked Jesus, "What's in it for *us*?"

What's in it for us is this: we get to be part of a kingdom where a fairness exists that allows *all people to flourish*. We get to be part of a kingdom where manifold gifts are for all, where care and well-being are for all, and where life is for all. Hear the good news: the last are first—all are first—in the kingdom of God. So let's live into the reality of the kingdom that we are part of now and will one day be part of in its perfection—to the glory of Christ our Lord. The kingdom of God, that kingdom we are a part of, is a beautiful kingdom *for everyone*. And that's fair. Amen.

24

Devouring Widows' Houses

November 9, 2003

> In the hearing of all the people he said to the disciples, "Beware of the scribes, who like to walk around in long robes, and love to be greeted with respect in the marketplaces, and to have the best seats in the synagogues and places of honor at banquets. They devour widows' houses and for the sake of appearances say long prayers. They will receive the greater condemnation." He looked up and saw rich people putting their gifts into the treasury; he also saw a poor widow put in two small copper coins. He said, "Truly I tell you, this poor widow has put in more than all of them; for all of them have contributed out of their abundance, but she out of her poverty has put in all she had to live on." (Luke 20:45–47, 21:1–4)

"Beware of the scribes who devour widow's houses." I was a Christian for years before I ever heard—I mean really heard—these words of Jesus. I was a Christian for years before I heard any words of Jesus that sounded like this at all. I was used to more standard themes like: "I am the way, the truth, and the light;"[1] "I and the Father are One;"[2] and,

---

1. John 3:16.
2. Ibid., 10:30.

"Believe in me—I will take you to myself."[3] These are the lines that rang in my ears about Jesus and about the call on my life.

The other themes on which I was raised had to do with charity: "Do unto others as you'd have them do to you;"[4] "Love your neighbor as yourself;"[5] and, "If you have two coats, give one away;"[6] I heard the lines about being generous, and I understood that generosity was part of what it meant to be a Christian. One of the first stories I remember that illustrated the notion of being a good person was the story about the woman who gave two pennies and how Jesus basically said, "That was a lot!" As I kid I remember thinking, "Great! I've only gotta give two pennies, and God will be pleased!"

"Beware of the scribes who devour widows' houses," was not something I had ever let sink into my Christian conscience. I'm not sure why not. Justice for all isn't some new idea that suddenly pops up in Mark chapter 12. Actually, it runs right through as a central theme. One of the first things Jesus said upon starting his ministry was, "The Spirit of the Lord is upon me, because he has anointed me to bring good news to the poor. He has sent me to proclaim release to the captives and recovery of sight to the blind, to let the oppressed go free."[7] I guess I hadn't let the "beware of scribes who devour widow's houses" line sink in because I'd never seen such injustice carried out by a church leader, by a church scribe. But, as I've looked at some of the identifying features of a Jerusalem scribe, I've decided that Jesus wasn't just saying beware of misguided church leaders, he was talking about politicians and business forces.

Scribes, at least those in Jerusalem in the first century where this story takes place, were some of the key figures in organized religion. Scribes were those who had a strong grasp of the law—the Torah. Social custom put them right near the top. Customary in those days was that in conversations a person less knowledgeable of the law was to initiate a greeting with one more knowledgeable, never the other way around. That explains why Jesus said, "Scribes like to walk around in long robes and be greeted with respect in the marketplace." Scribes were scholars who sat at

---

3. Ibid., 14:1–4.
4. Matt 7:12.
5. Mark 12:31.
6. Luke 3:11.
7. Luke 4:18.

Section Two—The Prepared Church Confronts the Issues of Its Day

the front in the synagogues; who sat at the seats of honor at meal times. They were honored by the larger public.

But according to Jesus, the scribes had other functions that we don't think of as primary roles of organized religion these days—for better or worse. The Jerusalem scribes were tied to power—governmental power—specifically, to the power of Rome.

Scribes and Sadducees worked together, as an aristocratic group of clerics, to run temple religion that satisfied the religious requirements of Jewish law and, yet, kept Roman rulers happy. Through their role as middlemen between Jewish religion and Roman authority, scribes and Sadducees maintained a level of privilege, authority, and wealth that was unprecedented in that society. Sadducees, scribes, and others tied into temple religion controlled money, land, and power. And Jesus says here that scribes, and presumably the other leaders, had one more function: "They devour widows' houses." Widows are often held up in Scripture as the most vulnerable group in society. Since women were not allowed any inheritance, a widow's home quickly became prized property that could be snatched out from under her without too much of a fight.[8]

Scribes were tied to religion—yes—but they were equally tied to politics, and Jesus says they carried out their political will with incredible injustice. And so, when I look for contemporary comparisons to Jesus' critiques, I don't look only inside the church, but at every political, governmental, economic, and social place of power to ask who it is that is devouring widows' houses.

Who are they who are finding ways to drive the poor and unwanted out of nice neighborhoods? Who controls the housing market that makes it almost impossible to afford to live in Highland Park? Who are they who create, but then don't adequately fund, governmental programs such as the Section 8 housing voucher designed to provide a rent subsidy to help families currently living in poverty. In Highland Park alone, there are 185 people on the waiting list for these vouchers, and I've been told anyone who is currently number one hundred or higher should expect to be on the list for another four years before being considered for help. In New Brunswick, the waiting list runs into the thousands. Who are they who knock down Palestinian neighborhoods? Who is it clearing jungles in South America for the sake of hamburgers? "Beware," says Jesus, "and be on the lookout for all those who devour widows' houses."

---

8. *Mercer Dictionary of the Bible*, s.v. "Widows," 959.

Devouring Widows' Houses

Jesus is teaching about faith. He's talking about the Christian life and what we're called to do. Part of our calling, as people of Jesus' way, is to beware of those who devour widows' houses—and to call them to task—in the public square, for the glory of God and the freedom of our neighbor. We are called to interrupt their long prayers, be they secular or religious prayers, and to insist that they live for justice.

I asked a friend the other day how her mother was doing in the little farmhouse where she lives down south. "Well, she's doing great healthwise, but I'm really worried about her because something's got her so upset." And she told me this story. A very wealthy contractor and owner of a number of businesses had plans to build a housing complex down her mother's road. The project itself was admirable enough. Well, there was no water or sewage system down that road, and it had to be in place in order to build such a facility. My friend's mother always had well water and a septic tank. The developer took it to the town council, and he now has permission to build a sewage system down the road. But here's the catch. The town says that everyone along that road now is required to tie into the sewage system. The cost is $8,000 per lot that touches the road. Well, grandma has a forty-acre piece of property, and a number of those acres touch the road. Her total bill might be around $64,000. She's eighty-three; she's been happy forever with well water and doesn't have $64,000 on hand for something like this. There's a clause in the law that says that if 51% of the people who own the lots that touch the road are against the plan, it needs to be resubmitted and extensively reviewed. Well, guess who owns 55% of the land on that road? You got it—the developer. Even if the other twenty homeowners on that road all dissented, they wouldn't be able to stop him. "Beware of those who devour widows' houses."

I asked my friend, "Have you brought this up in church?"

"Why church?" she asked me.

"Because this is a faith issue. This is a justice issue. Before God, in the community of faith, is just the place to talk about such matters."

"Well, the developer is a church member." she said, "That wouldn't go over so well."

My reply, "Even better. He needs to be talking about this with the people who are going to be impacted by his business ventures, most of whom are members of his same church. He needs to be talking to them because most of them cannot afford to pay anything close to what is being demanded. He needs to see their tears; he needs to know about their financial situations, he needs to know about the heartache that he's causing."

A couple of years ago, if you were standing in the right place in New Brunswick, you could hear the sound of a wrecking ball as it collided with tenement housing. In theory it made sense. The buildings weren't well kept, and were drug- and rat-infested, a breeding ground for asthma and disease. But two years after their homes were devoured by machinery and the politics behind the machinery, many of the previous residents still have not found anything half as nice nor affordable as those old buildings. Two years have past, plenty of time to have built beautiful, expensive condos on that old property, but somehow not enough time to help resettle many of the displaced folks who are still living out of hotel rooms along Route 1. Sure, there has been affordable housing built on George Street, but it isn't close to enough to make up for what was lost when those buildings came down, and many of the former residents of those buildings didn't meet the criteria for living in those new, low-income units.

As people of faith we need to get in the habit of asking tough questions to those who devour houses. A call to a house member, mayor, or a social work agency can reveal a lot. Stop by one of the shelters or at Elijah's Promise's Soup Kitchen and ask for a show of hands of how many of them used to live in those projects and are now homeless. I think you'll be shocked. It is part of the faith experience to keep our eyes open and our ears to the ground about who is devouring houses. It is the calling of Jesus Christ in each of our lives to be aware of such things.

Listen for the hum and the crushing sound of bulldozers devouring houses. In Israel, right now, it's the military of the government that is removing homes in the West Bank to make room for an eighteen-foot high security wall. Listen for the thud, thud of a rapidly beating heart, followed by heaving sobs, the behavior of many right here in our town who are overwhelmed with stress due to being behind on mortgage payments again. Listen for the gasps that accompany the ripping open of an envelope that holds an eviction notice that reads, "you have two weeks to vacate."

When we were living in Ecuador, Stephanie and I heard that many in the coastal region were losing their land. Police would suddenly show up and announce that the land the people had lived on for generations had been unclaimed until that day. They had lived there with no deed.

Suddenly, an international banana corporation was taking ownership of the land and demanding that everyone be off by the end of the week. People could either leave or negotiate with the corporation to be allowed to work the land for them.

Beware, Christians! Beware of those who devour widows' houses. And don't only *be wary* of unjust trends, but address them creatively and lovingly, for the sake of healing the world. Address injustice, not only so the oppressor may be healed, but for the sake of the widow. I hope that if your house is being devoured, or if you are concerned about what you see in terms of housing and other injustices, you will make church a place to address those issues, in response to the leading of our Lord.

I hadn't noticed, until preparing for this sermon, that the "beware of those who devour widows' houses" parable comes directly before the story of the widow who came to the temple to put money in the treasury, into the welfare box, that benefited orphans and widows. It's possible that Jesus saw her coming up to the treasury box even as he finished his "beware" speech.

I've always been impressed with this widow's generosity, giving the two coins—all she had to live on—to society. But in light of the previous story, this account takes on a whole new level of meaning. This widow, who could only come up with two leptas—the pennies of her economy—probably had had a house, husband, and a place to call her own not too long before this story. *But in the story, she was one of the persons whose home was devoured by the scribes.* She was now dirt poor, precisely because of the injustice of her religio-political community.

Jesus noticed her, and I wonder how he felt when he saw what she was doing. I can tell you how I feel. I feel bad about the whole thing. Here's a once self-sustaining woman who, through the death of her husband and the conniving of scribes, fell upon hard times and who could only get by now on the welfare system provided by the treasury. What's she doing? Why is she casting her only coins into the treasury—the common purse that was to serve the needs of the widow and orphan, but that was controlled by the same folks who devoured her house? I felt bad, too, that many of the people throwing large checks and bills into the treasury, and being admired by all, were likely the ones who grew rich off devouring her home, and the homes of others.

But Jesus said something to his disciples, and to me, about this woman, and it means so much. By highlighting her giving coins to the temple, Jesus said in effect, "Look to her, she's given us the best gift of all. In fact, she's given us something more than everyone who gave large sums of money. Against all odds, she's given all she has to live on, to the common cause of caring and loving everyone in her community." Regardless of how bad it was for this woman, regardless of how she'd been wronged, she insisted that it was still important to build up the community together. She refused to keep herself from doing what she could to help other widows and orphans. She had not lost hope that the common treasury that provided social services for those in need was a good thing to support.

The beauty of these two stories being combined in Scripture is that Jesus builds lesson upon lesson. We are first told to beware of those who devour houses and to address such injustices. But then we are called to put the same kind of energy into watching, listening, and learning from the acts of hope performed by those who have been victimized. We are called to pay attention to the widow's faith and action. Because, you see, victims of injustice—people whose homes have been devoured—are not problems to be fixed or issues to be resolved. Often, they are people who, when listened to, remind us of the antidote to a devouring human nature. The self-giving behavior of the widow, the desire she shows to give her all for others, is the kind of behavior that leads to the building of a new community based on the principles of self-giving love—God love.

You don't have to be a victim of injustice to offer truly self-giving gifts. Earlier in chapter 12 of Mark's gospel, Jesus commended a scribe who understood that loving one's neighbor was much more important than all other forms of religious sacrifices and ritual. Jesus tells him, "you are not far from the kingdom of God."[9]

But Jesus doesn't point to that good scribe as an example. Instead, he points to the oppressed widow giving coins. There is something about her *self-giving*, something about her *full commitment* to work for a better world that stood out to Jesus. Look at her and what she's doing—that is love!

Jesus himself ended up following the path of the widow. His life was devoured by the injustice doled out by scribes, Sadducees, and Roman authorities. He was ridiculed and tortured because he loved people, because he challenged injustice, because he accepted everyone. And yet, Jesus refused to stop loving, serving, and living for God and, instead,

---

9. Mark 12:34.

trusted that it was good and right to keep giving his all, even his life, for the treasury of true peace, justice, and righteousness. Jesus Christ, like the widow, gave his whole self to God's purpose of building a kingdom.

Let's become people who address the forces that devour the houses and lives of widows, orphans, seniors, the working class, immigrants, and poor nations. Let's pay close attention to those who have been victimized, because often there is a widow who throws all the coins she has to live on into a program that cares for the poor. Or sometimes, there is a homeless man who serves another homeless man lunch. Or sometimes there is a mom who asked the church for food who then shares that food with her needy neighbor. Or sometimes there is a person whose home has been demolished who spends his days participating in reconstruction efforts for others. Sometimes from a place of brokenness a person offers all she has to live on in order to serve the kingdom of God. Sometimes, that person is our best teacher, the biggest source of wisdom, the most helpful agent of the Spirit of God. Sometimes it is that person who will keep us from the temptation to be devourers ourselves, and who will, instead, encourage us to be builders.

The widow is the one who leads us in the way of Jesus Christ our Lord, right into the kingdom of God. Amen.

25

How Did You Respond When Herod Killed John the Baptist?

J uly 30, 2011

> The head was brought on a platter and given to the girl, who brought it to her mother. His disciples came and took the body and buried it; then they went and told Jesus. Now when Jesus heard this, he withdrew from there in a boat to a deserted place by himself. But when the crowds heard it, they followed him on foot from the towns. When he went ashore, he saw a great crowd; and he had compassion for them and cured their sick. When it was evening, the disciples came to him and said, "This is a deserted place, and the hour is now late; send the crowds away so that they may go into the villages and buy food for themselves." Jesus said to them, "They need not go away; you give them something to eat." (Matthew 14:11–16)

The debt ceiling, increased taxes, tax cuts, social programs getting hacked away—these are the questions weighing heavily on the American public these days. The topic dominates the media and conversations in all sorts of company. We worry for ourselves, our future, our children's future. We worry for communities.

Something is dying right now. Something is being lost. America is going through (and has been going through) an extended, financial train wreck—the political discourse surrounding the debt ceiling and

How Did You Respond When Herod Killed John the Baptist?

everything connected with it is just the latest manifestation of this ongoing, very serious issue.

I was in Camden recently with a group from our church—visiting an excellent inner-city ministry called HopeWorks 'N Camden. We met with a priest named Father Jeff who told us that most people have no idea how serious some of the federal and state budget cuts were. He explained that Camden and other extremely impoverished cities were spared the worst of the financial crisis of the past few years, thanks to the very basic social programs that at least provide *a safety net*. If those social programs were to be cut or dramatically reduced, he explained, Camden would become a nightmare. Father Jeff wondered aloud how the grandma who was raising four of her grandchildren was going to feed, clothe, and shelter them without that welfare check, the program that helps her do right by them. He predicts we haven't yet begun to see what desperation looks like.

This is a time of loss for many. It's been building for a long time. Maybe we'll stave it off again, but I think we are closer to a crisis point that *we'll feel in our households* than we have been for some time. It seems to me that governmental policies as well as the extremely elite in our country (with our passive support) have created a system that is bound to crumble for most everyone except the extreme elite. Brothers and sisters in Christ, what are *we* going to do, how are *we* going to behave in the face of loss?

Today's passage unfolds around the murder of John the Baptist. His death dealt a major blow to the already desperately lost common man and woman in first-century Palestine. Totally controlled by the Roman military, continually taxed into poverty, life was exceedingly tough. John had been a sign of hope during those troubled times.

Unlike Jesus—whose ministry had been extremely short, and his work, mainly with peasants in Galilee—John had a large following. His ministry appears to have lasted some years, and he was prophesying near the Jordan River, just outside the major metropolis of Jerusalem. John's life was highlighted favorably by the first-century historian, Josephus. Also, a passage from Acts of the Apostles references Paul interacting with disciples of John in faraway places in the Roman world.[1] John was widely considered to be a prophet of God. He was a bright light, a sign of repentance and recovery for a nation that was suffering in debt due to

---

1. Acts 19:3.

Section Two—The Prepared Church Confronts the Issues of Its Day

Roman behavior and the duplicity of the religious and national leaders of Palestine.

John called his fellow Jews to repent and turn away from corruption of all kinds. He warned that God was about to judge. Included in John's message was the notion that "one who is more powerful than I is coming after me; I am not worthy to carry his sandals."[2] As far as his people were concerned, though, John was as worthy and as holy as you could get. John the Baptist was a great prophetic leader.

John was so significant that it was to John that Jesus was drawn as he approached the age of thirty. It was after an interaction with John at the Jordan River that Jesus became more than a carpenter for those around him. And it was after John was arrested that Scripture tells us Jesus returned to Galilee and began his ministry.

Usually the gospel accounts move in a chronological order, but not today. At the beginning of Matthew 14, we are told that Herod heard reports about Jesus' ministry in Galilee, and his response was: "This is John the Baptist; he has been raised from the dead, and for this reason these powers are at work in him."[3] This is a surprising passage to us as readers, because we haven't yet heard about John's death. We thought he was in jail! That's what we'd been told just three chapters before: Last we knew, John was sending emissaries to Jesus, communicating from jail.

But then, for the rest of chapter 14, Matthew steps back and fills in the story for us. He tells us about John's gruesome murder that occurred after Jesus went back to Galilee to start his ministry. And then he tells us how Jesus immediately responded to the news.

That's what I want to look at today—how Jesus responded to loss, major loss that touched him personally and grieved the masses already crippled by oppression. How did Jesus respond to a situation that could have (maybe even should have) led to despair, fear, and silence? How did Jesus respond when Herod killed John the Baptist?

We are told that John's disciples went to Herod's place, took the body, and buried it; *then they went and told Jesus.* Their leader was dead, and the first thing they did was go to *another leader* to tell him what had happened. And Jesus wasn't just around the corner. It is likely they walked thirty or forty miles north—from near Jerusalem to Galilee—to communicate the news. This tells us a lot about the relationship between

2. Matt 3:11.
3. Ibid., 14:2.

How Did You Respond When Herod Killed John the Baptist?

John and Jesus. These followers of John knew that Jesus was to be trusted and that he'd know how to respond.

When Jesus heard about John's death, Matthew tells us, "he withdrew from there in a boat to a deserted place by himself," which, by now, is what we have come to expect of Jesus. He often went away by himself to pray. It was not a form of permanent escape, but was always a precursor to engagement.

Soon after Jesus heard of John's death, the crowds heard about it too—crowds that surely included Jesus' followers as well as John's. We are told that the crowds immediately followed Jesus to the deserted place—running around the lake toward the place where he was headed. They might have been following him just because he had always drawn a crowd, but I think they followed him there on that day, in such large numbers, because they wanted to be with him as together they faced John's death.

And when Jesus saw them, there on the shore, he didn't turn around and head back in his boat to continue grieving alone. No, he got out and compassionately cared for the crowd, curing their sick. Jesus' first response after loss, after spending some time in solitude, was to care for people and to engage with them in ways that showed that the business of the kingdom of God would continue as usual! John's death was not going to stop the ministry of compassion!

As the evening came, Jesus' disciples were concerned about the lack of food for this big crowd. "Send the crowds away so that they may go into the villages and buy food for themselves." But Jesus said, "They need not go away; you give them something to eat."

There has been a lot of attention given to trying to explain *how* Jesus was able to feed the five thousand. Was it terrific sharing or a straight-up miracle? Did they all get a tiny little bite—like we do when we have the Lord's Supper—but it was just a really satisfying bite? I'm not interested in any explanation today. Instead, I'm interested in the fact that on a day when the government had killed a prophet, and the disciples were realizing just how weak they actually were, Jesus conveyed to his disciples, "You've got the power to feed these people. You are organized as a new society! They don't need to spend money they don't have; they need not walk away from the community. God will provide!" Jesus wasn't suggesting that they would never again need to engage the food systems of the world—owned and operated by Herod—but on *that day*, when Herod had so betrayed them, Jesus was in a sense saying, "This new system, our community, can take care of all who are part of it!" Feeding the five thousand was a politically motivated miracle. We grieve John the Baptist, but don't think you can control us now, Herod.

It has always bothered me that this parable ends by saying, "and those who ate were five thousand men, besides women and children." It sounds so male-dominated, like it wasn't even worth adding up the women and children, their number didn't count. This week I got another read on this. In Mark's version, which is very close to Matthew's, Jesus asks the disciples to split up the men into groups of fifty and one hundred—this is what military sergeants would be asked to do by their commander. And then Mark names the total: five thousand. To name the total of men, after numbering them off by fifties and one hundreds is something that you do when you are giving an account of your troop strength—all soldiers in the first century were male.

Jesus was making platoons out of the crowd of men and Matthew gives us a troop count! Jesus then showed that this "army" could be fed by God, and so, too, could the soldiers' families! Herod might have his regime, but Jesus, immediately after John's murder, was showing that they had platoons of their own. They were gathering in a deserted place, mending their wounds, caring for themselves and their families, and preparing for some kind of battle.

Jesus and his movement miraculously fed five thousand soldiers and their families without draining a penny from their resource bank. They had all they needed, right there among themselves! Jesus pulled the masses out of reliance on the oppressor, and that is a sure step toward creating a new kingdom.

I imagine this is the report about Jesus that most terrified Herod. This is the report that most made him think that John, whom he'd beheaded, was somehow alive. His spirit, anyway, was clearly with Jesus, for the very day that Herod murdered John, Jesus' community radically grew. He performed one of his greatest miracles, and he did so in a way that looked like he was organizing an army.

Brothers and sisters, do you hear the good news? The moments after a loss can be a moment when the church comes together for Jesus to feed more than five thousand! The moment of loss might become—for us or others—a great moment of grace, or even a great moment of transformation or daring. A moment of loss is exactly the moment to claim the good news that nothing "will be able to separate us from the love of God in Christ Jesus our Lord."⁴ It may be the moment when Jesus helps us perform miracles. We have not caved in to the powers that cause loss, but have turned to God and each other—and when that has happened, blessings have been poured out—five thousand have been fed.

I have seen this reality play out time and again here in this place—and I want to take a moment to name examples. Almost ten years ago we gathered here in this sanctuary in disbelief, looking to God at a time when unthinkable violence occurred in New York City, just thirty miles away. We gathered, and people of faith similarly gathered in houses of worship all over this country, binding together for sustenance and strength from God and each other.

There are some of you whom we got to know through the events of 9/11. In your grief, you were part of the crowd that came and said, "God, please feed us, we're hungry." There was no way to erase the tragedy, but there were new ways to move forward out of it. This church grew in part because we refused to accept the feelings of despair in the air as normative and, instead, claimed peace, healing, and community! We held each other and God held us.

Over the course of the past ten years there have been other losses—the death of dear friends in the church. If I started naming them by name, I'd be too choked up to get through the list. Through these losses we've come together—all of us—to support spouses and children, colleagues, and neighbors. We've come together to be fed by God and to be fed by each other. Death has not been able to have the last laugh. Through loss we've chosen life.

We've faced other tough times together. We've faced illnesses of loved ones *together*. We've faced the Iraq War. We've faced immigration detention. Our response has been to come together at times like these, and, once together, ask God to feed us in ways that show oppressors (and us) who is Lord!

I frequently have people tell me, "Your congregation really pulls together to accomplish things, doesn't it?" I always nod enthusiastically. It is so true. But I think we especially pull together at times when something troubling is brewing in the world, or in one of our lives, at a time when the natural response might be to have the wind knocked out of our sails, or to try to make it on our own. It is at those crisis moments that

---

4. Rom 8:39.

we've learned to hustle to this deserted place together to find Jesus, and to sing songs to God and participate in healing each other as God in Christ heals us.

I have a hunch we'll become a church involved in shaping a new economy. I'm seeing signs of it already as we are more aware of job loss in the congregation, and we're rushing to help each other find solutions to fill the gaps. Most of us aren't job placement experts. Most of us aren't well connected with head hunting agencies, but what we are is *aware* of those who have chosen to be part of the kingdom community. In the past six months I know of at least seventeen "good jobs," full or regular part-time, that congregants have gained because of church connections. In addition, not a day goes by where someone who is doing OK right now doesn't hire someone in the church who is out of work—to paint a deck, to trim the shrubs, to watch their children, or whatever.

It is because we are one that we know when someone is hungry for work. It is because we are one that we are inspired to create and find opportunities. And, I believe, because we know Jesus feeds five thousand with a few loaves of bread and a couple of fish, we have the audacity to believe that maybe Jesus can create enough work for all to be satisfied. In fact, I want to go so far as to say in this church there should be a 0% unemployment rate for those seeking work. There should be enough jobs for all who want and need them.

Maybe it isn't just jobs that Jesus feeds us. Maybe God even feeds us creative vision for new economic policy. You know, Jesus fed five thousand in a deserted place, and that was a big deal, but it was when he went to Jerusalem, to the seat of power, and offered the bread of life to all, that the people in power really felt threatened. At some point, after we've done a good job of alternative economic recovery in our community, we've got to bring that energy to the world—making disciples of a new way.

I wonder if Herod will notice that Jesus Christ is creating jobs? I wonder if he'll think that John the Baptist has been raised from the dead? Amen.

Part Five

Faith Facing Creation and Environmental Degradation

26

The Breadth of the Covenant

February 22, 2006

> As for me, I am establishing my covenant with you and your descendants after you, and with every living creature that is with you, the birds, the domestic animals, and every animal of the Earth with you, as many as came out of the ark. I establish my covenant with you, that never again shall all flesh be cut off by the waters of a flood, and never again shall there be a flood to destroy the Earth. (Genesis 9:9–11)

> He is the image of the invisible God, the firstborn of all creation; for in him all things in heaven and on Earth were created, things visible and invisible, whether thrones or dominions, or rulers or powers—all things have been created through him and for him. He himself is before all things, and in him all things hold together. (Colossians 1:15–17)

Every time a child is born into this church family we stop as a church community and re-enact the covenant that God has made with this child. Our Reformed Church liturgy for baptism reads, "For you Jesus Christ came into the world; for you he died and for you he conquered death; All this he did for you, little one, though you know nothing of it as yet. We love because God first loved us."[1]

---

1. *Liturgy and Confession*, "Baptism," https://www.rca.org/sslpage.aspx?pid=1879.

Section Two—The Prepared Church Confronts the Issues of Its Day

I love that we baptize infants because it is a stunning reminder that God's love for us is not the result of our piety, perfection, or attempts at seeking God. God's love for us is prompted simply by God's desire to love—nothing else. The maker of the universe has made a covenant with you—before you even had a chance to respond! God's covenant promises to you are non-stop, through every beat of your heart, every day that unfolds before you, every pulse of love.

Our hope as a community of faith is that together we will embody the kind of love that will lead a child to grow into recognition and appreciation of God's promises. We hope and pray that youth in the church will get to a place where they say, "Yes, God, I am ready to commit to the covenant that you made and have been keeping since my first breath."

I love the covenantal language of our baptismal liturgy, and of our reformed faith, but I've come to believe that we ought to use that covenantal language in a much broader way than we do. Today I want to talk about the breadth of God's covenanting. I want to ask with whom is God in a covenantal relationship? And I want to talk about it from the perspective of the passages in Genesis 9 and Colossians 1.

Today we heard two passages about God's covenant with the world. The first is part of the primeval narrative at the beginning of Genesis. It comes on the tail end of the story of God getting fed up with human sinfulness and, in righteous anger, flooding the Earth, destroying all living things, except for Noah and his family and a remnant of animals. It's an awful story, really—God, annihilating all things out of anger for human sin. God apparently thought so, too, because at the end of it, God hangs up the bow and puts away the arrows. God explains that every time a rainbow appears, we should remember that God's never going to take that bow, or any weapon of destruction, off the shelf again.

God says, "As for me, I am establishing my covenant with you and your descendants after you, and with every living creature that is with you, the birds, the domestic animals, and every animal of the Earth with you, as many as came out of the ark. I establish my covenant with you, that never again shall all flesh be cut off by the waters of a flood, and never again shall there be a flood to destroy the Earth."[2]

There are many who look to this passage in Genesis 9 as the beginning of God's self-description as a God of Endless Grace. From this point on in the biblical narrative God's not going to deal with humanity

2. Gen 9:9–11.

The Breadth of the Covenant

according to its sins, but rather according to God's grace. As proof of this new approach by God, the biblical writer tells us in the very next verse that "righteous Noah," just getting off the boat, went and got really drunk and passed out in the tent and embarrassed himself and his family. God didn't flood the Earth again after Noah made a big mistake. God didn't even flood Noah's tent. No, God just kept living out God's covenantal promises: God brought light to the morning; God watered the Earth; God gave sun to grow plants and animals to eat those plants and pull plows; God gave otters river homes; God gave deer woods in which to roam; God gave silt and loam; God gave waters, salty and fresh; God gave seasons, dry and wet; God created Eden, not for two, but for all—a whole Earth-Eden that dripped with endless grace. This was God's commitment to humankind.

One way to read the biblical story is to see the dichotomy between God's continuing faithfulness to this covenant of love for every living thing, and humanity's continual failure to love God and every living thing. Humanity seems to keep forgetting about the covenant and fails to live in a loving relationship with all living things! This story line is addressed by God in the person of Jesus Christ. Let's look at the passage from Colossians.

Colossians 1, which was written some decades after Jesus' death, discusses the covenant with God that Christ (God in human flesh) restores. Through Christ, God reconciles all things (Paul says "all things" five times in verses 15–20) whether on Earth or in heaven. Friends, do you see what's happening here? In Genesis, God said, "Look, I'm making a covenant to do my part, regardless of whether humanity and all living creatures do their part." In Colossians 1, God seems to say, "I'm doing my part, and now I really want you to do your part so badly that I'm sending myself, in Christ, to help you do your part."

Friends, this is good news! God sent Jesus Christ, the very presence of God, to restore the covenant between God and "all things." Jesus Christ came, not just to save human souls, but to restore all things—flowers, mountains, trees, birds, bees, and the whole creation that God breathes into existence, supports, and upholds.

This isn't the only place where we hear that redemption brought about by Christ has benefits for more than just humankind. To the church in Rome, Paul writes that "the creation waits with eager longing for the revealing of the children of God . . . the whole creation has been groaning in labor pains until now; awaiting the redemption of [humankind]."[3] One of my college professors, Dr. Steven Bouma-Prediger, would always say that the world is waiting on tiptoe for humankind to get it right so that it can stop groaning in pain, and, instead, rejoice in God's graciousness!

Friends of Jesus Christ, it's time for us to start thinking of covenantal community in much broader terms than we usually do. If we want to talk about God's covenantal relationship, we've got to talk about all creation, all things. Maybe, as a sign, we ought to expand our baptismal practices. We could start with children who will not experience life in our community of faith. God covenants with them, and so should we. Maybe we should have a baptismal service each year that reminds us to care for all children, and to create a world where all children flourish. And then, let's go a step further. Let's imagine baptism for non-human covenant partners—How about a sapling, tomato plant, fawn, or kitten? How about a baptism for fish of the sea or birds of the air?

I'm not suggesting that baptism would mean something to a sapling, tomato plant, or fawn. But then, infant baptism really doesn't mean anything to an infant either. No. The act is about *God* showing love for the child, and for those who are moved to become more fully committed to covenanting with God—the parents, relatives, and the congregation. Baptisms call the community of faith to commit to the realization of the covenant for the recipient. That's why, in the baptismal liturgy, I always ask the church to stand and make vows to help the new baby experience the covenant of God's love. Today I want to think about what it would mean for us to make vows for the broader world with whom God covenants.

For children born into the world in smog-filled, drug-riddled urban poverty, we know God's vows to you. God is consistently going to get you up in the morning, fill your veins with pulsing blood, put thoughts, ideas, and the potential for wonder inside of you. Oh, the list could go on and on of what God will do for you! Now, what are *our* vows to God, on behalf of dear children living in poverty? Maybe our vow is to encourage affordable housing or job opportunities for financially stressed parents. Maybe our vow is to pass legislation that gets the smog down in those neighborhoods so that so many aren't prone to severe asthma. Maybe these are the vows that we'd make, when we have our baptism service for children from places of suffering.

---

3. Rom 8:19, 22, 23b.

The Breadth of the Covenant

But I want to go further today. As Genesis and Colossians show, this covenant expansion moves beyond human community and into all creation. For blue herons born in New Jersey, we know God's vow to you. God gave you an amazingly long neck, great eyes, and fast reflexes for catching fish. God gave you long legs, so you can get into deeper water, to get those bigger fish. God gave you graceful strides, God gave you a wonderful bill. Maybe our vow to God on your behalf is to commit to wetlands preservation in New Jersey, to read up on acidity levels in New Jersey streams, and to commit to making them healthier for you as you grow up. For the sapling, we know what God does for you as well. God waters you and gives you sun. God supplies the soil and proper dynamics for your growth. Our vow to you, young sapling, is that we'll let you grow to fullness, that we'll protect the water coming your way, and not destroy you.

This might all sound a bit absurd to you today, and if so, I'm sorry. I'm sorry that it sounds so "out there"—because it's not. What is absurd is that covenantal language has been kept for use within the walls of the church only. The Christian community needs to remember the breadth of God's covenant. I know I've been deficient, especially in regards to God's covenant with non-human things. Other than a few passing comments, I've rarely mentioned the natural world in my preaching. And that will change.

Now, on a practical level, we can't possibly hold a baptismal service, a covenanting service, for every tree frog and river otter, or even for every human being in the world. I think we've got nine church babies coming up for baptism in the next few weeks as it is! But, today I want to say that we've done something recently with our church facility that is about covenantal care for all things. Sitting over our head now while we worship God, are forty-two solar panels. When we go into the social hall for coffee hour (fairly traded, in reusable ceramic mugs, I might add) we sit under another eighty-six panels. All of that adds up to 10,000-kilowatt hours of renewable energy per year. That amount equals 28% of the light and power that we use to operate this building.

Up until now, all of our energy came from non-renewable sources such as fossil fuels. Fossil fuels are hypothetically renewable; they are made of ground up animal and plant particles, but they renew so slowly that they will be depleted beyond repair in the not-too-distant future unless something drastically changes in the way humans consume them.

Section Two—The Prepared Church Confronts the Issues of Its Day

Truly renewable energy is a resource that gets replaced relatively rapidly by a natural process, such as power generated from the sun, wind, or flowing water. That's what we're doing now, we're letting the light from the sun provide much of the energy needs for this ministry. We are leaving less of a permanent footprint on the Earth now, by making this change—sucking less fossil fuels from below the Earth's surface. Just as importantly, the renewable energy we are using is clean energy, meaning the conversion process is clean—no carbon is burned. The conversion process of making fossil fuels into useable energy has created an overabundance of carbon dioxide in the air.

Earth needs a certain level of carbon dioxide in the air. The right amount makes a thin and necessary greenhouse gas sheet that surrounds the Earth, trapping the warm air in the Earth's atmosphere. That "gas sheet" protects us from freezing to death, as the sheet keeps the Earth warm even when the sun isn't shining. But that sheet has now become a super thick "greenhouse down comforter," which is pressure cooking the Earth at temperatures that are doing irreparable damage. With these panels we've begun to try to thin the blanket of greenhouse gases.

I've heard it said that if all houses of worship transferred 30% of their light and power costs to renewable energy it would be the equivalent of taking one million cars off the road (and save them five hundred million dollars annually). Imagine if every person who worshiped in those churches went home and made adjustments to the type of energy they used to light and power their houses.

The panels on our roof now serve as a symbol to me of our church thinking about the breadth of God's covenant of love. I cannot think of a symbol with broader significance. Probably the most all-encompassing threat to the Earth that God made and sent Jesus Christ to reconcile to beauty and fullness is the emission of excessive amounts of carbon dioxide into the atmosphere. The first to see the effects will be the animal and plant species, whose existence depends on the Earth's natural climate control mechanisms. Second to see the effects will be the poor and oppressed—the very humans to whom God shows preferential treatment throughout Scripture. Eventually, we will all see the effects. Harnessing the sun for energy and power in ways that are clean, safe, and renewable, is one of the things we do now in response to God's covenant with the world. This is part of our vows on behalf of "all things." What will the rest of our vows be?

God has baptized all things, saying, "Yes, I love you." The fullness of God's "yes" will be realized when we say "yes" back with a breadth that matches the "yes" of God. Amen.

27

The Law, Earth, and Knowing God

N ovember 5, 2006

> One of the scribes came near and heard them disputing with one another, and seeing that he answered them well, he asked him, "Which commandment is the first of all?" Jesus answered, "The first is, 'Hear, O Israel: the Lord our God, the Lord is one; you shall love the Lord your God with all your heart, and with all your soul, and with all your mind, and with all your strength.' The second is this, 'you shall love your neighbor as yourself.' There is no other commandment greater than these." Then the scribe said to him, "You are right, Teacher; you have truly said that 'he is one, and besides him there is no other'; and 'to love him with all the heart, and with all the understanding, and with all the strength', and 'to love one's neighbor as oneself,'—this is much more important than all whole burnt offerings and sacrifices.' When Jesus saw that he answered wisely, he said to him, "You are not far from the kingdom of God." After that no one dared to ask him any question. (Mark 12:28–34)

The other day the winds were whipping around in town, and a number of trees toppled to the ground. You've seen them down around here, haven't you? I was walking home from a visit to see the new twins we've been praying about each week and I passed a section of road with three trees lying in it. As I came to one tree, where public works was on the job, I heard a squealing noise. And then I watched as this big, burly guy in an orange public works coat gently lifted from the fallen tree a baby squirrel, bringing it out of the road and away from the chain saws. I watched him gently set it down, where it would at least have a chance to make it. He was telling everyone not to touch it in the hopes that its mother would still take it back. "The less human hands on it the better," he said as he looked lovingly upon that squirrel. I remember thinking, "My, oh my! His gaze looks like the gaze those parents just had as they looked upon their twins!" All right, that's a bit of an exaggeration, but it *was* similar. It warmed my heart to see this happen, and you know, even though he was sad about what happened to that little squirrel, it clearly warmed his heart too—to care so much for it. I wouldn't be a bit surprised if that man came back in the morning, found the squirrel unclaimed by its mother, took it home, and fed it with a baby bottle. This week, as I thought back on that event, I realized he was living out the most important commandments—the heart of the law—he was loving his neighbor and God.

A scribe, one versed in the Law of Moses, came to Jesus and asked him one of the questions hotly debated in their day: "Which commandment is the first of all?"

Jesus answered, "The first is, 'Hear, O Israel, the Lord our God, the Lord is one; you shall love the Lord your God with all your heart, and with all your soul, and with all your mind, and with all your strength.' The second is this, 'You shall love your neighbor as yourself.' There is no commandment greater than these."

The scribe said, "You are right, Teacher. . . . this is much more important than all whole burnt offerings and sacrifices."

The other scribes were shocked, not because of Jesus' answer about the first commandment—many in Jesus' day were stating the same first commandments, a combination of Deuteronomy 6:4–5 and Leviticus 19:18—but because of his suggestion that sacred acts of worship, sacrifices, and offerings, were not part of the equation of the most important commandment. To compound the matter, Jesus tells the scribe who affirmed the secondary nature of these acts of public worship: "*You* are not far from the kingdom of God."[1]

I can see why this bothered the scribes and others who were gathered there. It kind of bothers me. This passage suggests that the first and second linked commandments are much more important than sacrifices and many aspects, therefore, of organized religion. Any other form of

---

1. Mark 12:34b, emphasis the author's.

Section Two—The Prepared Church Confronts the Issues of Its Day

expressing love for God, such as that which takes place in public worship, is a second-rate form of loving God. We'll come back to this aspect of the passage at the end.

This story, like many, is told in all three of the synoptic gospels: Matthew, Mark, and Luke. Luke's version of this same story is longer than the others. After Jesus states the greatest commandments, it ends with the lawyer (it's a lawyer rather than a scribe in his account) saying to Jesus, "Who is my neighbor?"[2] Jesus responds by telling the story of the Good Samaritan, who showed neighborliness to a beaten and downtrodden man. He walked up to the man in the ditch, cleaned him up, carried him on his donkey to a shelter, and paid for his stay there. There are multiple layers to the meaning of that parable, but the plain message is that the man in the ditch is your neighbor; go all out in caring for him.

The Good Samaritan story is not an Old Testament story that had always been part of Jewish law, one of the commandments of the people of Israel. No, it was Jesus' creative first-century rendering of the heart of the Old Testament law. Mark, in today's parallel story, gives us no story like the Good Samaritan; but the teaching about the greatest commandment begs for one. And so, in light of the Good Samaritan story in Luke, I see Mark's absence of a descriptive story as an invitation to other Christians—you and me—to write creative renderings that awaken us to forgotten neighbors. And today, I want to talk about our forgotten non-human neighbors—squirrels, feral cats, and all of creation.

Yes, you heard me right, feral cats—wild, mangy cats. When I was a student minister in Brooklyn there was a woman named Faye who used to write her prayer request each week (that was the church's style—to write prayers) and put it in the offering tray. The minister would then pull the prayer requests out and read them aloud to the congregation. Faye's were special: "God, please bless all cats that are cold and lonely tonight, and protect those who rescue them;" "God, our rescue team found two feral cats yesterday. We pray for good homes for both of them—help us come up with the money for shots;" "God, help me, I've got twelve feral cats in my living room this week. You've got to find homes for them!" When it was my week to do prayers, I always was a bit apprehensive to read Faye's requests. To be honest, these were always a bit embarrassing to read. I would sometimes mumble through them, sometimes speed through them, sometimes only read portions of the request that

2. Luke 10:27b.

didn't sound embarrassing to me. But while I hemmed and hawed and protected my public image, Faye just went about living out the greatest commandment day after day. Someday, when Faye dies, her minister will speak of how she experienced God through those cats—and about how much fun she had caring for cats and getting to know them.

Practicing the greatest commandment benefits both the practitioner and the recipient. Just ask Faye, or those cats! I think we know that it benefited the cats, but sometimes we forget what a benefit commandment keeping has for the commandment keeper. Practicing commandments is a joyous task. Just ask the author of Psalm 119 who, 176 times, says some version of the line, "Happy are those who keep God's commandments." Or ask the author of Deuteronomy who wrote, "Keep his statutes and his commandments, which I am commanding you today for your own well-being and that of your descendants after you."[3] It is utterly true for anyone who keeps the greatest commandment in a consistent way in terms of creation. Caring for creation leads to great joy. Friends of Jesus Christ, hear the gospel. Live the law, draw close in a caring way to your non-human neighbors, and draw close to God.

This week as I was listening to NPR in the car I was moved by a report on the environment. The story quoted a *Washington Post* article entitled, "Warming Called Threat to Global Economy."[4] Julie Eilperin wrote, "Failing to curb the impact of climate change could damage the global economy on the scale of the Great Depression or the world wars by spawning environmental devastation that could cost 5 to 20 percent of the world's annual gross domestic product, according to a report issued yesterday by the British government."

She continued, "The report by Nicholas Stern—who heads Britain's Government Economic Service and was formerly the chief economist at the World Bank—calls for a new round of international collaboration to cut greenhouse gas emissions linked to global warming. 'There's still time to avoid the worst impacts of climate change, if we act now and act internationally,' Stern said in a statement. 'But the task is urgent. Delaying action, even by a decade or two, will take us into dangerous territory. We must not let this window of opportunity close.'"

---

3. Deut 4:40a.

4. Eilperin, "Warming Called Threat to Global Economy," http://www.washingtonpost.com/wp-dyn/content/article/2006/10/30/AR2006103000269.html.

Section Two—The Prepared Church Confronts the Issues of Its Day

I'm sure you've all heard reports like this in recent times—whether it's in the 2006 documentary, *An Inconvenient Truth* by David Guggenheim that features Al Gore presenting scientific data about human climatic impact, or in any of the many scary books that highlight the pain the Earth is experiencing, and how much damage the Earth's injuries will, in the very near future, cause *us*. Scary truths and hard facts about the doom that will come to humanity as a result of creation abuse are important; they sometimes prompt voters, and therefore governments, into action. But today, I want to suggest that a Christian approach—a greatest commandment approach—to this Earth neighbor looks very different than the report I read to you from the *Washington Post*. We care for our non-human neighbors not because it's pragmatic to do so, although it is, but rather because we are commandment followers—and God commanded us to love our neighbors. And the more we love our non-human neighbors, the more we will find that we connect, also, with God.

October

> I watched mosaic colors warm a distant hill, and ferns turn brown along a motley trail. My path gave whispered messages from shuffling feet. A bend revealed the opulence of one red tree, and slim black branches dangled yellow jewels. Like kettles boiling pickles, beans, and jam my camera tried to seal this harvest feast and keep it shelved until Earth's constant cycle yields beauty of another lovely new October.[5]

That's a poem my grandmother published that tells of a day on the path near her house where she walked each month, year after year. These were her thoughts one October. My grandmother knew that stretch of woods, and many more. She could identify every tree species in upstate New York. She knew every bird, by look and song. She knew her wildflowers and butterflies.

She knew and loved her non-human neighbors, connecting to them relationally. She knew them so well that she could identify when they were in trouble. My grandfather loves to tell the story of when she, a first-year teacher in 1945, stared down the principal of her elementary school as he tried to explain that he wanted to cut down the woods by the school in order to help the church meet its budget that year. Those woods are still there.

---

5. Dale, "My Special World," 22.

Her advocacy for her neighbor, creation, took the form of teaching adult education classes in her church on sustainable living, where, among other things, she presented photos of department store aisles alongside her photographs of algae fungi, complete with a poem, "Symbiosis," to highlight the superiority of algae over materialism:

> Orange splashes on black rock can be likened to man's hypothetical utopian community. Their algae-fungi vie for space and light but temper rivalry with some impunity. Recyclers of the Earth, they decompose in symphonies of close harmonic unity.[6]

All of this commandment keeping to creation led to great joy. Just before she died she wrote, "My Balance Sheet":

> For me the sun came up near 30,000 times—my world a blend of constant love, few passing shadows. While birds trilled praises overhead, the trail through sheltering pines was edged by flowers. The entries show but twenty aches and pains and twenty million blessings. To tally up these years four score, no reckoner could wish for more.[7]

In her last days she spoke of her own death from a peaceful place, likening it to the algae-fungi she had written about; she felt a close, harmonic unity with the Earth. I tell you about my grandmother today because loving planet Earth and all non-human neighbors was at the core of her relationship with God. Following the laws of God as they pertained to creation, her days went well. She was blessed by keeping the law, and she was a blessing to her neighbor, creation, in the process.

Friends of Jesus Christ, we've been told today that there's something much more important than "whole burnt offerings and sacrifices," or any of the other "sacrifices" that we make by coming to church. It is more important to love God and your neighbor with all your heart, soul, and mind—and that neighbor includes creation itself. But there *is* something absolutely essential about being *here* together in this sanctuary on Sundays. Here is where we come together, not to sacrifice, but to receive God's neighbor love for us. In this place, we experience God living out the greatest commandment—to love vulnerable us, even as God loves God's very self.

---

6. Ibid., 106.
7. Ibid., 119.

Don't come here to "make a sacrifice for God"—you're better off going straight to the soup kitchen, or to spend an hour recycling. But do keep coming here. Come here to be fed by God—for that is, I believe, something that will help you live the commandments even more fully. It's only when you've been nourished by God that you'll be ready to care for squirrels and feral cats, wooded trails, and trilliums. Amen.

Part Six

Faith Facing Sexual Orientation

28

The Way of the Cross

Addressing Homosexuality

February 20, 2005

> For the wrath of God is revealed from heaven against all ungodliness and wickedness of those who by their wickedness suppress the truth. For what can be known about God is plain to them, because God has shown it to them. Ever since the creation of the world his eternal power and divine nature, invisible though they are, have been understood and seen through the things he has made. So they are without excuse; for though they knew God, they did not honor him as God or give thanks to him, but they became futile in their thinking, and their senseless minds were darkened. Claiming to be wise, they became fools; and they exchanged the glory of the immortal God for images resembling a mortal human being or birds or four-footed animals or reptiles. Therefore God gave them up in the lusts of their hearts to impurity, to the degrading of their bodies among themselves, because they exchanged the truth about God for a lie and worshiped and served the creature rather than the Creator, who is blessed forever! Amen. For this reason God gave them up to the degrading passions. Their women exchanged natural intercourse for unnatural, and in the same way also the men, giving up natural intercourse with women, were consumed with passion for one

Section Two—The Prepared Church Confronts the Issues of Its Day

another. Men committed shameless acts with men and received in their own persons the due penalty for their error. And since they did not see fit to acknowledge God, God gave them up to a debated mind and to things that should not be done. They were filled with every kid of wickedness, evil, covetousness, malice. Full of envy, murder, strife, deceit, craftiness, they are gossips, slanderers, God-haters, insolent, haughty, boastful, investors of evil, rebellious toward parents, foolish, faithless, heartless, ruthless. They know God's decree, that those who practice such things deserve to die—yet they not only do them but even applaud others who practice them. (Romans 1:18–32)

Lent is about the way of the cross. The way of the cross is about Jesus loving and serving God regardless of the ramifications, and finding, in that perfect love, resurrection from fear and even death. The way of the cross is Jesus clearing money changers out of the temple; it's Jesus standing steadfast on the side of the poor, the despised and diseased; it's Jesus challenging religious and political authorities. Jesus didn't die for claiming to be the Son of God. He didn't die to forgive our sins. He did do that of course—but he didn't go up to Jerusalem and say, "Kill me, so I can forgive sin." No, Jesus died for acting with *radical love* in response to God, even when church and state didn't like it. During Lent, we draw close to Jesus who is on his way to the cross.

But Lent shouldn't just be about remembering Jesus and the cross. Lent is also about "taking up our own cross," the particular cross that defines our historical and political moment. We are Christians, made like our namesake by the power of God. We are full of the same Spirit as Jesus Christ now, receiving that Spirit as we travel on the road we call faith—a road that weaves its way through real history. This Lent, take up the crosses that are on the faith road you are walking in the year 2005.

The cross I want to pick up from the faith road today is the topic of homosexuality and Christian faithfulness. This is an issue that is dividing Christian denominations throughout the country and world. Episcopalians, Methodists, Lutherans, Presbyterians, and now, the Reformed Church in America (RCA), are all in the throes of very heated debates and deliberations about this issue. For some here in this sanctuary, homosexuality is something that is not at all an issue for you. It might even bother you that it need be addressed. "What's the big deal? Are Christians still talking about this like it's a problem?" For others, the fact that the word "homosexuality" is uttered from the pulpit is disturbing and inappropriate. "How dare the church address something that is so wrong and that the Bible so clearly rejects?"

There is one aspect of the current debate that I'm not going to enter into today, and I thought I'd just make that clear from the beginning. I'm not going to talk about whether or not "marriage" should be the word used to define same-sex unions as well as heterosexual unions. I'm not going to address it because it is, to my mind, a "second-tier" issue. I hear good arguments on both sides of this debate, and I hope that it is one in which the church can soon engage. But for now, in our denomination in the year 2005, there is a much more basic question—a first-tier issue that the church must address, which is whether or not it is appropriate for people of faith to live in life-long monogamous relationships with persons of the same sex.

I chose to address the passage from Romans today, because it is generally considered the most compelling passage condemning homosexuality. Jesus never speaks explicitly about homosexuality; Paul mentions it three times. Romans chapter 1 is Paul's clearest statement. It is also the only reference to both male and female homosexuality. All other references in Scripture are addressed only to men.

In Romans 1, verses 26 and 27, Paul calls homosexual passions and acts "degrading, unnatural, and shameless." For many, this is the end of the story—"the Bible is clear." But to read the Bible out of context is dangerous sometimes—and this is one such time. Acclaimed biblical scholar, Ernst Käsemann, tells us that we should examine the whole, then execute the parts. He says, "in true theology there is no place for global judgments, and concreteness is always required. Awareness of the provisional nature of the solutions offered at any time and expected from theology does not release it from, but obligates it to, unceasing labor. Each of its statements is to be thought through by the reader either in assent or rejection, and it thus remains a question instead of lulling to sleep or granting secure possession."[1]

The first thing to say about this passage is that neither the letter to the Romans, nor the argument in which the verses about homosexuality are found, are about homosexuality. I think acknowledging this reality is essential. Paul was not writing with the intent of giving his full thoughts on homosexuality; rather, he was just using homosexuality as a means to bolster a much bigger argument.

1. Käsemann, *Commentary*, viii.

Section Two—The Prepared Church Confronts the Issues of Its Day

I want to take time this morning to look at "the bigger argument" in which these verses are found, so that together we might understand the placement of the passages about homosexuality. The letter to the Romans is Paul's attempt to explain to Jewish and Gentile followers in Rome why it is that he is proud of the gospel of Jesus Christ. In chapter 1:16–17 Paul states his thesis: "I am not ashamed of the gospel . . . for in it the righteousness of God is revealed through faith for faith." The letter to the Romans is about the righteousness of God, as revealed through Christ, and about what that revelation means for those who live by faith.

Paul's argument about God's righteousness is really eleven chapters long. Theme grows on top of theme. Much of those eleven chapters are about the details of God's new way of being righteous, brought about by Christ. But before he gets to the "new righteousness," he presents his understanding of the way that God, in the past and before the coming of Christ, maintained divine righteousness in the face of human sin and corruption.

This argument about divine righteousness was absolutely essential for the Jewish believers among the community to whom Paul was writing. You see, God's righteous judgment, also called "God's wrath," was understood in Hebrew Scripture to be part of what made God, God. God's wrath was part of God's righteousness. In his ministry, Paul must have frequently been accused of writing off wrath and righteousness, with all his preaching about Jesus' love for sinners. To combat those accusations, Paul, in Romans 1:18—3:20, lays out his understanding of how God, throughout the ages, maintained divine righteousness through "wrath." While this argument might sound strange to many of us today, it was a necessary piece of theological understanding for Paul's religious audience.

Paul first emphasizes how God has exhibited wrath toward Gentiles, those without the law, and then, how God has exhibited wrath toward Jews, who have been given the law. In a summary section in Romans 3:1–20, Paul concludes that "no one is righteous, not even one," and therefore God's wrath is appropriately placed upon all.

Let me delve into the section about God's wrath toward Gentiles, as it is in these verses that references to homosexuality come up. Paul explains that Gentiles had the opportunity to know God through the natural world and through invisible power, and so righteousness was expected of them—even though they weren't given the law, like the Jews had been.[2]

2. Rom 1:18–32.

The Way of the Cross

In a sweeping generalization he says all failed to give honor and thanks to God, and the result was that they started to commit idolatry, choosing random four-footed animals or birds to worship. This idolatry, according to Paul, was an affront to God's righteousness. Therefore, Paul says, God had to pay them back for what they had done, in order to protect God's righteousness. God's way of carrying out "wrath" at that time was to "give them up;" to give them freedom to indulge in behaviors that were unnatural and destructive. That, according to Paul, is how God, throughout the ages, protected God's righteousness.

Paul lists here the kinds of things that people indulged in after God "gave them up." He begins his rhetoric with something he felt would be *clearly* seen as unnatural, speaking of homosexuality. Why did Paul feel so strongly about homosexuality that he chose to use it as an example of unnatural acts? First, he was writing to the Romans from the port city of Corinth, a city notorious for its "thousand sacred prostitutes."[3] Paul might very well have been exposed to a truly sinful climate of sexuality. Second, for Paul, there was a natural/created pattern of things—heterosexuality—which, it seems, he assumed was true for all people.

After referencing homosexuality, Paul goes on to list "every kind of wickedness"—envy, murder, strife, deceit, craftiness, evil, heartlessness, and ruthlessness—saying that these, too, are unnatural in that they go against our created order. Paul's point in Romans 1:18—3:20 is to show that the world is under God's wrath, and therefore God's righteousness is maintained.

Paul's argument about God's use of wrath in the past was a set up so he could say, "That was then, this is now!" The wonder of Jesus Christ is that God's righteousness need not be held up by "wrath" any longer! In Jesus, God has replaced wrath with suffering love as the way to maintain righteousness. God has replaced wrath with divine graciousness! Hear Paul's conclusion to the argument. "But now, apart from the law, the righteousness of God has been disclosed . . . the righteousness of God through faith in Jesus Christ for all who believe . . . God put forward [Jesus] as a sacrifice of atonement by his blood, effective through faith. [God] did this to show his righteousness, because in his divine forbearance he had passed over the sins previously committed; it was to prove at the present time that he himself is righteous and that he justifies the one who has faith in Jesus."[4]

3. Freedman, *Eerdman's Dictionary*, "Corinth," 280.
4. Rom 3:21a, 22a, 25–26.

This is the "whole argument" that Paul is making in the first chapters of Romans. It's an argument about God's righteousness, and how faith in Jesus is the new way that God's righteousness is maintained. God doesn't "give people up" any longer—at least not those who come to God in faith, seeking to be made new.

Read in the context of "the whole argument," this is what we can say about homosexuality from Paul's perspective: Paul believed homosexual passion and acts were sinful results of idolatry, allowed by God as God "gave people up" to their own destruction; and Paul believed that through the gift of Jesus Christ, idolatry falls away, sins are forgiven, and followers are filled with the Spirit of God—led to newness of life. Through faith, believers come to follow Christ, not idols, and find themselves stepping away from wickedness, evil, covetousness, malice, and homosexual desire. It won't happen automatically (we learn from later chapters), but there will be, in the believer, at least a recognition of sin, and the desire to change.

It is at this point that it becomes clear that Paul's argument cannot address our current questions about homosexuality. While all Christians, as they live and grow in faith, work to correct most of the sins Paul listed in Romans 1, such as lying, cheating, stealing, covetousness, malice, gossip, etc., there are endless numbers of Christians for whom the inclination for a partner of the same sex just will not go away. Indeed, many people were walking with Jesus when they first discovered their sexual orientation.

Paul says later in his letter that after one is "in Christ," sinful inclinations *will fall away*. But as we know, for many people, those inclinations do not fall away, and they never will. They are an integral part of God-given identity. Is faith in God not strong enough, then, to "correct" homosexuality? Is there some deficiency in God's grace? Or might it be that homosexuality is natural for some people, not in need of correction, for it is not sin. If that is the case then homosexual orientation ought to be celebrated, for it is a person's God-given image.

Some of the most wonderful Christians I know, some of the most Spirit-filled ministers, are gay men and lesbian women. They are undoubtedly "in Christ," recipients of the "new righteousness," and they are gay. Their sexual orientation is not a result of God "giving them up" to sin, for God hasn't "given them up," at all. On the contract, God has guided many of them into holy relationships! This reality that some believers are homosexual in orientation and led to others of the same sex is not something that Paul understood. He didn't know to acknowledge the distinction between homosexual perversity (which he had in mind in the Romans argument) and same-sex love expressed by those "in Christ." *But we must acknowledge it.* I find it totally inappropriate that this passage from Romans, about a large theological argument about God's righteousness, has become grounds for the condemnation of holy relationships between persons of homosexual orientation.

I want to tell you this morning about my journey on this issue. In my freshman year in college I read *Uncommon Decency,* a book about how Christians are called to decency toward all people when it comes to moral deliberations, especially those with whom we disagree. I was struck by the chapter entitled, "How to Be Decent about Sexuality."[5] It called Christians to task for the ways they had become full of hatred toward gay and lesbian persons. The author basically says, "Shame on you" to the church for the fact that there was more acceptance and love in the gay bar scene than there was in the church of Jesus Christ. And as I read this, I came to say, "Shame on me." I remember reading that book and feeling my face go flush. I thought it was embarrassment, but in retrospect, maybe it was embarrassment coupled with the hot winds of the Holy Spirit, my own Pentecostal event. That moment was one in which I felt the weight of sinful judgment alive in my life. I remembered saying in a casual conversation in the high school cafeteria, "God made Adam and Eve, not Adam and Steve," as if that simple joke summed up the truth about homosexuality. I can remember laughing at gay jokes on the baseball bus. I didn't think I'd ever known a gay person, but after reading that chapter, I realized that probably 5–9% of the kids in my class were oriented toward persons of the same sex, and just afraid to admit it because of people holding views like mine. I realized, reading that chapter, that in my ignorance I had probably hurt people and exhibited great prejudice. As one of the few practicing Christians in my high school, I had probably turned them off to the church as well.

When, in my freshman year of college, I realized that it was verses from my own Bible that had been the backbone of my bigotry, I knew I had to do something. While I still didn't know whether or not I believed homosexual physical relationships were appropriate, I knew I had to read the passages critically for myself. I took an independent study with

---

5. Mouw, "How to Be Decent about Sexuality," chap. 7.

a professor at the college, carefully studying the passages referencing homosexuality in Scripture, and reading any current essay or book I could get my hands on regarding the scientific or psycho/social aspects of the issue. Simultaneously, I attended a gay Bible study, meeting regularly with the minister who led the group. I needed to meet people who were both gay and Christian. And I did. I met wonderful men and women living out committed lives of love with a life-long partner, struggling and rejoicing in the same way that heterosexual couples do, except without the support of a broad community base; certainly without the support of a congregation. I learned that the backbone of these relationships was mutuality, respect, and a shared faith. Paul didn't know homosexual Christians, but I do, and I cannot read Scripture without that new knowledge any longer.

So, as I turned to Scripture, I had Gary and Brian (a couple in the Bible study) in my mind. I read Genesis 19, a gang rape in Sodom. This is a horrific biblical story, and the story that gave birth to the term "sodomy." However, Gary and Brian, a couple together for fourteen years when I met them, certainly weren't the mark of the violent, perverse, inhospitable men in that passage from Genesis. Neither can I hold Romans 1 over Gary and Brian, nor over any other homosexual person who is seeking to live in a holy relationship. Guidance from Scripture concerning sexual relationships is going to have to come from different places in the Bible. It is not faithful to the text, nor helpful to the kingdom of God, to appeal to passages that just don't apply to the situation at hand.

Here's my proposal: Instead of looking to the negative passages about homosexuality in Scripture, none of which seem to apply to the reality of sexual orientation, let's look to Jesus Christ for positive guidance about all holy relationships. Jesus lived his life close to God, and in so doing, emanated holy qualities; qualities of mutuality, respect, compassion, commitment, listening, interest, and love. Holy relationships, whether they are heterosexual or homosexual, are opportunities in this world in which to experience some of those holy qualities of God-like covenant. In the giving and receiving of intimate, embodied love—love laced with mutuality and respect—we have one of our greatest opportunities to experience the kingdom now in our lives.

May the church of Jesus Christ become a place that helps same-sex couples reflect heaven in their relationships. In fact, may it be that the church encourages healthy relationships of all kinds: marriages, unions, friendships, and community relationships—that we might all have the opportunity to experience something of the kingdom of heaven. Amen.

Part Seven

Faith Facing American Mass Shootings

29

Don't Go Fishing Again

A pril 22, 2007

> After these things Jesus showed himself again to the disciples by the Sea of Tiberias; and he showed himself in this way. Gathered there together were Simon Peter, Thomas called the Twin, Nathanael of Cana in Galilee, the sons of Zebedee, and two others of his disciples. Simon Peter said to them, "I am going fishing." They said to him, "We will go with you." (John 21:1–3a)

"I am going fishing." That's what Peter said to the other disciples by the Sea of Galilee just a few weeks after the resurrection of Jesus. John's gospel does not tell us about Jesus' ascension to heaven, but from the other gospels we are told that the ascension happened forty days or so after Easter. So, sticking with that timeline, and having a couple of other post-Easter stories from John that come before this one, this *fishing* story probably happened thirty days or so after Jesus was raised from the dead.

"Let's go fishing." It sounds benign enough, even restful and enjoyable.

"I'm taking a day off, throwing a line in the water, anybody want to come?"

"Yeah, we'll join you!"

That's what it would sound like to me, if my dad were to say, "Let's go fishing." But it was something altogether different when those words came from Peter. You see, fishing was Peter's job—and the job of many of the other disciples—or at least it had been until Jesus changed their vocation. Jesus said to them, "Follow me, and I will make you fish for people."[6] For the entire time of Jesus' ministry, Peter had not put net to lake, had not gone back to his old line of work. There was nothing wrong with a career in fishing; it was admirable. It just wasn't the right career for Peter or the other disciples anymore. Their vocational instructions had been clearly given by Jesus.

Hear how Luke describes the disciples' new job: "Jesus called the twelve together and gave them power and authority over all demons and to cure diseases, and he sent them out to proclaim the kingdom of God and to heal."[7] In Matthew's account, we read that Jesus called them together after the resurrection and said, "All authority in heaven and on earth has been given to me. Go therefore and make disciples.[8] In Matthew, Mark, and Luke, Jesus warned them it would be hard: "Deny yourselves, take up your cross daily, follow me."[9]

Peter's response to his new call was, "I am going fishing, going back to my old job." Can you blame him, and them, for wanting to get out to the country and go back to what they knew and where they felt safe? I remember when Pastor Stephanie and I lived in Ecuador and we took a weekend away at the beach. We got up early and walked the shore, picking up shells in the town of Salinas. As we walked, we could see a fleet of small wooden canoes heading in from the ocean, with their night catch. It's hard work out there, fishing in the night, but at least nobody's trying to take your life, like the authorities were in Jerusalem after Jesus died and rose. At least you don't have this sinking feeling that you're being watched.

Before deciding to go back and fish, we hear that the disciples were behind locked doors whenever they gathered for fear of the authorities.[10] Even after the resurrected Jesus appeared to them in a locked room, breathing the Holy Spirit upon them, they were still anxiety ridden on a daily basis. The second time he appeared to them they were hiding out again, behind doors.

"I am going fishing," Peter said. Others followed.

6. Matt 4:19.
7. Luke 9:1–2.
8. Matt 28:18b–19a.
9. Luke 9:23; Matthew 16:24; Mark 8:34.
10. John 20:19.

Don't Go Fishing Again

We are a couple of weeks removed from Easter and from the radical hope that springs from the resurrection. We might be just a few days less removed from Easter than the original disciples were removed from the first Easter when Peter said, "Let's go fishing." We are supposed to be on the Easter high, the Easter tide, riding it for all its worth. Catch a wave! We're sitting on top of the world knowing that our savior lives!

But then this week came along and I'm starting to understand why Peter and the other disciples were ready to go back to an old way of life; old forms of self protection and smaller, safer dreams.

You've read the papers; you've seen the reports. A lonely, hurt, and very violent young child of God got up on the 16th of April and went on a rampage of death and destruction. By the time he finished, thirty-three were dead, "stamping the campus in the picturesque Blue Ridge mountains with unspeakable tragedy, perhaps forever."[11] The obituaries of the people who died, the stories of their budding lives, are just heartbreaking; surgeons, scientists, artists, and farmers, being molded and formed at Virginia Tech University—all dead.

As I worked on this sermon this past Wednesday, 223 people died in Iraq from bombs and gun violence. That was third-page news, understandably, on that day, behind a page about Virginia Tech and then another about the thousands of locals, including members of this church, who were evacuated due to Monday's raging floodwaters.

Let's go fishing, Christians. Let's forget this different way of being in the world. Let's put self-protection, me and mine and all that kind of stuff, at the top of our list because the hope that the kingdom of God is coming—and it is a message of peace, hope, joy, and love—is just too hard to work for, and even believe in.

The disciples were out there fishing, having no luck by the way, and Jesus called to them from the shore. "Hey, you haven't caught anything yet, huh?"

"No."

"Why don't you cast on the other side?"

"Ok."

So they cast again, and they weren't able to haul the net in because there were so many fish.

Friends, Jesus visited them. He visited them while they were retreating, scared, uncertain, and making a choice to give up their vocation. He

---

11. "Questions Raised," http://diverseeducation.com/article/7240/#.

Section Two—The Prepared Church Confronts the Issues of Its Day

visited them not to chastise them, but rather to gently care for them. He even helped them catch some fish, 153 of them! He helped them catch fish, and then he sat with them, and fed them fish from his own grill—and bread (and probably wine too). And he empowered them again for their new vocation, saying things like, "You know, I really want you to feed my sheep. . . . If you love me, feed my sheep."

Friends of Jesus Christ, hear the good news today: Jesus *is* on the loose, and he won't let us slip away from our vocation. He's not going to let us fish again—at least not permanently. He knows it's not good for us and certainly not good for the world. He wants us to show love by feeding and tending all people as we travel toward the kingdom of God.

And with Jesus committed to visiting us when we are feeling down about our job, we're going to have this job for the long haul. And this new vocation that Christ keeps us in is the only one from which we ought to operate in order to face Monday's massacre and all suffering. We face the Virginia Tech tragedy as Easter people, constantly renewed by a risen Lord. We face Virginia Tech as the church, not as people in retreat, going back to old positions of reasoning, and fear.

Easter people are rushing forward, rushing toward the kingdom of God that is moving quickly toward us. We're rushing toward it because Christ was rushing there ahead of us while he lived among us. We might have stopped when he was killed and buried, but then he got up, rushed onward, faster now, rushed onward and is now there, at the right hand of God. So we rush. We rush onward, toward the prize, joyously colliding with it throughout our lives as it breaks in upon us.

And we might stop again, overwhelmed by massacres, wars, and floods, but Jesus comes to us again, showing up at the old jobs, patterns, addictions, and fears to which we return, tending to us and loving us back into our new vocations. So we rush on again, even today, toward the kingdom, and over and over it breaks in upon us and we see it! We point it out to those around us. We welcome it and become transformed as we let the rules and ways of the in-breaking kingdom envelop us even as we rush on.

I remember when the Columbine shootings occurred, eight years ago today. I was really shocked by it all—defeat is the word I'd use to explain how I felt. I woke up in the morning, the day after the shooting, and the clock radio was going off. From NPR I heard, "Jesus, Lamb of God, worthy is your name. Jesus, Lamb of God, worthy is your name." It was the sound of Columbine High School students singing a Natalie Grant praise song that I learned to love at our college chapel services. It was as if Jesus visited me while I was lying in bed. And just like that it somehow made it possible for me to believe that there was more than destruction in Columbine.

It didn't take away the sadness, it didn't in any way undercut or undervalue the losses, it just became, for me, a healthy place to start; solid ground on which to stand. That moment gave me back my vocation. Praying for Columbine became meaningful.

A few months later, I was fortunate enough to be asked to speak at Columbine Reformed Church, not about the shootings, but about the children's home where Pastor Stephanie and I had lived in Ecuador. I had a wonderful visit with families in Columbine—families with high school students who had suffered so—and I applauded their interest in Ecuadorian kids. I had a chance to give them something—an affirmation about their Christian love and hope. Making that affirmation to them sprang from my vocation as a disciple of Jesus Christ.

Friends of Jesus Christ, it is my prayer this week that Jesus would encourage you in your vocation as disciples. Don't go fishing—don't go back to old vocations if you are in despair. Instead, turn even more fully toward your new vocation—your everyday, new vocation—of being disciples of the Christ who is ushering in the kingdom of God. That's what you have to offer people at Virginia Tech, and those around you who have been shaken by the massacre.

There are key ways that being a hope-filled disciple can help you face the atrocities of this week, and can help those in Virginia and throughout the country as well. Firstly, your hope in God erases fear. There is a fear-based media and political heyday going on right now. Arm the public, ban all guns, restrict foreign student visas, put hidden cameras in dorm rooms, fire the school president, increase security on campuses nationwide. Fearless ones, any statement that sounds fear-driven, you can unveil as such. Any policy that seems to be borne from anxiety, you can reject. The world needs fear-stoppers—and in Christ you are fearless. No more duct tape and codes orange. No more locked-down living. Decisions borne of fear are not Christian decisions. Encourage the world to operate out of hope—not fear—especially now.

And secondly, and just as importantly, your Easter-born fearlessness leads you to be compassionate and fully present with those who mourn. Having no worries about crosses and the like you have no need to immediately deal with anxiety-based questions of policy and culpability, and are instead freed up to listen for those who are deeply saddened and scared, and to offer them care and support. In addition to the caring that you can do on your own, I'd like to encourage us to care together. Here are two ways we can do this now:

A. Catherine is a graduate of Virginia Tech, and I asked her to help us begin the process of really caring by writing a card from our church to the school, simply stating our love for them, the victims, and expressing our hope that God's love will sustain them at this time.

B. I also want to invite you to Wednesday morning prayer when we will be praying, by name, for all who lost their lives in Virginia. We will also begin the practice of praying by name for all those (whose names we can track), American and Iraqi, who have died during the week. That prayer time will run from 7 to 8 am on Wednesday.

John ends his book basically saying, "You know what? This book I wrote contains just a sampling of what Jesus did. I suppose that the world itself could not contain the disks and CDs it would take to record what Jesus did and does." Plan on some of those recordings being of the times he appeared to you, and brought you back to your new vocation—or kept you firmly planted in it. Maybe he'll appear that way for you now. Amen.

Part Eight

Faith Facing Natural Disasters

30

Caring before Katrina

October 30, 2005

> He has told you, O mortal, what is good; and what does the Lord require of you but to do justice, and to love kindness, and to walk humbly with your God? (Micah 6:8)

> Woe to you, scribes and Pharisees, hypocrites! For you tithe mint, dill, and cumin, and have neglected the weightier matters of the law: justice and mercy and faith. It is these you ought to have practiced without neglecting the others. (Matthew 23:23)

The cover of a Christian journal I receive each month, called *Sojourners*, has a picture of a weeping mother (African-American) in New Orleans with her very serious looking toddler in her arms. The headline reads, "Can you see me now?"[1] The article inside, like so many other provocative articles I've read in recent weeks, speaks of the way that Hurricane Katrina, while tearing off roofs and taking lives, also tore the cover off the twin blemishes of racism and poverty that are perpetuated in this country.

We saw it on CNN; fellow Americans, children of God, black and poor, sitting on roofs and bridges, waiting for help. Many are describing the slow federal response to Katrina as genocide. Folks around the world saw what was happening too. I went on the Internet and typed in

---

1. *Sojourners*, cover.

Section Two—The Prepared Church Confronts the Issues of Its Day

"Katrina and racism" and thousands of references from articles around the world jumped onto the screen.

There have been a lot of historians talking too; pointing to the fact that natural disasters like this one, which expose great sins of our nation, have played a role in bringing about social change and correction in the past. The *Sojourners* article I mentioned spoke about how a great flood in Johnston, Pennsylvania, in 1889, killed hundreds of poor people, mainly because the dam of a fishing pond built by the "new industrialists," the "robber barons," had overflowed its banks. A pond of wealthy pleasure became a source of death—and the outrage of a nation over this event helped catalyze the populist movement that resulted in new labor laws, unions, and anti-trust regulations. Maybe Katrina and Rita will have a positive impact—we can only hope so.

But as a follower of Christ, all this talk of how historical disasters prompt the change of heart in a nation seems particularly tragic. Yes, I hope this Katrina relief debacle serves as a wake-up call to care for brothers and sisters by overcoming racism and poverty. Yes, I hope this war will be a wake-up call to care for brothers and sisters by overcoming racism, poverty, and American hubris. But it shouldn't take a hurricane or a war gone sour for us to love all brothers and sisters in the world community enough to be able to "see them." We should care before Katrina, and before we know there are no weapons of mass destruction.

I almost didn't preach on the lectionary gospel lesson this morning. I'm tired of talking about Pharisees and about Jesus' other historical antagonists. Usually we read about Jesus' actions in Jerusalem for one solid week during the church year—Holy Week. The lectionary has had me preaching about Jesus' actions and harsh parables and statements spoken in Jerusalem directed at Pharisees, scribes, and others, for seven weeks now!

I don't like the way that constant reference to Pharisees makes *them* seem to be the archetypal sinners. But you know I'm glad I stuck with it because by the end of the week something good had happened. I stopped seeing the Pharisees in their historical context—I'd had enough of that. Instead, the Pharisees are us, organized Christian religion in our nation. Jesus is talking to us. And as he speaks to us, we've got a choice about whether we will remain who we are, or whether we will join Jesus as he travels through our Jerusalem.

Jesus was not in ministry after a hurricane, or after the start of a war. For Palestine, it was a fairly normal time—not a good time, but normal nonetheless. Palestine was under occupation, but times had been worse for sure. Under occupation, yes, but allowed at least a level of self-rule, as long as they rendered taxes to Caesar. Under occupation, but still fishing, still having family carpentry businesses, still carrying out lives of relative independence. There weren't outside nations coming in to attack since Rome, the occupying force, was the world power of the day. Politically, things were oppressive, but stable. There were no political or social hurricanes.

There were no "religious hurricanes" either when Jesus entered the city of Jerusalem on Palm Sunday. Sadducees were the stability of temple religion and had close ties to the political regime. Pharisaic scribes were the magesterium of religion, The Torah was the guideline that they interpreted. If you took a poll of the folks in Jerusalem the day before Palm Sunday trying to get a pulse of the people about the religious climate of the town, they would have likely said, "It's a day like any other day." There was a lot that wasn't right, but nothing exceptionally wrong. The Torah was being followed, the leaders were doing their work, and temple life was good.

This insight is one that I'd never really reflected on until the lectionary forced me to think about Pharisees week in and week out. Friends, they weren't all that bad. In fact, they were good. There was little trouble in Jerusalem and it was largely because of their stable leadership.

Sometimes I think we read the New Testament and picture the religious leaders of Jesus' day to be particularly corrupt. I think we picture throngs of people just waiting for a savior like Jesus to come along and cleanse the temple and make all things right. Sure, there were folks who wanted changes in religion and society. Zealots, the name given to a variety of small resistance movements, shared the common belief that Palestine needed to be freed from Roman control. Essenes were Jews who wanted to see a rededication to purity and adherence to Jewish law beyond what Pharisees required (John the Baptist was possibly an Essene, by the way). This movement was relatively small too.

Palestine in the first century was not a "burn baby burn" kind of environment. College students weren't burning their draft cards and cities weren't clashing with continual racial tensions. In fact, organized resistance movements were few and far between. The poor, weak, and lame

Section Two—The Prepared Church Confronts the Issues of Its Day

weren't organizing rallies and unions. From any outsider's perspective, it wasn't a *kairos* ("time ripe for change") moment.

But don't tell Jesus that. He came saying exactly the opposite: "The time is at hand, the time is now!" According to Jesus, the time was ripe for change. Now, now, now! There was no time like now. He, like the prophets before him, insisted on dealing with societal sinfulness *before* the general populous woke up and saw there was a crisis at hand.

We heard this morning from one of those earlier prophets, the 8th-century BC prophet, Micah. Micah wrote at a time when Judah was thriving, but would you think that from his prophetic words? Micah wrote, "Hear this, you rulers of the house of Jacob and chiefs of the house of Israel, who abhor justice and pervert all equity, who build Zion with blood and Jerusalem with wrong! . . . because of you Zion shall be plowed as a field; Jerusalem shall become a heap of ruins."[2] Now, do you think that was the assessment of the heads of the nation of Judah, or even of most of the common folks who were benefiting from a decently organized governmental and religious structure? No. But to Micah, the time was at hand to repent and walk closely with God!

Micah and Jesus have an ability to see the truth about injustice *before* a disaster. The cover on the front of *Sojourners*, "Can You See Me Now?" doesn't have to be asked to Jesus and Micah, because they saw and voiced the truth long before Katrina struck.

I got to asking myself this week what Micah and Jesus had in common, and as I looked at these texts side by side, I suddenly realized something amazing. The most famous line in Micah's prophecy is Micah 6. The voice of everyman asks, "With what shall I come before the Lord, and bow myself before God on high? Shall I come before him with burnt offerings, with calves a year old? Will the Lord be pleased with thousands of rams?"[3] The voice goes on and on with questions about proper offering and ceremony.

And the prophet responds, "He has told you, O mortal, what is good; and what does the Lord require of you but to do justice, and to love kindness, and to walk humbly with your God?"[4]

Micah *qualifies the law of God*. There is a lot in the Old Testament about proper offerings for transgressions, but Micah says in effect, "Put

2. Mic 3:9–10, 12.
3. Ibid., 6:6–7a.
4. Ibid., 6:8.

justice, mercy, and walking with God as your priority—period. That's what God wants."

The Scripture reading from Matthew today included many angry statements about Pharisaic behavior; but to my mind the most significant line aimed at them today was, "You've neglected the weightier matters of the law: justice and mercy and faith." Do you hear it? Jesus repeats the core of Micah's prophecy, telling the Pharisees to remember what is weightiest—most important—to God: justice, mercy, and faith.

Justice means to make something right or fair. Fairness is the thing that Micah and Jesus list first. At the core of the Torah is fairness and equality for all persons. Justice is about offering equality to others, and restraining oneself from excess, in any way necessary, to allow for fairness to be realized.

Mercy, or kindness, is a step beyond fairness, and a step toward friendship and love. Jesus and Micah call us not only to be concerned with fair treatment for all but to get close to people; to be able to truly extend compassion to the "other."

Faith means walking humbly with God. It's interesting to me that faith is listed third by both Micah and Jesus. Maybe it's virtually impossible to walk with God—I mean really walk humbly—if you don't care about justice or mercy. I truly believe it was because Jesus knew what was "weightiest" about the law that he behaved as he did when he arrived in Jerusalem.

Jerusalem was calm.

It might not have seemed like a time to flip tables in the temple, but Jesus had met blind Bartimeus, and he knew how badly Bartimeus wanted to go to temple and couldn't because it was against the law.

Jerusalem was peaceful.

It might not have seemed like a time to lambaste a fairly balanced and middle of the road religious hierarchy, but Jesus had met tax collectors who wanted to worship God in community; tax collectors, who with the right support, could be encouraged to change the way they did business—yet they were all rejected.

Jerusalem was a well-ordered city, politically and religiously.

It might not have seemed like a good time to tell stories that all ended with religious hierarchy being criticized and "uninvited" to God's community, but Jesus had gotten to know lepers who longed to be in full communion with society, but who were not invited.

Section Two—The Prepared Church Confronts the Issues of Its Day

Jerusalem was doing well.

It might not have seemed like a good time to yell, "You hypocrites!" at the top of his lungs in the temple; but he'd seen people begging for food, day in and day out, and he saw that the social system wasn't empowering those who were down. It just kept them down—and nobody seemed to care to fix it.

Jesus' actions in Jerusalem were the result of his prioritizing justice and mercy, and thereby giving voice to the voiceless. These are priorities that our society, and I dare say our religious society, doesn't put as priorities until a hurricane, or a long slow war, leaves us no alternative but to take action.

Healthy economy? Jesus didn't check the stock market, he checked for bloated bellies on the children of the working poor.

Decent health care? He wasn't asking those who could afford it about the amount of their co-pay; he was concerned, rather, with those who couldn't even afford fresh bandages on their missing limbs.

Decent development in the cities? Jesus wasn't checking out the new malls or the high-end developments; he was interested in whether the man who had been begging for forty years at the pools at the temple gate was going to be taken seriously and cared for in a more humane way.

Spirit-filled followers of Jesus Christ and the Torah, we are called to care for all people, and to employ the tools of justice, mercy, and humble faith. Christ calls us to put justice and mercy at the front of our list of what it means to follow God. Walking in faith with God is all tied up with fairness and intentional compassion for our neighbor. We will be doing well, I think, if people get annoyed with us, saying, "Why are you creating a problem where there is none? Why are you criticizing religion and society? We've got a system that the world envies." When such things are said they are voiced by those who are not the victims. We're to give voice to the voiceless.

Organized religion today, like in the first century, is primarily a good thing. It brings order and stability to many people's lives. It serves as a conduit for living relationships with God. It creates community for many. But unfortunately, organized Christian religion of the late twentieth and early twenty-first centuries has been very complacent about justice and mercy, and I dare say that this complacency has even negatively impacted the personal faith of many believers. We have carried on our business, week in and week out, in relative silence as injustice upon injustice has been heaped upon the poor and voiceless in our country and around the world through our national policies, which Christian religion seems to sometimes loudly, and sometimes silently, endorse.

We haven't had too many Rosa Parks or Martin Luther King Juniors of late, rising up out of our congregations. We need Jesus to wake us up again. Come flip our proverbial "money changing tables" upside down. Come speak your mind to us about the ways we have forgotten to care for some of your children who are left out of the system. Jesus, come yell, "Woe hypocrites," at us, if that's what it takes—awaken us, organized Christianity, from our slumber. For we've got to get the weightiest matters of the law back where they belong—at the beginning of our consciousness and action—the time is always at hand to implement those weighty actions for the sake of the world.

"Sometimes it takes a natural disaster to expose a social disaster"—that's what I read this week in the *Sojourners* article.[5] It's sad, but true. But we Christians have a higher calling— to care before Katrina. We are called to question tax cuts for the rich when there apparently isn't money available for low-income housing vouchers. We are called to care for Iraqis, *before* more than one hundred thousand are dead. We are called to care before two thousand US soldiers, largely from the poor underbelly of America, are killed in combat. We are called to question trade laws like Central American Trade Agreement before it is signed into law. We are called to question harsh immigration laws, when simultaneously American businesses thrive because of the hard work of undocumented laborers. We are called to do some serious soul searching about laws prohibiting same-sex civil unions or marriage before the results of those laws lead to continued and strengthened injustice and lack of mercy. We've got work to do to bring the weighty matters of the law of God to bear on all things. Amen.

---

5. Wallis, "Sometimes," http://sojo.net/magazine/2005/11/what-waters-revealed.

31

Living in Light of Rachel's Cry after the Tsunami

January 2, 2005

> Thus says the LORD: "A voice is heard in Ramah, lamentation and bitter weeping. Rachel is weeping for her children; she refuses to be comforted for her children, because they are no more." (Jeremiah 31:15)

For a month we've been unpacking, examining, and rediscovering the meaning of Christmas together as a congregation. For a month we've been getting ready to receive baby Jesus, a flicker of light in a world that sometimes acts like a giant candle snuffer. After Christmas each year, I turn back to the Scripture and examine what happened next.

It took all of three or four weeks after Jesus' birth before the first real challenge came. Some astrologers showed up in Jerusalem and told Herod that they came to see the new infant king of the Jews. Herod was scared. He hadn't had a kid recently. Who could they possibly mean was "born king of the Jews?" Was someone attempting to rise up against him in power? After encouraging them to pay a visit to Bethlehem to see this new infant king he sent an army into that little village himself, systematically killing every child under the age of two. The wise men had said they'd come to see an infant king, but just to be sure he didn't miss the right kid, Herod set the death age as two years old. Sociologists estimate that approximately two thousand people lived in Bethlehem at the time. There were probably about twenty male babies under the age of two killed that night.

Jesus lived through it. Warned in a dream, Joseph and Mary got out of town, out of the country, actually, fleeing to Egypt. You wonder if Joseph and Mary should have warned other families in Bethlehem, but they probably had no idea that Herod was so obsessed with killing Jesus that he was willing to carry out mass murder in order to get the right child.

To describe the destruction, Matthew uses a formula that he often employs—he calls on language of the Hebrew Scripture to describe the current reality. "Then was fulfilled what had been spoken by the prophet Jeremiah, 'A voice is heard in Ramah, lamentation and bitter weeping. Rachel is weeping for her children; she refuses to be comforted for her children, because they are no more.'"[1] Matthew, being a scholar of the Hebrew Scripture, would have known that Jeremiah's words were not originally written about this occasion. Jeremiah was writing almost six hundred years before Jesus' birth, and in his day there were plenty of reasons to wail and lament. In the days of Jeremiah, in the town of Ramah, not too far from Bethlehem, Jews had been brutally killed, and those that lived through the killing were lined up and loaded into wagons, forced into exile in Babylon.

Jeremiah's words about the suffering in Ramah were poetic words of suffering. The woman, Rachel, to whom he refers, is Rachel the wife of Jacob, dead one thousand years at the time of Jeremiah. Jacob and Rachel were considered patriarch and matriarch of the twelve tribes of Israel. The devastation in Ramah evoked global wailing—even from the matriarch whose body lay below the ground. Even bones cry out.

A few weeks after Jesus' birth, Matthew tells us it's happening again. Jeremiah's poem has become pertinent, suffering has returned. People in Bethlehem now cry out, and it's as if they can hear Rachel crying from her tomb. Abominable suffering has befallen the people, even in the days immediately after God has entered the world in a new and radically loving way. Not even the arrival of Christ could stop atrocity. In Matthew's account we are reminded that Jesus' entry into the world and into our lives is not a quick fix to disaster and suffering.

Two thousand years later the prophet's words have been fulfilled again. A voice can be heard from Gall, Phuket, Sri Lanka, Chenai,

---

1. Jer 31:15.

Thailand, and Indonesia. A cry has come up that is so sustained, so piercing, that we can even hear it in our living rooms, in our minds and hearts as we lay in bed at night. "Rachel weeping for her children; she refuses to be consoled, because they are no more."

She weeps in other places too. She weeps in Iraq and the dilapidated high-rise housing of American cities—worlds that collide as the children of those impoverished neighborhoods become our soldiers fighting in that nation. She weeps in abusive homes. Rachel weeps for those incarcerated, and for their families outside. The prophecy is fulfilled over and over again. But this time, as a world community, we're hearing her loud and clear in South Asia.

And we need to hear her weep. Weeping is the beginning of any legitimate healing.

Yes, there is healing. Jeremiah—the prophet often called the "wailing prophet" because of his continual expressions of grief—begins to get hopeful just one chapter after the lament about Rachel. God tells him to buy a piece of property in Ramah, which had been overrun by Babylon. Go and take out a mortgage, go to the bank and get this thing signed. Jeremiah gives us details about the business transaction, "I bought the field at Anathoth, from my cousin Hanamel, and weighed out the money to him, seventeen shekels of silver. I signed the deed, sealed it, got witnesses, and weighed the money on scales."[2] After carrying out God's wish, Jeremiah sat down to think, and he got raving mad at God. I paraphrase, "God, you created the whole world, you are Lord of all, nothing is too hard for you, you show steadfast love . . ." the list goes on and on. "Yet you, O Lord God, you said to me, buy the field for money and get witnesses—though the city had been given into the hands of the Babylonians!" God, what were you thinking?

God says to Jeremiah, who still hears Rachel weeping, "I'm gonna do something new here in Ramah. You will see my glory in this place again. Invest in hope. Buy some land, soon others will be doing so too."

Six hundred years after Jeremiah, God essentially says, "Hold out hope in Bethlehem too. For see, I have protected Jesus my Son. Joseph and Mary, bring him up in Egypt, come back when you can. In him I will renew all things! Don't stop mourning the loss of babies in Bethlehem, continue to hear their parent's cry out, but work in hope too!"

---

2. Ibid., 32:10.

Sometimes, when devastation befalls the world, we're left to wonder, "Is it all for naught?" The thought of rebuilding feels overwhelming and futile. To rebuild knowing that the 150,000 people who had been working as world builders only two weeks before dead; to rebuild, knowing that tomorrow another wave might roll—that is hard.

But friends, the good news today is this. We worship a God who cries with Rachel, and yet who continues to be a builder; and by the power of the Spirit leads us to be mourning-builders too! God will lead us back to hope-filled work.

What will follow your grief about this tsunami? I should say, what first flickers of hope will start pulsing for you simultaneously with the cry you are hearing from South Asia, the cry that has even welled up in your own eyes and choked your breath?

Friends, with sounds of Rachel in your ears go buy a plot of land in Sri Lanka for a family who has lost it all. Go buy a toothbrush and washcloth, and send it to the living. Send money to the Red Cross. Skip a meal and send the money saved to Church World Service. Adopt a child. Or, let Rachel's cry from South Asia open your ears to the cries in New Brunswick or Harlem. Start hearing Rachel cry out from places within your reach, where you can, in person, bring about great change.

Hear Rachel's cry and respond by going to medical school, starting a helpful program in your community, picking up the neighborhood, taking a kid to her first Rutgers basketball game, or teaching a child to read. Do the absurd—embrace life even while crying with Rachel.

Jesus, too, lived with atrocity. His demise didn't sneak up like a vicious wave. Long before he was arrested, the writing was on the wall that his days were numbered. He even said so to his closest friends. But in the morning, the day after telling his friends he would be rejected, and would suffer, and die, he went and healed a leper, converted a CEO, and taught and expressed compassion. Rachel's cry and a hope-joy cry are both found inside Jesus.

Hear the cry, "Why have you forsaken us?" Cry that yourself. But also live like light has come into the world, and into your body through the one who lived and died to live again and to help us live again. Here we have a broken body, spilled blood, a torture scene, massive devastation. Here we have hope, peace, love, joy, Spirit, and nourishment. In this meal, there is sadness and grief, but it is a meal defined as "death overcome."

Section Two—The Prepared Church Confronts the Issues of Its Day

Here is the meal that can make us world-builders, or kingdom-bringers, once again. Amen.

Part Nine

Faith Facing Darfur

32

Darfur in Light of Easter

April 30, 2006

> But Peter said, "I have no silver or gold, but what I have I give you; in the name of Jesus Christ of Nazareth, stand up and walk." (Acts 3:6)

I was sitting in the doctor's office a couple of weeks ago and had one of those endlessly long waits. I'd read *Sports Illustrated* going back to the Super Bowl. I'd even flipped through the gardening and home magazines. Finally, I picked up the local New Jersey Jewish newspaper, *The Jewish State*. I wish I'd picked it up first.

The entire cover page was about Jewish concern about the genocide in Darfur, Sudan. Under the heading "'Never Again' is Now," I read about Jewish efforts to raise awareness and help with humanitarian relief. I read about a Jewish lobby pushing for the US government and world community to intervene in Darfur with peacekeeping troops. I read about a Jewish doctor from Princeton who closed his practice for half a year to go live and work in refugee camps there.

Last week, just a few days after reading the article at the doctor's office, I got an email from Anshe Emeth Conservative Temple here in town. Under the same heading, "Never Again," our Jewish neighbors were extending an invitation for concerned citizens to join them in a bus trip to Washington, DC. There, an interfaith group would be calling on the president and Congress to take action to end the genocide in Darfur.

Section Two—The Prepared Church Confronts the Issues of Its Day

At least one of our congregants took the invitation. Our dear friend Elsie is traveling to Washington as we speak.

"Never again," refers, of course, to the holocaust, the event that has become the symbol of large-scale, man-made horror over the past sixty-one years. In article after article this week, I read Jewish authors who said that in light of the holocaust, Jews have an imperative to do something in the face of genocide. Dr. Efraim Zuroff wrote, "So as we face the terrible crimes being committed in Darfur and its vicinity by Arab militias supported by the Sudanese government, we have a Jewish obligation to speak out against the murders and try our utmost to facilitate prompt action to save those targeted by the killers." He went on, "If 'never again' is to have real meaning, the lessons [of the holocaust] have to be taken seriously by Jewish people who, today, are in a position to render meaningful assistance in the fight against these crimes."[3]

"Never again." It's a great theme that grows out of the awful experience of the holocaust. It's a mantra that tells a story, and it's a story that leads to action on behalf of Darfurian victims of 2006. Skepticism creeps into my mind. It's good to care, but what can a relatively small number of American Jews possibly do about the situation in the Darfur region of Sudan—even if they successfully recruit concerned Christians, Muslims, and humanists? It's so far away, the politics are confusing, and the power players hold all the cards. China won't help because they want to keep access to Sudanese oil reserves. We won't help with our troops, because our troops are overextended guarding Iraqi oil reserves. Everyone has their own agenda for not stopping the destruction.

But Jewish communities in America haven't let the tremendously difficult road ahead stop them. Their *story*, their formative story of the holocaust, is so strong that it leads them to try to beat the odds, to think the unthinkable. "Our humanity is at stake," writes famous Jewish author, Elie Wiesel. He says, "We must be involved. How can we reproach the indifference of non-Jews to Jewish suffering if we remain indifferent to another people's plight?"[4]

I hope that the story of the holocaust is not just a Jewish story but one that the world community joins in on. We should all say together, "Never again." But as Christians, there is another story that we have. And

---

3. Zuroff, "A Plea," http://www.edah.org/zuroff.cfm.
4. Wiesel, "Atrocities in Sudan," http://www.ushmm.org/wic/end/article.php?ModuleId=10007205.

Darfur in Light of Easter

as I thought this week about the power of "never again," and how it is impacting the global political discourse about Darfur in 2006, I felt strongly that it was time to address Darfur in light of *our* formative story. We've got a story that needs to sink into our beings, and then we've got to live in its light. That story is "He is risen, and so are we." It's an earth-shattering story; a story that has so much hope in it that it should lead us to strive to overcome all negatives with radical positives. He is risen, and so are we, and we are filled by the Holy Spirit, and empowered to be in the presence of God for Darfur.

Think about what the formative story did to Peter. Do you remember the stories we were sharing about Peter, and the other disciples, just sixteen days ago, on Maundy Thursday and Good Friday? Soldiers came to arrest Jesus to drag him off to prison and "the disciples deserted him and fled."[5] When Jesus was before the council, and Peter was waiting quietly outside in the courtyard, a servant girl came up to him and a dialogue ensued that went something like this:

She questioned if he was one of the disciples.
"I do not know what you are talking about."
"But you were with him."
"I do not know the man!"
"People, this man was with Jesus, listen to his accent, he's a Galilean."
"I swear to you that I do not know the man."[6]

Can you blame the disciples, and Peter? Church and state came down on their Lord with one crushing blow, and all hope was gone.

Even an empty tomb didn't immediately lead them to radical new ways of being in the world. I said a couple of weeks ago at the Easter service that the women who were at the tomb were overcome, put in an ecstatic state over the events of Easter. It took them a while to share the story—they had to take it in. Then last week we read that one of the disciples' first acts upon hearing that Jesus was raised from the dead was to go and lock a door, for fear of those same powerful rulers who had killed Jesus. It took multiple visits from Jesus, and the breath of the Holy Spirit, to get them fully on board with what God had done in the resurrection, to get them fully committed to the story.

We hear about Peter again today. Maybe this Peter is a different guy.

---

5. Matt 26:56.
6. Ibid., 26:69–74.

Section Two—The Prepared Church Confronts the Issues of Its Day

The first thing we read is that Peter goes back to the temple. Back to the temple—what's he thinking? That's where Jesus got in trouble just before his death. Hardly any time has passed, maybe seven weeks, and Peter's back? No way. People know Peter's face now. Pentecost has occurred, and thousands have started trusting in Jesus and identifying Peter as the outspoken leader of the Jesus movement. Going to the temple is risky.

And he doesn't go there quietly. Peter goes and heals somebody who was carried on a stretcher to the gates of the temple each day to beg. That's the kind of crazy business that got Jesus killed. Peter got close to that man in his grave-like state. He stopped, looked the man right in the eye, stretched out his hand, and said, "I have no silver or gold, but what I have I give you; In the name of Jesus Christ of Nazareth, rise up and walk."[7]

When his action of healing the crippled man led to a gathering crowd, presumably of commoners and the temple authorities, he addressed them boldly, telling them they had handed over and rejected Jesus, the one sent by God. He named Jesus, claimed that the rabble rouser Lord was present in his followers, still causing a raucous of unmitigated love by the power of the resurrection.

"He is risen—and so are we." That's our story. Once it sinks in, it should start changing us. Once it's our story, it ought to allow us to dream big dreams, stand up against great evil and take giant risks in love. Once it's our story, we should all have our names changed to Petros: Peter, the rock.

When you live in light of this story you care more, you dare more, you worry less, and you are up for any test that comes your way. For Christ is risen from the grave, and so are you! But it's hard to experience being raised without first going to the grave. Today is about going to the grave.

I don't mean your own, end-of-life grave. I mean go to the graves, prisons, and refugee camps of the world. Go to the bombed-out neighborhoods of Iraq or the famine-ridden neighborhoods of Malawi. Go to the grave of tears on the face of the kid who got beat up on the playgroup, the grave of fear of the gay teenager who is lonely and afraid of the upcoming prom. Go to the graves of the world and tell the story there, "He is risen, and so am I, and you can be too." Go to the graves of the world,

---

7. Ibid., 3:6.

Darfur in Light of Easter

and rise from the graves of the world: the Nazi Germany grave; the Palestinian/Israeli grave; the Haitian grave; the Darfur grave.

Some graves we face in our family life, our community life, our national life. Some graves we face together as a world. Today, moved by the plea of our Jewish neighbors, I want to get specific and talk about Darfur, and about the suffering of brothers and sisters of ours, for God is parent of all. Maybe the skepticism I voiced earlier is on *your* mind. "What's Darfur got to do with me?" Or, "It's so complicated and big, let me work on the things in my own life that need fixing."

Friends of the God who covenants with the world and revealed that covenant through the death and resurrection of Jesus, every broken place has to do with all of us. Every grave needs Easter. Will we ever be able to do everything for everyone? No, and God doesn't expect that. God's the only one with "omni" before the list of personality traits. But the story of the New Testament disciples is the story of people going to every grave-like situation and saying, "He is risen—watch, I'll show you how!" I believe this is what Jesus wanted when he said, "Go therefore and make disciples of all the nations, baptizing them [bringing them from death to life], in the name of the Father, Son, and Holy Spirit."[8] Go to graves, and reenact the story represented by the words, "Christ is risen and so are we."

Let's first visit the graves. In 2003, in Darfur, the western region of Sudan, an armed group of African Sudanese Darfurians began to actively protest against what they viewed as oppression by Sudan's Arab-dominated government. This came near the end of a twelve-year civil war between northern and southern Sudan. The government responded by arming militias known as *janjaweed*, to go on campaigns of murder, rape, and arson against entire tribes. This was a shocking way to respond to a political challenge. Since 2003, four hundred thousand people have been killed, and an estimated two million have been displaced. The victims have primarily been Muslim villagers, mainly of the Fur, Zaghawa, Massalit, Jebel, and Aranga groups.

Many of the survivors have been displaced within Sudan, but hundreds of thousands of people have spilled over into Chad, a country that has tremendous troubles of its own. A few weeks ago, the ruler of Chad indicated that by June, all Darfur refugees will need to be out of Chad. Chad can't handle it.

---

8. Ibid., 28:19.

Section Two—The Prepared Church Confronts the Issues of Its Day

Just yesterday, the UN World Food Program announced that, beginning tomorrow, it will cut daily rations in half due to lack of funding. The 6.1 million people being fed by the program will have their daily rations reduced to 1,050 calories per day. James Morris, the executive director of the UN program said, "Food must come first. We cannot put families who have lost their homes and loved ones on a 1,000 calorie a day diet."[9] In the same article another spokesman said that the reduction in rations will eliminate any gains made a year ago, when malnutrition in Darfur was cut almost in half because of adequate funding.

Friends, have hope—don't be overwhelmed. I say that almost against my will. It feels overwhelming, but there is one who overwhelms our overwhelmed realities. Those tombs can be empty. We've got a God who empties tombs. So let's work on that assumption!

I'm going to ask you today to consider making some commitments to those in grave-like situations in Darfur:

Call or visit Frank Pallone. He's our congressman. He's got an email; he's got an office on Bayard Street. Thank him for supporting House Bill 3127, the Darfur Peace and Accountability Act. Also, ask him to please support the additional $514 million of emergency supplemental funding requested for humanitarian relief and peacekeeping purposes.

Call Robert Menendez and Frank Lautenberg, our senators. Thank them for their work on Senate Bill 1462, the Senate version of the Darfur Peace and Accountability Act. Also, ask them to support the additional $514 million of emergency supplemental funding requested for humanitarian relief and peacekeeping purposes.

Go to Somerville, New Jersey, from 2 to 4 pm today. On the courthouse lawn on Main Street there will be a "Save Darfur" rally. There will be activities for the whole family. Visit the website www.millionvoicesfordarfur.com and sign your name to the petition being circulated.

Make a financial offering to Church World Services "Dear Sudan" food program. Church World Service is our ecumenical organization for humanitarian relief. It costs 16 cents per day to feed a person through CWS's program. Consider your family size, and make a donation equivalent to a week or a month. For Stephanie and I, that would be a donation of about $20 for a month of food for a family of four.

---

9. "Huge Donor," http://www.un.org/apps/news/story.asp?NewsID=18278&Cr=Sudan&Cr1#.Ug4ZAN13tUo.

Talk to each other in the church about what you've done, or about ideas you have for congregational involvement, and report back to me—so we can praise God together for all that is being done and to be inspired to do more.

Jesus Christ is risen today; that's our story. We have hope where we should not. It's foolish hope—to choose non-violent love—but it's the only love I know that has the power to open tombs. Let's live as if we're risen—because we are. In Christ the world can be risen indeed! Amen.

Part Ten

A New Day
The Election of Barack Obama

33

At What Point Do We Give up "Waiting In Anticipation"?

November 9, 2008

> May the God of peace himself sanctify you entirely; and may your spirit and soul and body be kept sound and blameless at the coming of our Lord Jesus Christ. The one who calls you is faithful, and he will do this. (1 Thessalonians 5:23–24)

Between last Sunday when we met here for worship and this Sunday, a lot has changed in America. There is a new communal spirit alive in the country, and indeed, it's not an exaggeration to say that much of the world is joining in jubilation. Regardless of whether you cast your vote for Obama or McCain, I think there is a shared sense that a profound shift has taken place. There is a "lightness" to things, an awareness that there's a new approach coming to a huge range of issues—and a new understanding of what "power" looks like. On election night, I was moved not only by Obama, but almost equally by McCain, who gave one of the most gracious and heartfelt concession speeches and endorsements of an opponent that I've ever heard. For one of the first times in my life, I'm experiencing overwhelming emotion and joy over politics that has me crying almost uncontrollably. I'm sure I won't get through this sermon.

Section Two—The Prepared Church Confronts the Issues of Its Day

I've seen your tear-stained faces too. In addition to all the historic hurdles overcome, in terms of race, something else amazing has happened. There are a few "themes" that can control a nation. From 9/11 until Tuesday night, it seemed that *fear* was the controlling theme. On Tuesday, a new controlling meta-narrative took over—hope. Suddenly hope abounds.

But Tuesday night wouldn't have happened if hope hadn't abounded first in the lives of various persons in the political realm and in the hearts of millions upon millions of people. Tuesday was the result of hope-driven people working hard, in a variety of public and private ways during this past "fear-dominated," red-alert period in American history.

Hope-driven people are people who have caught a glimpse of a new day—people who see something wonderful out in front of them. Hope-driven people see a day when there is peace, when there is joy, when the fighting stops, and who work for that day even before it seems feasible. Hope-driven people won't let barriers get in the way of what should be. In our public discourse it seems that many say their hope springs from having a picture of "a more perfect union" in their mind. The great experiment called "America" is a "hopeful one," and so aiming at a vision of a renewed and restored America, prompts hopeful action.

Regardless of your political leanings, we Christians ought to be excited to see *hope* as a motivator for our country, for our faith is about hope. Of course, Christian faith is about a particular hope. It isn't, first, a hope for America; our hope is about something much bigger. Christian hope starts with the promise above all promises: that all of life is *eternally connected to God, and this promise is the result of love initiated by God! We have hope for resurrected life beyond the grave; life with God forever!* "Who can separate us from the love of Christ? Will hardship, or distress, or persecution, or famine, or nakedness, or peril, or sword? . . . I am convinced that neither death, nor life, nor rulers, nor things present, nor things to come, nor powers, nor height, nor depth, nor anything else in all creation, will be able to separate us from the love of God in Christ Jesus our Lord!"[1]

And if that's our starting point, then we don't need to fear anything. If that's our starting point, that out in front of us is a God who is not just out there as a "great ideal" but is moving in our direction in love, then our bar is set radically high, and we cannot be satisfied with anything

---

1. Rom 8:35, 38.

less than "your kingdom come. Your will be done, on Earth as it is in heaven!"[2] If that hope is our starting point, then things like a vision for "a more perfect union" can become important sub-visions—visions that fit within the bigger vision of hope for life with God. These can be visions that we join in with others, as part of our faith.

I must admit that sometimes over these last years I've felt pretty overwhelmed with despair—the day bombing began in Baghdad, the day Abu Graib abuses were publicized, the day we learned about a series of global prisons in addition to Guantanamo Bay—these were hard days. Life has been under siege by death, and death has even picked away at *my* hope. I'm really thankful that during these years we've had each other and we've reminded each other on a weekly basis of our shared hope. Jesus is always in front of us, but we've had enough experiences of actually feeling his presence among us, and inside us, that it's helped keep our hope alive.

But Christian hope as *a dynamic motivational force* for changing us, or changing the world, wasn't an "automatic" feature of early Christianity. It took some time for it to develop—"hope" had some rocky years in the early days. The text I want to share with you today comes from 1 Thessalonians. This little five-chapter letter, tucked among Paul's collection, is the earliest document we have in our New Testament. Written in the year 51 AD, it was composed just twenty years or so after Christ's death. And, by virtue of being early, it addressed some important "early" questions.

First, a bit about the church in Thessalonica and Paul's relationship to it: Paul writes that Silvanus, Timothy, and he (the church founders) send their greetings in the name of God and the Lord Jesus. He recalls the Thessalonians' beautiful reception of God's message. And Paul also writes to applaud the Thessalonians for their steadfastness in faith. "Timothy has just now come to us from [visiting] you, and has brought us the good news of your faith and love . . . for this reason, brothers and sisters, during all our distress and persecution we have been encouraged about you through your faith. . . . How can we thank God enough for you in return for all the joy we feel before our God because of you?"[3]

After heaping well-deserved praise on a new church that is off to a good start, Paul focuses on addressing some of the concerns Timothy picked up on during their visit that stemmed from Paul's teaching that Christ would return soon. Wherever he went, Paul taught that the time

2. Matt 6:10.
3. 1 Thess 3:6a, 7, 9.

Section Two—The Prepared Church Confronts the Issues of Its Day

is coming soon! Stay on your toes. "Keep awake."[4] Like the parable Jesus told of the bridesmaids needing to keep the lamps lit, Paul had given such a message to the church in Thessalonica. But they'd been waiting years! You wonder how many of Paul's early church starts were built on the promise that Jesus would return *any time*. It was a campaign promise hard to keep, and yet it was so compelling. The hope for that immediate return dominated the minds and behaviors of the people.

It had been at least five years since Paul first was in Thessalonica, and Jesus hadn't come back yet. Compared to our two thousand-year wait, five is nothing; but they'd been waiting, and watching, and trying to truly conform their lives to the soon-to-arrive Jesus. And Paul learns people were concerned about the delay, concerned for many reasons—practical, emotional, and theological. The answers he gives in chapter 4:1–12 suggest some of the questions that were being asked:

Paul, I thought Christ was coming right away, so I chose not to marry, and to instead be celibate. I thought it would help me stay focused on Jesus, but I'm beginning to rethink that decision. This is getting cruel. How much longer until Christ returns?

Paul, I haven't been *working* because, well, I thought he was coming soon! I thought I ought to be out telling everyone the good news, sort of like you, Paul. I've got a family to feed and the non-Christians in our town are beginning to think we're lazy. The "we-don't-want-to-get-jobs-because-we're-busy-waiting-for-Jesus excuse" is getting old!

The questions made sense. If the return of Christ was imminent, then waiting with eyes open to the skies, encouraging others to believe, might seem appropriate. But if he was delayed, well, what did that mean? They had human lives to live—should they go about them?

I imagine Paul appreciating the questions, as he doesn't chastise anyone here. Paul is known for speaking boldly and critically in his letters. Paul's answer to the first question about marriage is basically "don't live with lustful passions like those who do not know God, but do live a sexual life in controlled and honorable ways, and don't wrong or exploit anyone. Honor God in and through your sexual relations." This is a *huge* statement. I imagine the Thessalonians receiving *this word* with a sigh of relief on one level, but also heard the sobering reality from Paul that Christ's delay might be long enough so that a future generation of children could be born and grow up. Paul was encouraging them to bring a

4. Ibid., 5:6.

new generation forth—I guess the time might not be drawing to a close after all!

His second answer to their question about work was, "Yes, you're right to commit to loving one another, and prioritizing that, do it more and more, but also, in your day-to-day life, live quietly, mind your own affairs and work with your hands (get a job!). Don't be dependent on others. Show the world that Christians are responsible in community." This answer, too, suggests Christ's return might be delayed.

Finally, there was a third question. While the community wanted to have clarity about marriage and work, the deepest concern of the community was about death: "What should we think about death? We didn't think anyone from our community would die before Jesus returned. We thought the Lord was coming to save us all. Some of our most caring saints have passed on now, and still no Jesus!"

Paul answers this way: "Brothers and sisters, you need not grieve as others who have no hope." He says, "This we declare to you by the word of the Lord . . . We believe Jesus died and rose again, and so it will be for those who have 'fallen asleep'" (that's the actual phrase Paul uses instead of "died").[5] Christ died, and in and through his death he eradicated death forever. Now, because of him there is sleep (*koimao*), not death. The Greek word "*koimeterion*" is the root of our "cemetery" (place of sleep). Paul says that Christ will descend from heaven, and when he descends "the sleeping" will rise first and meet him in a cloud above the Earth. When a royal ambassador pays a visit, you go forth to meet him. That's what the "sleeping ones" will do. And after the sleeping ones rise, the living, too, shall rise to him, to join in that official gathering of the entourage of the coming Christ, soon to see the establishment of his kingdom. Brothers and sisters, Paul says, "Encourage one another with these words."[6]

I don't know where Paul gets his information, and to be frank, I have a hard time picturing how what he says will happen will actually take place, but this is what I gain from Paul. He is telling them not to lose hope in the radical promise that Christ is out in front of us, and he's breaking in our way, and he'll transform everything. Don't deny marriage, don't fear work and engagement, and don't even fear death. Don't grieve as others

---

5. Ibid., 4:15.
6. Ibid., 4:18.

Section Two—The Prepared Church Confronts the Issues of Its Day

who have no hope, rather engage in everything, even death, as one who is full of Christ's promise of radical love and eventual arrival.

With their series of questions, the Thessalonians may have been asking, "At what point do we give up *waiting in anticipation* for Christ's arrival?"

Paul's answer: "Never."

"How long do we need to keep the lamps trimmed and burning?"

"Forever."

Christian hope and the promise of God's good future is rock solid. But with those lamps trimmed and burning, pointing hopefully toward God's future, and with the confidence that we don't even need to fear death, let's let hope influence day-to-day life—for life sure needs that kind of hope.

You know who modeled this perfectly?—Jesus Christ. Jesus knew something major was going to happen. God was doing something and it was imminent. Jesus anticipated the end of the story. But he didn't spend his "waiting time" standing still, looking for God breaking in. Free from anxiety about the end, because of his connection to God, he spent his "waiting time" looking out at others, looking out for ways to heal and help. He did all this with the hope that God was going to be coming soon, in some way, and bringing his kingdom with power.

There is a Christian brother of ours who seems to recognize the power of Christian hope for the transformation of the world; President-elect Barack Obama:

> I am a Christian, and I am a devout Christian. I believe in the redemptive death and resurrection of Jesus Christ. I believe that that faith gives me a path to be cleansed of sin and have eternal life. But most importantly, I believe in the example that Jesus set by feeding the hungry and healing the sick and always prioritizing the least of these over the powerful . . . [some years ago] there was a very strong awakening in me of the importance of these issues in my life. I didn't want to walk alone on this journey. Accepting Jesus Christ in my life has been a powerful guide for my conduct, and my values, and ideals.[7]

Friends of Jesus Christ, ultimately at the end of the age, we are in the arms of God—God will embrace us forever—so says much of Christian

---

7. Sarah Pulliam and Ted Olson, Barack Obama interview, http://www.christianitytoday.com/ct/2008/januaryweb-only/104-32.0.html.

Scripture. But I'm thankful that we don't have to wait until the end of the age to see big things happen; to see God's Spirit breaking in. For every time you live in Christian hope for what will be, and your decisions for your neighbor are driven by that hope, God breaks in, in small and large ways, through you. When we truly live with lamps trimmed and burning toward God's future, and that future frees us from anxiety, we start seeing things change. I think that's what happened on Tuesday night. Hope won. Hope won!

By setting eyes on a new day, a better day, the country has started living into that new day. God, you did return! Not for good though; not to take us with you. You just stopped in to bless our hope! You're here; I can feel the tremors of your Spirit, but you're still out in front of us, with a more perfect vision. Stay out there in front; don't return yet, for we're just starting to get the idea of what "waiting hopefully" looks like, and what it can mean for the life of the world. God, I think you'll be proud of us. Amen.

34

The Servant of the Lord

Does Anyone Have a President Who Is Bothering Them?

February 27, 2011

> Listen to me, O Coastlands, pay attention, you peoples from far away! The Lord called me before I was born, while I was in my mother's womb he named me. He made my mouth like a sharp sword, in the shadow of his hand he hid me; he made me a polished arrow, in his quiver he hid me away. And he said to me, "You are my servant, Israel, in whom I will be glorified." (Isaiah 49:1–3)

The New York Times Middle East Correspondent Anthony Shadid wrote of a cell phone message being passed around a couple of weeks ago in Egypt. "From Tahrir Square to our brothers [and sisters] in fellow countries . . . is there anyone who has a president bothering them?"[1] People are calling those young social media wielding servants with government toppling abilities! They are calling from Bahrain. They are calling from Libya. For in those places, and in so many more, the good news of an overthrown dictator is ringing through mountains and across dry

---

1. Shadid, "Uncharted Ground," http://www.nytimes.com/2011/02/12/world/middleeast/12revolution.html?pagewanted=all&_r=0.

land. There are presidents, dictators, and military generals, propped up by the global hunger for oil, goods, and power, who have been bothering the poor of the Middle East for years—and somehow, this week, a way has been cleared.

Finally, the structures have begun to flip upside down. Finally one can say, "Blessed are the poor, for they shall inherit this new Egypt. Blessed are those who mourn, for they shall be comforted. Blessed are the captives—they shall be set free!" Already it is coming to be.

Tahrir Square is becoming a symbol—a servant symbol for a new world. As President Obama said on February 11th:

> Today belongs to the people of Egypt, and the American people are moved by these scenes in Cairo and across Egypt because of who we are as a people and the kind of world that we want our children to grow up in. . . . The word "*tahrir*" means "liberation." It is a word that speaks to that something in our souls that cries out for freedom. And forevermore it will remind us of the Egyptian people—of what they did, of the things that they stood for, and how they changed their country, and in doing so changed the world."[2]

Brothers and sisters, Egypt's road to transformation has become a symbol for other nations in the Middle East, but hopefully it is also a humbling symbol for us in the United States. It took hundreds of thousands of unnecessary deaths (Iraqi and American) and hundreds of billions of US dollars so far (probably trillions) to "build" a democracy in Iraq—a democracy that is shaky at best, and doesn't really seem to have the backing of the people. It took 2½ weeks of nationwide protest, following months of quiet stirring and preparation, and the loss of very few lives (and virtually no U.S. or Egyptian dollars) to change Egypt and the Middle East forever.

When Egypt paused for a day to mourn for the handful of people killed in the mostly peaceful demonstrations, I wept. I wept for the deceased, but I also wept with joy at the thought that a country of eighty million could so dramatically change with so little bloodshed that it was actually possible to pause as a nation to remember them by name!

All around the Middle East there are *servant peoples* rising up, showing their force without drawing a sword, showing their force against

---

2. Obama, "Remarks By The President on Egypt," http://www.whitehouse.gov/the-press-office/2011/02/11/remarks-president-egypt.

Section Two—The Prepared Church Confronts the Issues of Its Day

Saddam Hussein-sized dictators who have been ruling for approximately forty years. Thank you, God, that they are choosing the Egyptian people's model of democracy building! And thank you, God, that we, the United States, who frequently promote democracy differently, are keeping our bombers, and fighter planes, and tanks out of the airspace and off their roads. We are exercising great responsibility and power by not jumping into the fray.

Might it be that we, too, are coming to believe that Tahrir Square is a more effective way—your way, O God? Let's hope so. If there comes a time when we must enter Libya or elsewhere to assist, may it be that we do so with the great restraint and servant leadership that has been recently modeled for us in Egypt.

Does it feel strange to talk of and to God in the midst of this modern-day political event? Isn't it only radicals of other faiths that do that? If it feels strange to reflect like this, it's only because we are not in the practice of doing what was commonplace for Israel's prophets—reflecting on God's place in real political history. God is the omnipotent one, the actor of all actors. How can we not seek to understand God's part in things? If the prophet we'll refer to as Second Isaiah had watched what unfolded in Egypt, he likely would have called Egypt's cell phone/twitter/facebook wielding actors the Messianic Servant Community of freedom. In and through their actions he would have definitely seen the hand of God at work. I'll say more about that in a moment.

Our passage today is set in the year 540 BC. At that time the population of Judah had been living in Babylonian captivity for close to fifty years. Many had assimilated into Babylonian society—some keeping their Jewishness alive, and some letting that slip from them. There was still oppression, still a real sense of being second-class citizens or worse, but gains had been made, at least by some. Some prophets kept crying out for the community to stay strong, and to keep its identity, in exile. This is the time of the prophet Jeremiah, and especially the time of the prophet Ezekiel. They wept and wailed along with the people, and tried to help them see the face of God in and through their suffering.

And then, almost fifty years into exile, along came a superpower greater than Babylon—Persia. Babylon quaked at its arrival, and without drawing a drop of blood, King Cyrus of Persia and his military took over the mighty city. In a dramatic instant, the political climate changed. And there was a prophet of Israel, who we will call II Isaiah, *ready to speak to that change.* Apparently he'd already been speaking to Israel in exile, under the Babylonians. He admitted in chapter 49:4 that most of the time he felt his words fell on deaf ears. He said, "I have labored in vain, I have spent my strength for nothing and vanity."

The prophetic book of Isaiah is written in at least two (maybe three) distinct historical periods. The first thirty-nine chapters wrap up around the year 700 BC, one hundred years before Judah is exiled to Babylon. Chapters 40 through 55 (and maybe the chapters beyond) are all written 150 years later, in one historical moment—this instant when Babylon itself, the oppressor who destroyed Jerusalem in 587 and took the inhabitants as booty, was overthrown. Today's passage is found in the middle of this second section, written by II Isaiah.

As political realities changed, here was a prophet, a servant-voice, ready to interpret history in the light of God's activity. Here was a prophet who saw what God was doing with Persia and Babylon and who spoke of God's involvement. Chapter 45 claims that King Cyrus of Persia—definitely not Jewish—is God's Messiah, God's anointed one! I'm sure this was news to Cyrus! You wonder whether it might have been Isaiah's spoken word, his *naming* of Cyrus as Messiah, which prompted Cyrus to think about himself as such, and led him to act justly toward Jews in exile, sending them home.

From the perspective of the prophet this big superpower takeover, this real political event, served a particular God-purpose. It was God's ways of restoring God's little tribe Judah to Jerusalem, to the city that was supposed to shine with heavenly light, the city that was supposed to be organized for the greater purpose of God's reign that will be a blessing for the whole Earth!

The chapters of II Isaiah are full of flowing descriptions of the grandeur and power of God and about God's plans to move history. But they are also full of something else that is particularly highlighted in our passage from Isaiah 49—*the servant motif.* The work that God intends to carry out for all of Israel, and indeed for all of the world, is going to happen through God's servant agent.

There is debate and uncertainty about the identity of the servant. Is it the prophet? Is it someone else? Is it Israel as a whole? Is it a group or community within Israel?

Understandably Christians have hung on these images and have tied them to images of Jesus. Handel's "Messiah" sure helped that tradition

Section Two—The Prepared Church Confronts the Issues of Its Day

along—with numerous quotes from Isaiah. While it is fine to describe Jesus through texts of old, and we'll do so ourselves further along in this sermon, Jesus was not the servant that Second Isaiah had in mind in 540 BC.

"Listen to me, O Coastlands, pay attention, you peoples from far away! The Lord called me before I was born, while I was in my mother's womb he named me. He made my mouth like a sharp sword, in the shadow of his hand he hid me; he made me a polished arrow, in his quiver he hid me away. And he said to me, "You are my servant, Israel, in whom I will be glorified.""

For myself, I believe the servant being addressed here is a *servant community within exiled Israel*. The task that is described for the servant is too daunting for one person—but it is possible for a community. I believe God is saying that there is a servant community Israel within full Israel. There is a servant Israel called by God who hears the voice of God and whose message is razor sharp in articulating God's word and whose presence will bring about glorious results for all. God goes on to say to the servant community who is within Israel, who is for Israel, "You know, it is too light a thing that you should be my servant to raise up the tribes of Jacob and to restore the survivors of Israel; I will give you as a light to the nations, that my salvation may reach to the end of the Earth!"[3] The task for the servant community to bring about liberation and transformation is a global one!

In Isaiah chapter 49 God goes on to say, and I paraphrase, "I've kept you through all this, and I've cleared a path for you now, so that you can establish the land again, apportion the desolate heritages; say to prisoners 'come out!' and to those who are in darkness, 'show yourselves.' And I will protect you as you travel out of captivity and back to your homeland. I'll protect pastures for your animals. I'll keep you from hunger and thirst, scorching wind and sun. By springs of water I will guide you."[4]

It is impossible to say definitively when it was that words like this would have been uttered. So, I want to imagine the scene. I imagine God, through the prophet, proclaiming these words to a gathering of exilic Jews *after* the fall of the Babylonian empire, but *before* Cyrus of Persia announced he was releasing all Jews to return to their homeland: "Servants of Israel, people connected closely with God, are you ready to announce

---

3. Isa 49:6.
4. Ibid., 49:8b–10.

to Cyrus that he is God's Messiah, called to send us home? Servants of Israel, planted among Israel in exile, people connected closely with God, are you ready to lead your people back? Servants of Israel, your previous efforts may have felt futile, but the time is at hand! God is moving through human history, and *this* moment in God's human history is a time for freedom!"

Almost six hundred years later another prophet picked up this scroll of Isaiah. He picked up a section that also contained Isaiah's servant language. In his first recorded public sermon, Jesus picked up the scroll of Isaiah and said from chapter 61:1–2a, "The Spirit of the Lord God is upon me, because the LORD has anointed me . . . to bring good news to the oppressed, to bind up the brokenhearted, to proclaim release to the captives . . . and to proclaim the year of the Lord's favor."

To the people around Jesus, their particular historical moment had the usual oppression in the air—they did not see any sign that this was a historic moment of reality-altering release. But to Jesus, this was the moment for gospel—for *euangelion*. As Walter Brueggemann says it, "gospel" means "release for captives who are held by exploitative powers."[5] Jesus proclaimed it, like II Isaiah had many years before, and he started sharing that he was servant of the message, and he started looking for other servants to join him, that Israel might be freed again and so all the world might be blessed.

Brothers and sisters, it is time for us to join Isaiah and Jesus in their servant community. And in addition to joining Isaiah and Jesus, I believe we should look to contemporary servants of God too—agents of God's history making power that are alive in our historical moment.

Maybe it is time that we join with those powerful servants who are shouting, "Leave office!" to dictators, and "Come out!" to prisoners, and "Enter the light!" to those who live in darkness. Maybe we should join with the powerful servants who are shouting about "bargaining rights" in Wisconsin. Might it be that they, too, are part of God's servant communities? Maybe one thing we can offer them is a greater awareness of the sacredness of their contemporary political revolutions.

In addition, maybe *we* are also called to be the *servant-leader-instigators* of new revolutions, called to draw others to join us in the efforts God breathes into our collective life. In our congregation, at this moment, we've been charged with unique tasks: we've been charged to

---

5. Brueggeman, *Isaiah*, 12.

Section Two—The Prepared Church Confronts the Issues of Its Day

care for victims of human trafficking; we've been charged to work with victims who fear returning to their countries; we've been charged to speak about a more sustainable eco-friendly world, a world where there is less waste and more respect for God's creation; we've been charged with insisting on housing for vulnerable people; we've been charged with saying that all people be celebrated and loved, regardless of sexual orientation; we've been charged to help build a school in Zambia; we've been charged to walk for flooding victims in Pakistan; we've been charged to care for each other in our illnesses; and, we've been charged to help each other find jobs. In short, we are servants charged with tasks that are the gospel, the good news.

Second Isaiah saw God moving in history, and heard God speaking in history to become a servant—to form a community of servants—that the whole community of God might be saved. Jesus saw God moving in history; heard God telling him to become a servant and to form a community of servants—that the whole world might be saved.

Brothers and sisters, with Jesus Christ within and beside us, it is our turn now—to join and support servant movements and to start some movements ourselves. There are presidents and principalities and powers that are bothering the world—let's rise up, servants of God, and join God and God's servant communities, in ushering them out, and ushering God's love and peace back in. Amen.

Bibliography

Achtemeier, Paul J., ed. *Harpers Bible Dictionary.* 1st ed. San Francisco: Harper & Row, 1985.
Bauer, Water, et al. *Greek-English Lexicon of the New Testament and Other Early Christian Literature.* 2nd ed. Chicago: University of Chicago, 1979.
Bernstein, Richard. "U.S. Accuses Iran of Deceiving U.N. Inspectors." *The New York Times* (2 Mar 2005). No pages. Online: http://www.nytimes.com/2005/03/02/international/europe/02cnd-nuke.html.
Brueggeman, Walter. *Isaiah: 40–66.* Westminster: John Knox, 1998.
Bush, George W. "State of the Union Speech." *The Washington Post* (28 Jan 2003). No pages. Online: http://www.washingtonpost.com/wp-srv/onpolitics/transcripts/bushtext_012803.html.
Craddock, Fred. *Luke: Interpretation: A Bible Commentary for Teaching and Preaching.* Louisville, KY: John Knox, 1990.
Dale, Jack, ed. *My Special World: Poems and Photographs of Dorothy Forsythe Dale.* New York: North Point, 2005.
Eilperin, Juliet. "Warming Called Threat to Global Economy." *The Washington Post* (31 Oct 2006). No pages. Online: http://www.washingtonpost.com/wpdyn/content/article/2006/10/30/AR2006103000269.html.
Freedman, David Noel, ed. *Eerdmans Dictionary of the Bible.* 1st ed. Grand Rapids, MI: Wm. B. Eerdmans, 2000.
Gutteres, Antonio. "Millions Leave Home in Iraqi Refugee Crisis: Interview with Antonio Guterres." By Simon Scott. *Weekend Edition Saturday* (17 Feb 2007). No pages. Online: http://www.npr.org/templates/story/story.php?storyId=7466089&from=mobile.
Harrison, Rick. "Feds Round up Fugitives: Edison, Metuchen, Woodbridge Raids Net 35 Illegals." *Home News Tribune* (25 May 2006) 1.
"Huge Donor Shortfall Forces Drastic Food Cuts for Millions of Sudanese." *UN News Centre* (28 Apr 2006). No pages. Online: http://www.un.org/apps/news/story.asp?NewsID=18278&Cr=Sudan&Cr1#.Ug4ZAN13tUo.
Johnson, Lyndon B. "Remarks at Gettysburg on Civil Rights." (30 May 1963). No pages. Online: http://www.lbjlib.utexas.edu/johnson/archives.hom/speeches.hom/selected_speeches.asp.
Käsemann, Ernst. *Commentary on Romans.* Grand Rapids, MI: Wm. B. Eerdmans, 1980.
Khavkine, Richard. "Essex County to Receive New Detention Center for Illegal Immigrants." *The Star-Ledger* (21 Dec. 2010). No pages. Online: http://www.nj.com/news/index.ssf/2010/12/essex_county_to_receive_new_de.html.
King, Jr., Martin Luther. "Eulogy for the Young Victims of the Sixteenth Street Church Bombing." In *A Call to Conscience: The Landmark Speeches of Dr. Martin Luther*

Bibliography

King Jr., edited by Clayborne Carson and Kris Shepard, 18 Sept 1963. New York: Hachette, 2001.

Mangan, Dan. "Donald Trump Makes Bid for Proposed Mosque Building," *New York Post* (9 Sept 2010) 4:34.

Matthews, Karen and Beth Fouhy. "NYC Panel Clears Way for Prayer Center near Ground Zero" (3 Aug 2010). No pages. Online: http://www.salon.com/2010/08/03/panel_clears_way_for_ground_zero_mosque/.

Mills, Watson E., ed. *Mercer Dictionary of the Bible*. Macon, GA: Mercer University, 1991.

Mouw, Richard J. *Uncommon Decency: Christian Civility in an Uncivil World*. 1st ed. Downer's Grove, IL: InterVarsity, 1992.

Obama, Barack. "Remarks By The President on Egypt" (11 Feb. 2011). No pages. Online: http://www.whitehouse.gov/the-press-office/2011/02/11/remarks-president-egypt.

Pulliam, Sarah and Ted Olson. "Q&A: Barack Obama." *Christianity Today* (23 Jan 2008). No pages. Online: http://www.christianitytoday.com/ct/2008/januarywebonly/104-32.0.html.

"Questions Raised About Virginia Tech's Response to Shootings." *Diverse: Issues in Higher Education* (16 Apr 2007). No pages. Online: http://diverseeducation.com/article/7240/#.

Pagels, Elaine and C. Welton Gaddy. "Audio News Conference on the President's Irresponsible Use of Religious Language" (11 Feb. 2003). No pages. Online: http://www.religionandpluralism.org/ANC_transcript_President_or_Preacher.htm.

Phillips, Joseph. "Tolerance and the Ground Zero Mosque" (16 Aug 2010). No pages. Online: http://townhall.com/columnists/josephcphillips/2010/08/16/tolerance_and_the_ground_zero_mosque/page/full.

Ratnesar, Romesh. "Ground Zero: Exaggerating the Jihadist Threat." *Time: U.S.* (18 Aug 2010). No pages. Online: http://www.time.com/time/nation/article/0,8599,2011400,00.html.

Reformed Church of America. *Liturgy and Confessions: Baptism* (1994). No pages. Online: https://www.rca.org/sslpage.aspx?pid=1879.

Richard, Pablo. *Apocalypse: A People's Commentary on the Book of Revelation*. Maryknoll, NY: Orbis Books, 1995.

Shadid, Anthony. "Uncharted Ground After End of Egyptian Regime." *The New York Times* (11 Feb 2011). No pages. Online: http://www.nytimes.com/2011/02/12/world/middleeast/12revolution.html?pagewanted=all&_r=0.

Wallis, Jim. "Sometimes It Takes a Natural Disaster To Expose a Social Disaster." *Sojourners Magazine* 34, no. 10: No pages. Online: http://sojo.net/magazine/2005/11/what-waters-revealed.

Wiesel, Elie. "On The Atrocities in Sudan." Darfur Emergency Summit (14 July 2004). No pages. Online: http://www.ushmm.org/wic/end/article.php?ModuleId=10007205.

Whipp, Margaret. "Covenant and Care: From Law to Loving-Kindness: A Response to Robin Gill." In *Covenant Theology: Contemporary Approaches*, edited by Mark J. Cartledge and David Mills, 117. Carlisle, UK: Paternoster, 2001.

Wright, N. T. "Paul's Gospel and Caesar's Empire." No pages. Online: http://ntwrightpage.com/Wright_Paul_Caesar_Empire.pdf.

Zuroff, Efraim. "A Plea for Jewish Action Against the Crimes Being Committed in Darfur." EDAH. No pages. Online: http://www.edah.org/zuroff.cfm.

www.ingramcontent.com/pod-product-compliance
Lightning Source LLC
Chambersburg PA
CBHW051104230426
43667CB00013B/2443